Unsettling Thoreau

Unsettling Thoreau

NATIVE AMERICANS,
SETTLER COLONIALISM, AND
THE POWER OF PLACE

JOHN J. KUCICH

University of Massachusetts Press
Amherst and Boston

The electronic version has been made freely available under a Creative Commons (CC BY-NC-ND 4.0) license, which permits noncommercial use, distribution, and reproduction provided the author and University of Massachusetts Press are fully cited and no modifications or adaptations are made. Details of the license can be viewed at https://creativecommons.org/licenses/by-nc-nd/4.0/.

This book will be made open access within three years of publication thanks to Path to Open, a program developed in partnership between JSTOR, the American Council of Learned Societies (ACLS), University of Michigan Press, and The University of North Carolina Press to bring about equitable access and impact for the entire scholarly community, including authors, researchers, libraries, and university presses around the world. Learn more at https://about.jstor.org/path-to-open/.

Copyright © 2024 by University of Massachusetts Press
All rights reserved
Printed in the United States of America

ISBN 978-1-62534-834-0 (paper); 835-7 (hardcover)

Designed by Sally Nichols
Set in Adobe Garamond Pro
Printed and bound by Books International, Inc.

Cover design by adam b. bohannon
Cover art by Conrad Bakker, *Thoreau's Cabin at Walden Pond*, engraving c. 1854.
WikiMedia Commons / Public Domain.

Library of Congress Cataloging-in-Publication Data
A catalog record for this book is available from the Library of Congress.

British Library Cataloguing-in-Publication Data
A catalog record for this book is available from the British Library.

Portions of this book previously appeared in *The Concord Saunterer: A Journal of Thoreau Studies* 19/20 (2011/12); *Thoreau beyond Borders: New International Essays on America's Most Famous Nature Writer*, ed. François Specq, Laura Dassow Walls, and Julien Nègre (Amherst: University of Massachusetts Press, 2020); and *Thoreau in an Age of Crisis: Uses and Abuses of an American Icon*, ed. Kristen Case, Rochelle L. Johnson, and Henrik Otterberg (Leiden: Brill, 2021).

For Monica, Alexander, and Christopher

Contents

Illustrations ix
Preface: Reading Thoreau on Native Ground xi
Acknowledgments xix
Abbreviations xxiii

INTRODUCTION
Thoreau's Indian Problem
1

CHAPTER 1
Ghosts of Musketaquid
Playing Indian, Local History, and A Week on the Concord and Merrimack Rivers
25

CHAPTER 2
Savagism and Its Discontents
The Indian Notebooks
57

CHAPTER 3
Becoming Native
Walden, *"Walking," and the Poetry of Place*
86

CHAPTER 4
Indians in Massachusetts
Cape Cod, *Colonialism, and Wampanoag Revitalization*
115

CHAPTER 5
Lost in the Maine Woods
Henry Thoreau, Joseph Nicolar, and the Penobscot World
140

CHAPTER 6
Succession
Wild Fruits, The Dispersion of Seeds, *and Thoreau's Indian Afterlife*
169

Notes 193

Index 217

Illustrations

FIGURE 1: Wicker creel from Thoreau's Journal (Morgan Library & Museum)   12
FIGURE 2: Page from the Indian Notebooks (Morgan Library & Museum)   61
FIGURE 3: Albert Bierstadt, "Last of the Narragansetts" / Martha Simons (Millicent Library)   121
FIGURE 4: Thoreau's map of Cape Cod (Concord Free Public Library)   126
FIGURE 5: William Apess portrait and title page, from *A Son of the Forest* (New York Public Library)   131
FIGURE 6: Photograph of Solomon Attaquin (public domain)   138
FIGURE 7: Thoreau's map of Maine (Concord Free Public Library)   142
FIGURE 8: Photograph of Joseph Nicolar from 1893 edition of *Life and Traditions of the Red Man* (public domain)   153
FIGURE 9: Photograph of Joseph Attean (University of Maine Folger Library and Penobscot Nation)   156
FIGURE 10: Portrait of Joseph Polis by Charles Bird King (Gilcrease Museum)   161

Preface
Reading Thoreau on Native Ground

Several years ago, I took part in a canoe trip retracing Thoreau's 1857 journey through the Maine Woods. The trip brought together major landholders, wilderness guides, conservation advocates, members of the Penobscot tribe, and several Thoreau scholars, along with a host of photographers, filmmakers, and travel writers.[1] These individuals had varying ideas about how to manage the large swaths of land being sold off by paper and timber companies and how to bring sustainable development to an economically ravaged region, and the canoe trip was an effort to bring these advocates for the Maine Woods together on the 150th anniversary of the publication of Thoreau's landmark book. As we paddled and portaged and sat around campfires in the late spring evenings in the narrow window between black-fly and mosquito seasons, we shared different visions for these lands and waters: as conservation land; as hunting and fishing grounds; as exciting opportunities for river rafting, hiking, snowmobiling, dogsledding, and skiing; for real estate development; or as a rare opportunity to restore tribal territory. We read from *The Maine Woods*, both to mark what had changed and what had not in the stretches of river and lake through which we traveled and to see how Thoreau's ideas about this landscape resonated with our own. The Thoreau that emerged in these conversations wasn't an unambiguous hero—his often racist comments about the Penobscot people he met and his status as a short-term visitor from out of state made that stance untenable. Nor was he a villain—his detailed and largely sympathetic portraits of two revered Penobscot leaders; his profound response to the magic of the mountains, lakes, and rivers that we also felt; and his incisive account of a complex and fluid human landscape in nineteenth-century Maine were simply too compelling to dismiss. Thoreau, instead, became a focal point of a rich and often charged conversation, a point of reference for a range of ideas and visions that we worked through over many days and evenings without ever fully resolving. Reading Thoreau was, in short, unsettling to our assumptions and expectations about the land we traveled through and the people we met. His writings didn't offer any clear answers about the future of the Maine Woods in the twenty-first century, though they played a part in the establishment of the Katahdin Woods and Waters National Monument in 2016.[2] Instead, they lent a shape and depth to difficult conversations and, in particular, helped everyone better see what was at stake for the land through which we traveled and for the people who have lived in these lands since long before the first European ships arrived on its rocky coast.

What was true in the Maine Woods is true as well in Concord, where visitors gather from all walks of life and from all parts of the world to see if their own world can look newer, sharper, and more promising when glimpsed through the eyes of a writer who traveled widely in the woods and waters of Musketaquid more than a century and a half ago, the region Thoreau called, in *A Week on the Concord and Merrimack Rivers*, the "Grass-ground River." Some come as pilgrims to a shrine, eager to add a stone to the cairn at the site of the small house by the shore of Walden Pond or to leave a pencil on the modest headstone on Author's Ridge in Sleepy Hollow Cemetery. I have done this, too, leaving a rock from Katahdin near where Thoreau himself sat at his front door, gazing at the pond and mulling over what he himself had seen on the mountain. But most engage in some form of the conversation that took place during the canoe trip, wondering how the efforts of this writer to live more simply, more ethically, and with more awareness of the more-than-human world can help us confront the wicked nexus of environmental, economic, and racial problems that shapes our world. They, too, find Thoreau unsettling in entirely fruitful ways. His stock has risen in recent years as people seek alternatives to the ravages of late capitalism and the environmental crises that threaten us all. As the United States has begun to confront its legacy of systemic racism, Thoreau's strident condemnation of slavery and his model of civil disobedience has reemerged as a key touchstone in moving that work forward. He went to jail, he worked on the Underground Railroad, he spoke alongside Frederick Douglass and Sojourner Truth, and he fiercely defended John Brown.

Yet as the national conversation turned to addressing America's other original sin, the legacy of Indigenous dispossession, genocide, and ongoing colonization, Thoreau's writing has offered less clarity. While some admirers have long noted his interest in Native people and often celebrated him as a "friend of the Indian," others have shown that he was deeply enmeshed in a settler colonial world and often advanced the savagism that rationalized Native dispossession. In his published writings, in his Journal, and in his vast Indian Notebooks, Thoreau copied and crafted a dizzying range of attitudes about Indigenous people. At times, he saw the full humanity within Native communities and recognized the richness and sophistication of their many cultures; at times, he bore stark witness to the savage machinery of colonization. At other times, he parroted the darkest stereotypes of savagism and seemed to accept the inevitability of Indian vanishing and the naturalness of white settlement. If his more typical stance was a Romantic view of Native people as a primitive counterpoint to a modernizing United States, and if he pursued a lifelong interest in learning from the traditional ecological knowledge of Native cultures so as to better help the settlers who displaced them live more mindfully on stolen land, those are hardly decolonial positions. Most striking is Thoreau's comparative silence on Native dispossession in his time and his lack of interest in Native communities that struggled, and survived, in his region. Thoreau himself needs unsettling, to be lifted off his podium of environmental and social justice sainthood and seen as a writer very much caught up in the conflicting currents of his own time. Teasing apart these different positions, tracking their course in his writings, weighing what Thoreau did say and what he didn't, and trying to measure his place and his impact in a settler colonial world is the project of this book.

Thoreau does not emerge from this study as a nineteenth-century advocate of decolonization; indeed, decolonizing Thoreau is something *we* must do, by looking in part at how he participated in the settler colonial efforts of his day, how he struggled against them, and how he engaged (or didn't) with his Native neighbors.[3] Thoreau was able to speak so powerfully against slavery and capitalism by standing (at least in part) outside those systems. He was more complicit in Indigenous dispossession and genocide, and so from this view, he is less a hero than a very human writer, caught up in something he at time critiques, at times accepts, and is never able to fully resolve. This conclusion may not be comfortable for anyone who (like me) has long turned to Thoreau's work as an inspiration and a touchstone for resisting racial injustice, for imagining alternatives to capitalism's quiet desperation and not-so-quiet devastation, for seeing and valuing the more-than-human world, for an example of simplicity, attention, and spiritual probing, for being, as he says in "Resistance to Civil Government," a bad subject and a good neighbor. Decolonizing Thoreau means seeing these contributions to building a better world alongside his shortcomings and, perhaps, learning to face our own.

This work would be impossible without the growth of Native American and Indigenous Studies (NAIS) in recent decades. Native and nonnative scholars have recovered an enormous amount of writing by Native people before the twentieth century that allows us to better contextualize writers like Thoreau; they have also insisted that such scholarship engage with the Native communities whose interests are very much at stake in this work. This particular book draws heavily on NAIS work—over the years, I've benefited from the insights and generosity of scholars at Native American literature and NAIS conferences, and my study of Thoreau is deeply informed by key works of NAIS, especially Jean O'Brien's *Firsting and Lasting*, an incredibly rich synthesis of settler histories in the nineteenth century; Lisa Brooks's *The Common Pot*, a powerful exploration of the durable place-world Native people built in the Northeast; and Robin Wall Kimmerer's *Braiding Sweetgrass*, an endlessly rewarding resource for applying Indigenous knowledge to a broken world. But a study of Thoreau is an uneasy fit within NAIS. Although I include extensive discussion of two Native writers, Joseph Nicolar and William Apess, my focus is very much on a settler writer who, quite frankly, is of lesser interest to Native scholars and writers. An NAIS project that focuses on similar themes—one that takes as its topic Native American writers in New England during the long nineteenth century, with a particular interest in the environment and the role it plays in shaping Native communities—is certainly imaginable (and, indeed, Lisa Brooks's *The Common Pot* and Siobhan Senier's *Sovereignty and Sustainability* offer powerful models of this crucial work), but in such a project, Thoreau would play, at best, a minor role.[4]

In addition to learning from a growing body of NAIS scholarship, I've benefited from the generosity and wisdom of Native people outside the scholarly community. Some of the members of the Penobscot Nation I first met on the canoe trip mentioned above—James Francis, Chris Sockalexis, Jenny Neptune, Jason Pardilla, and Charlie Brown—have shared their own work on Penobscot revitalization in publications, presentations, visits to the tribal museum, and travels through Penobscot territory. In my academic community, Bridgewater State University, located in the Wampanoag homeland, I've learned a tremendous amount from my colleague Joyce Rain Anderson, a key scholar of cultural rhetorics and an active member of the Wampanoag community. She has kindly introduced me to Wampanoag scholars, elders, and culture keepers, including Linda Coombs, Donna Mitchell, and Kerri Helme, each of whom has taught both me and my students something of what it means to live on Native land. Through Bridgewater State University, I have also been privileged to work for many years with the *Maȟpíya Lúta Owáyawa*/Red Cloud Indian School on the Oglala Lakota reservation in South Dakota, which helps prepare students for college while deepening their ties to their Lakota language and community. Among the remarkable people who serve these students, Moira Coombs and Maka Black Elk have been particularly generous in welcoming me to this work. From each of these relationships, I've gained a richer sense of both the joy and the struggle that make up the continuing revitalization efforts throughout the Native community, of the long legacy of colonization and the incredible resilience that underlies efforts to rebuild communities, reclaim languages, and restore the many forms of sovereignty that had long been stripped away. It's been a privilege to witness some of these efforts up close, but I've also been able to see this effort is one in which Native people necessarily take the lead.

Yet while Thoreau is hardly central to the ongoing project of Native revitalization, it remains crucially important to interrogate the role such cultural icons play in creating the society in which we live, as well as to explore how they might help our nation live up to its promise. I've been fortunate to work on this project as a member of the Thoreau Society, an author society that, rather than trying to burnish the legacy of this writer, has welcomed a rich, critical inquiry into his relationship to the settler colonial world. I've learned a great deal from Joshua Bellin and Richard Schneider, two exemplary scholars who have written extensively about Thoreau's relationship to settler colonial ideologies, and I've benefited from Brent Ranalli's imaginative, insightful work on Thoreau's interest in Native Americans. These colleagues, and many others in the community of Thoreau scholars, have encouraged me to think more deeply about Thoreau's writing and to ask difficult questions about what his work meant in his own time and what it means in ours. Thoreau hardly emerges as a hero of decolonization in this book. Some readers may like him less after considering these questions. I certainly did. But I hope they find, as I did, that his work remains intensely interesting—full, from our current perspective, of good and bad and, in the manner of the best literature, continually raising new questions and complications. Thoreau's continued relevance, I suggest, does not depend on naming and excising the bad bits in his work so as to preserve the good—they are interwoven. His critique of capitalism, his effort to live simply, his deep connection to the environment, and his stirring arguments for abolitionism are entwined with a complicated and often deeply problematic attitude toward Native people that I believe makes his work more relevant to our era. It is easier to see, looking back from the vantage point of a century and a half, Thoreau's entanglements with settler colonialism; seeing them clearly, I hope, helps us better see our own.

Certainly, my interest in Thoreau has grown more complicated over the course of writing this book. Living, as I do, on the edge of Thoreau country, I've learned to see my own home with much more richness and detail through the pages of his writing. And if his efforts to engage with his Black, Irish, and Native neighbors were at once full of promise and rife with problems, they have been occasions for me to interrogate my relations with neighbors near and far. I hope that this book, and my life, are better for it.

A note on terms: Thoreau used the term "Indian" throughout his writing, and I use it when quoting or referring specifically to Thoreau's writing projects. I use the terms Native American, or Native, or Indigenous, depending on the context, as equivalents, though I recognize that some scholars and activists use these with important differences. I use "Native people" when referring to individuals within a group, or to Indigenous people in general, in contrast to European settlers; I use "Native peoples" when referring to distinct national or tribal groups. Settlers, including Thoreau, often tried to claim these terms for themselves; I use quotation marks ("native" and "indigenous") when referring to such instances of replacement. When the dynamic of replacement is not in the foreground (as in an indigenous plant or one's native town), I use the lower case. Where possible, I use the tribal name and spelling preferred by a Native community with as much specificity as possible—thus "Wampanoag," "Mashpee," "Penobscot," "Penacook," "Nashobah," or "Nipmuc." Some of the Native people mentioned by Thoreau were part of communities that are very much extant today; others are not, and I have tried to be mindful of the often ambiguous history that shaped these peoples. "Musketaquid" is the name of the community that long inhabited what became Concord; early colonial accounts identify them as part of the Massachusett tribe with strong ties to the neighboring Pawtucket and Nipmuc nations. They relocated to nearby Nashobah after leaving Concord, and after Metacom's Rebellion, many joined relatives in the Natick community, whereas others, likely, joined Nipmuc and Abenaki communities. Their descendants remain very much a part of the Native Northeast.

Acknowledgments

This book is the result of a long conversation with many people about Thoreau's complicated legacy, beginning in a high school English class, where reading *Walden* helped me realize there were other ways of living than the one I knew growing up in late-twentieth-century suburban Connecticut. That conversation has continued ever since. *Unsettling Thoreau* had its roots in graduate school, when my adviser, Elizabeth Ammons, wisely suggested I leave a chapter on Thoreau out of my dissertation and return to it at a later date—it struck her as a separate project that needed more thought, and so here it is, twenty-odd-years later. When I was ready to return to it a decade ago, I was extremely fortunate to fall into conversation with Laura Dassow Walls and Kristen Case, who encouraged me to develop some conference papers into an article on *The Maine Woods* and, eventually, this book. They have welcomed me into the richly informed and rigorous ongoing conversation at the heart of the Thoreau Society. Rochelle Johnson, James Finley, Stan Tag, Henrik Otterberg, Brent Ranalli, Lawrence Buell, Richard Schneider, Joshua Bellin, William Rossi, Robert Sattelmeyer, Rebecca Gould, Robert Thorson, Robert Gross, Jeffrey Kramer, Alex Moskowitz, Kathleen Kelly, Richard Higgins, and many, many others have asked good questions and given welcome encouragement at different stages of my work.

I am grateful that Kristen Case passed my name along to Mike Wilson of the Northern Forest Center, who invited me to take part in the Thoreau-Wabanaki Anniversary Tour, a canoe trip retracing Thoreau's last journey along the Allagash and Penobscot Rivers in 2014. I met a wide range of scholars and stakeholders on that trip, including several members of the Penobscot Nation. I am deeply grateful to James Francis, Chris Sockalexis, Jason Pardilla, Jenny Neptune, Charlie Brown, and many others in the Penobscot community for welcoming me to their homeland and sharing their stories and wisdom.

I've been fortunate to do this work while serving in the English Department at Bridgewater State University (BSU). My students have engaged enthusiastically and critically with many of the texts and ideas presented in this book, and I am thankful for their willingness to help me think through this material. My colleagues at Bridgewater have also been an incredible support, giving immensely helpful feedback on portions of my work and, more generally, offering inspiring models of how to build a life that balances teaching, research, and family in ways that nourish each sphere. I don't have space to name everyone I've learned from over my many years in the BSU community; the few names I can mention represent an extraordinary group of teacher-scholars. Ann Brunjes has been both a cheerleader and a critical sounding board. Kim Davis, Ben Carson, Matt Bell, Jim Crowley, Heidi Bean, Lee Torda, Brian Payne, and many others have contributed to the rich intellectual community in Tillinghast Hall. Joyce Rain Anderson has generously shared her deep knowledge of Native American and Indigenous Studies and introduced me to some remarkable people in the Wampanoag and Nipmuck communities—I'm grateful to have learned from Donna Mitchell's grace and wisdom in her later years, and both Linda Coombs and Kerri Helme have taught my students and me invaluable lessons about what it takes to revitalize and nurture an Indigenous community.

I am grateful to the excellent staff at both the Monroe Special Collections at the Concord Free Public Library and the Morgan Library for making accessible their carefully stewarded Thoreau manuscripts, as well as the staff of the Maxwell Library at Bridgewater State University for gathering scholarly sources from near and far. I am especially grateful for the patient guidance of Brian Halley at the University of Massachusetts Press, who began discussing book ideas with me some fifteen years ago and carefully guided my earlier collection, *Rediscovering the Maine Woods: Thoreau's Legacy in an Unsettled Land*, from inception to print. He has been a deft guide through this project as well. I've benefited enormously from the careful reading and hard questions from my anonymous readers and from the impeccable editing of Nancy Raynor. I've done my best to take up their questions and address the many concerns and complications inherent in my topic, but I know mine won't be the last word on Thoreau's relationship to Native America.

Finally, I owe my deepest debt to my family. Alexander and Christopher were children when I began this book, learning their way around the streets, playing fields, and woods of our hometown, not far from Musketaquid; as it drew to a close, they became increasingly thoughtful contributors in our ongoing conversation about what it means to live and grow on Native land. And to my wife, Monica, my partner in all things, I can only express a gratitude beyond words.

Maynard, Massachusetts, September 15, 2023

Abbreviations

CC   Henry David Thoreau. *Cape Cod*. Edited by Joseph J. Moldenhauer. Princeton, NJ: Princeton University Press, 1988.

Corr   *The Correspondence of Henry David Thoreau*. Edited by Walter Harding and Carl Bode. New York: New York University Press, 1958.

Exc   Henry David Thoreau. *Excursions*. Edited by Joseph J. Moldenhauer. Princeton, NJ: Princeton University Press, 2007.

FS   Henry David Thoreau. *Faith in a Seed: The Dispersion of Seeds, and Other late Natural History Writings*. Edited by Bradley P. Dean. Washington, DC: Island Press, 1993.

IN   Indian Notebooks. Extracts Relating to the Indians, MA 596–606, Morgan Library, New York, NY. Citations follow Robert Sayre's numbering in *Thoreau and the American Indians*. Princeton, NJ: Princeton University Press, 1977. See also the appendix to chapter 2.

JM   "Online Journal Transcripts," The Writings of Henry D. Thoreau. University of Santa Barbara. https://thoreau.library.ucsb.edu/writings_journals.html.

LTRM   Joseph Nicolar. *The Life and Traditions of the Red Man: A Rediscovered Treasure of Native American Literature*. Edited by Annette Kolodny. Durham, NC: Duke University Press, 2007.

MW   Henry David Thoreau. *The Maine Woods*. Edited by Joseph J. Moldenhauer. Princeton, NJ: Princeton University Press, 1983.

PJ   Henry David Thoreau. *Journal*. The Writings of Henry D. Thoreau. Edited by Elizabeth Hall Witherell et al. 8 vols. to date. Princeton, NJ: Princeton University Press, 1981–. [Volumes indicated by Arabic numerals.]

RP   Henry David Thoreau. *Reform Papers*. Edited by Wendell Glick. Princeton, NJ: Princeton University Press, 1973.

W	Henry David Thoreau. *Walden*. Edited by J. Lyndon Shanley. Princeton, NJ: Princeton University Press, 1971.
Week	Henry David Thoreau. *A Week on the Concord and Merrimack Rivers*. Edited by Carl F. Hovde Princeton, NJ: Princeton University Press, 1980.
WF	Henry David Thoreau. *Wild Fruits: Thoreau's Rediscovered Last Manuscript*. Edited by Bradley P. Dean. New York: Norton, 2000.

Unsettling Thoreau

INTRODUCTION

Thoreau's Indian Problem

> Now I ask if degradation has not been heaped long enough upon the Indians? Is it right to hold and promote prejudices?
> —William Apess, "An Indian's Looking-Glass for Whites" (1833)

In a journal entry from March 19, 1842, Thoreau walks over the newly bare fields of Concord and is everywhere reminded that he walks in "the tracks of the Indian": "Where this strange people once had their dwelling place. Another species of mortal men but little less wild to me than the musquash they hunted—Strange spirits—daemons—whose eyes could never meet mine. With another nature—and another fate than mine—The crows flew over the edge of the woods, and wheeling over my head seemed to rebuke—as dark winged spirits more akin to the Indian than I. Perhaps only the present disguise of the Indian—If the new has a meaning so has the old" (*PJ* 1:381). He calls them "daemons," an ambivalent word denoting a supernatural being between the status of gods and humans; for the ancient Greeks, a daemon might be a tutelary spirit or a force of evil. "Daemon" captures both the power Native people held for Thoreau and their fraught legacy for someone trying to live justly in an era rife with injustice. It captures as well his difficulty in seeing through this thick colonial aura to recognize them as real people struggling, as he did, with what it meant to be a part of nineteenth-century America.

In his eulogy for Thoreau, Ralph Waldo Emerson notes that "every circumstance touching the Indian was important in his eyes," and some years later, he told a visitor to Concord that Thoreau was "more like an Indian . . . than a white man." Emerson was not alone in this view. Nathaniel Hawthorne, having just moved to Concord in 1842, observed in his journal that "Mr. Thorow . . . leads a kind of Indian life among civilized men."

Brent Ranalli has explored why so many in Thoreau's circle saw him as Indian—in his attitudes, his actions, his stolidity, even his gait.[1] This habit of mind, I argue, gets to the heart of Thoreau's Indian problem. It was a problem in Thoreau's time, when too many in his circle were eager to celebrate his uncanny "Indian wisdom" while doing little to protest the systematic dispossession of Indian people across the country. And it is a problem today, when many scholars and admirers of Thoreau remain unsure of how to square his deep interest in Native American history and culture with his conspicuous silence on his country's colonization and genocide of Native people. Some point out Thoreau's deep immersion in the savagist writing of the era and his frequent and persistent comments about the inevitable vanishing of the "red race"; others point out that few whites of the era approached Native culture with such sympathy, had such deep respect for Native knowledge, so thoroughly punctured notions of European American superiority, and proved so willing learn from Native people. Thoreau's Indian problem is that both these stances are true and that most of his readers focus on one stance at the expense of the other. In this book I would like to examine how the two fit together.

First, savagism. Joshua Bellin and Richard Schneider have laid out a clear case that Thoreau fully absorbed the ideology of Indian vanishing that permeated just about every ethnographic account of Native peoples in Thoreau's era.[2] The nineteenth-century sources that Thoreau carefully read and copied into his Indian Notebooks hewed closely to a narrative that began with an essential racial difference between the European and the Indian, quickly moved to the innate inferiority of the latter, and ended with the inevitable Indian decline when the two came into contact. Such accounts framed this encounter not as what it was, that is, one of brute conquest, but as a natural process couched in the dispassionate language of science. Savagism was often horrific at the point of contact, marked by massacres and death marches at its most brutal and by systematic dispossession, imprisonment, servitude, sexual exploitation, poverty, disease, and alcoholism in more "normal" conditions of U.S. hegemony. Thoreau's life was bracketed by major Indian wars: the First Seminole War from 1815 to 1817 and the Dakota War of 1862. In between, through his college years and the heart of his writing life, were Black Hawk's War (1832); the Creek, Choctaw, Chickasaw, and Cherokee Trails of Tears (1831–38); and the systematic genocide of California Native peoples during the 1850s. It is important to keep in mind that regions of the country far removed from the blood-soaked frontier played their part. Nostalgia for a vanished Indian past in places like New England both naturalized the violence of dispossession and obscured Native peoples who remained on the margins. As "real" Indians vanished, whites began what Philip Deloria describes as "playing Indian," adopting the various accoutrements of Indian drag as a way of asserting their claims as natives to their region, often in the face of newly arriving immigrants from Europe.[3] Playing Indian was a key feature, in other words, of settler colonialism. Patrick Wolfe has argued that settler colonialism was a long-term structure rather than a singular event, a complex of political policies and cultural practices that sought to normalize the systematic dispossession and genocide of the people whose land settler societies claimed as theirs. As Mark Rifkin notes, settler colonialism was not a rigid ideological formation but a structure of feeling that was (and is) never fixed; Jodi Byrd describes it as a cacophony, always threatening to unravel, and hence needing to be constantly refashioned, a common sense that gives shape to a stolen world and is prone to the kind of haunting Thoreau describes in his journal entry above—an example of what Renée Bergland has called "the national uncanny." Narratives of savagism, of Indian vanishing, were an effort to put these ghosts to rest.[4]

Not everyone in Thoreau's circle fully bought into this narrative, of course. Like any ideological structure, settler colonialism was never monolithic, and it always struggled to contain contradictory voices. Ralph Waldo Emerson's "Letter to Martin van Buren" (1838) was a strident plea for justice to the Cherokee Nation, written just as Thoreau fell under his mentorship. Lydia Maria Child, in *Hobomok* (1824) and *An Appeal for Indians* (1868), and Margaret Fuller, in *A Summer on the Lakes, 1843* (1844), protested various aspects of U.S. Indian policy, its savagist underpinnings, and its brutal human toll. Yet none of these writers made Native issues central to their work, and none offered a sustained rebuke to others in the Boston literary world who traced out the contours of savagist ideology in greater and greater detail. John Augustus Stone (born in Concord in 1801) helped popularize the fashion for stories of the tragic, vanishing Indian with his wildly popular play *Metamora: Last of the Wampanoags* (1827), a fashion enshrined at the heart of a new American literature by James Fenimore Cooper's Leatherstocking novels. Closer to Thoreau's own writing life, Henry Wadsworth Longfellow's *Song of Hiawatha* (1855) acted out in trochaic tetrameter the inevitable vanishing of the "noble savage" traced by George Bancroft in his *History of the United States* (1834–1874). Francis Parkman, in *The Oregon Trail* (1849), offered a firsthand view of the march of settlement; in his portrait, the Lakota "savages" were anything but noble. It is important to keep in mind, too, that the cadre of liberal Eastern advocates for Indians were the ones who developed the Dawes Act of 1887 and the Indian boarding school system later in the century, advocating what might be termed a "soft version" of savagism that had devastating effects.

There is no shortage of evidence that places Thoreau within this savagist framework. Several of his comments about members of the Penobscot Nation in "Ktaadn" (1848) are full of scorn. An early one establishes a framework for the essay: "I observed a short, shabby, washerwoman-looking Indian—they commonly have the look of the girl that cried for spilt milk—just from 'up river' . . . take out a bundle of skins in one hand, and an empty keg or barrel in the other, and scramble up the bank with them. This picture will do to put before the Indian's history—that is, the history of his extinction" (*MW* 6). Even at the end of "Ktaadn," after Thoreau has vented his anger at Louis Neptune for what he simply assumes is a bout of drinking, the most sympathy Thoreau can muster for Neptune remains fully within the logic of Indian vanishing, as an "ancient and primitive man" who is "but dim and misty to me, obscured by the aeons that lie between the bark canoe and the batteau" (*MW* 79). Most of his comments about Native people throughout his work fall into this nostalgic mode of savagism: one of his earliest journals rhapsodizes Tahattawan's memory on the banks of Musketaquid on October 29, 1837, and as late as January 23, 1858, Thoreau mourned the inevitable vanishing of the Indian. "Who can doubt," he writes, "this essential & innate difference between man & man—when he considers a whole race—like the *Indian*, inevitably & resignedly passing away?" (*PJ* 1:8–9; JM 25:55). Thoreau's encounters with his Penobscot guides, Joe Attean and Joe Polis, may have powerfully shifted his thinking, but they did not lift him out of the orbit of savagism, and although Thoreau was attentive to the lesson on Penobscot politics offered by Polis, he was not moved, as he was with slavery, to call his nation and his neighbors to account for their role in Native dispossession. Thoreau wrote "Resistance to Civil Government" to explain his act of civil disobedience, but while he did not approve of a government that waged war against Native peoples, violated treaties, and uprooted tribes, he spent his night in jail to protest slavery, not colonialism. His journal documents several occasions when he helped fugitive slaves to freedom, but he did not risk arrest or worse by helping Native individuals escape an unjust law.[5] He criticized his countrymen for seeking gold in California in

"Life without Principle" (1863) but not for the appalling string of massacres of California Natives; he criticized his neighbors for being too attached to their property in *Walden*, but he didn't make the connection between their foolish pursuit of wealth and the impoverished Native people who lived on the margins of New England society. Thoreau sought out Indigenous people on occasion, but he seemed most comfortable with the vanished ghosts of Musketaquid—happiest when he added their relics to his growing collection of lifeless artifacts.

Yet while this is all true, it is not entirely fair to Thoreau. He was, for one, deeply interested in Native culture and history at a time when most saw it as mere savagery. The Indian Notebooks, for all the savagism they reproduce, also reveal a deep, sustained interest in Indigenous people. There, he wrote down many of the oral traditions that the kind Polis tried to tell him while crossing Moosehead Lake, gathered by white ethnographers like Ephraim Squier and Henry Rowe Schoolcraft. There, he gained an awareness that what came to him from contemporary white ethnographers was deeply limited. He increasingly sought out books by people who had spent significant time in Native communities, including several by Native writers. Thoreau read widely among the savagist ethnographers of the era, yet he also notes in these authors evidence of the sophistication of Indigenous cultures, from Peruvian highways to the extensive mounds of the Ohio Valley. Thoreau also notes his skepticism about more extreme ideas, juxtaposing Alexander von Humboldt's caution about judging Native capacity based on a colonized population with Samuel George Morton's dismissive summary of Indian ability and adding four exclamation marks where Schoolcraft posited an Old Testament ancestry for a Native group. Clearly, while Thoreau was fully immersed in the savagist norms of the most popular ethnographers, he remained a critical reader.[6]

Thoreau's ambivalence was apparent in his few meetings with Native people in Massachusetts. Daniel Ricketson, his friend in New Bedford, was eager to show Thoreau some of the local Natives, and on visits in 1855 and 1856, the pair tracked down some members of the Wampanoag community in the area: Sepit and Thomas Smith and Martha Simons. It is clear that Thoreau sees these people as relics, the last of a vanishing race. He passes the small but thriving Wampanoag village of Herring Pond on his way to Cape Cod in 1857, but Thoreau barely pauses before proceeding on to Sandwich.[7] After the intrusive encounters with the Smiths and Martha Simons, this meeting is more respectful, but it may also signal Thoreau's lack of interest in Native people who lived comfortably in nineteenth-century Massachusetts.

This may also explain why Thoreau never visited the place in Massachusetts most likely to upend Indian stereotypes. Mashpee, on Cape Cod, was the largest Native community in the state, a town of several hundred Wampanoags who, in 1834, with the aid of the Pequot minister William Apess, won the right of self-government after a long campaign of civil disobedience that included, for Apess, a month in a Cape Cod jail. Their struggle seemed perfectly suited to capture Thoreau's attention—a combined political, spiritual, and environmental declaration of independence. The woods and waters the Mashpee fought to preserve were not simply economic resources for the tribe; they were an ecosystem foundational to the tribe's being.[8] Thoreau should have been drawn to it like a magnet. And yet he passed twice within a few miles of Mashpee, never even mentioning the tribe or the town. For a view of Thoreau as an enlightened social justice advocate in a dark era of American history, it's a problem.

Thoreau's most sustained encounters with Native Americans were with his Penobscot guides in Maine. The wide range of Thoreau's attitudes are on display in the essays collected in *The Maine Woods*, from savagist scorn to deep respect for Indigenous knowledge and a growing awareness of how people like Joe Attean and Joe Polis could integrate a rich and comprehensive Native world into a rapidly developing United States. While there is a general trajectory in Thoreau's view of Native people away from savagist caricature, it's not an even one, as his 1858 comment about racial distinction suggests. Without the example of Joe Polis stepping from his birchbark canoe to his neat framed house right before him, Thoreau falls too easily back into the well-worn savagist groove.

Yet Attean and Polis had given him plenty to think about, and I suggest that these encounters helped illustrate a fundamental tension in Thoreau's interest in Native Americans. On the one hand, his encounters with Native people often shifted him out of his savagist certainties, helped him critique the settler colonial norms that shaped nineteenth-century America, and enabled him to see them (at times) as neighbors struggling to secure their place in a troubled society. On the other hand, Native people were, for Thoreau, more often a means for him to explore what it means to be "native" in America. Part of this project was learning to better understand the land he called home. Early in his career, in "Natural History of Massachusetts," Thoreau held out a vision of a science informed by what he termed "a more perfect Indian wisdom," and Thoreau's long study of Native Americans might be better seen not as a disappointing counterpoint to his antislavery writing but as a component of his interest in natural history (*Exc* 28). Robert Sattelmeyer makes the following point: "This interest in the pre-history of American Indians was really an interest in the possibility of recovering whatever primal wisdom and knowledge that the Indian might have possessed and that the civilized man had lost." Sattelmeyer suggests that if Thoreau had ever planned to write a book about Native people, he gave it up by 1859 as his interest in phenology grew, but it would be more accurate to see these two pursuits as increasingly intertwined.[9] They fed into a larger project that might be termed, to draw on the Potawatomi botanist Robin Wall Kimmerer's phrase, "becoming indigenous to a place": a deep understanding of interconnectedness and reciprocity that extends to all members of the human world, and far beyond it.[10] This concept is powerful and a bit amorphous, but it indicates the complex process of learning to live responsibly in a certain place, becoming a mindful member of a community that treats all its members—human and more-than-human—with respect.

Thoreau's Indian project transformed into what might be termed, following Kimmerer, his "indigenous" project, an effort not to redress a specific evil in human society, as his antislavery work tried to do but to refashion ethics by reaching beyond the human world and establish an alternative way of being in place different from what he saw around him in nineteenth-century America. The term "indigenous" is a problematic one when used to describe the work of a European American writer, and I use it to highlight such concerns. Thoreau never applied it to himself, though he notes, in his late "Succession of Forest Trees" (1860), that the farmers of Concord "come as near to being indigenous to the soil as a white man can be" (*Exc* 165). One key feature of settler colonialism, as Jace Weaver, Jean O'Brien, and Jodi Byrd note, is the process of settlers claiming indigeneity for themselves in order to fully erase a Native claim to their land, to separate themselves from their European homelands, and to establish priority over more recent immigrants. This is not, of course, how Native people use the term themselves. Byrd draws on the definition by Taiaiake Alfred and Jeff Corntassel: "The communities, clans, nations and tribes we call Indigenous peoples are just that: indigenous to the lands they inhabit, in contrast to and in contention with colonial societies and states that have spread out from Europe and other centres of empire. It is this oppositional, place-based existence, along with the consciousness of being in struggle against the dispossessing and demeaning fact of colonization by foreign peoples, that fundamentally distinguishes Indigenous peoples from other peoples of the world."[11] As Kimmerer notes, "indigenous" is a birthright term fully available only to people rooted in Native communities, and she offers "naturalized" as a better alternative for non-Native people who want to live responsibly in their new home. But this word, too, comes with strong ethical imperatives.[12] If a naturalized person wants to learn from the deep-rooted wisdom of Native peoples how to live more ethically and sustainably on one's home ground, that person must fully acknowledge the history that brought a settler society to a land they are just beginning to fully see and to partner with Native communities as they work to survive—and thrive—in lands from which they had long been dispossessed. Otherwise, an effort by a white writer to become more "indigenous" to place is another act of replacement, another step in the ongoing genocide of Indigenous people.

How far Thoreau went in meeting these obligations is the subject of this book. There is no question that he sought to learn from Native people, that he valued their knowledge and sought to understand how to remake American society along more ethical and sustainable lines. He learned, too, to see and to cherish the long stewardship of Native peoples for the land he also loved. Yet while he at times acknowledged the long violence of colonial dispossession that allowed him to make Concord and New England his home, it was never central in his work and never sparked the political outrage that fueled his abolitionist writing. And though he sought out Native people, he had a difficult time seeing them as anything more than relics of a primitive age, and it never seems to have occurred to him that he might work *with* them rather than simply write *about* them. Thoreau's Indian project, in short, was bound up with the settler colonial ideologies of his era, and although he pushed against these bounds more than many of his contemporaries, he never shook free of them. If we can see his limits with greater clarity more than a century and a half later, we can also recognize how they continue to shape our world.

Thoreau's encounters with Indigenous people were almost always problematic, indelibly marked by the pervasive ideology of savagism. One way he was able to break out of the deep ruts of racial prejudice was to focus on the more-than-human members of the Indigenous community. Thoreau's deep interest in botany—particularly the native plants of Musketaquid—offered him a different way of thinking about place and, ultimately, people. We glimpse this in Thoreau's encounter with Martha Simons, "the only pure-blooded Indian left about N. Bedford," on June 26, 1856, where a thoroughly colonial exchange is suddenly shifted when the conversation turns to the plants Thoreau has stuck in his hat band (JM 21:137). In *Walden*, Thoreau turns from the village to the woods and waters on the edge of town, weaving both the former human inhabitants (Black, Irish, French Canadian, white and Native) and his many brute neighbors into a community rooted in a very different environmental ethos from the one shaping Concord. Once he has lost the world, he begins to "discover the infinite extent of his relations" and to speak the language of Musketaquid (*W* 171).

In *Walden*, Thoreau learns to listen closely to what the woods have to tell him. Native people themselves have little to say. Thoreau did not model his life at Walden Pond on Native examples—his own experiment in simplified agriculture centered on raising white beans to trade for rice, rather than an effort to re-create the Three Sisters method that had sustained Native people along the Musketaquid for centuries. It is possible that he had not learned about such methods when he started hoeing his beans; more likely, his lack of interest in Native farming suggests that Thoreau was less focused on reproducing Native technologies than he was in reimagining his relationship to the land he called home. His is an indigeneity not of politics or economics but of poetry—a way of using "Indian wisdom" to reimagine settler connections to place rather than to deal justly with the specific people who had long inhabited it and with their relatives and descendants still living on New England's margins.

His encounters with Native people underscores this distinction during the period. In terms of cultural contact in his years at Walden Pond, Thoreau had more direct and extensive engagement with his Irish and African American neighbors—people better termed "arrivants" rather than "settlers."[13] His contacts with Penobscots during his 1846 trip to Maine were abortive, tending to affirm the savagist notions that permeated his reading about Indigenous people. Although Thoreau sought out Native people who lectured in the Boston area or traveled through Concord, including a Penobscot family who camped near town in November 1850 (Concord, it turns out, was an outer edge of the Penobscot world), deeper engagement with Native people in their own homelands, captured in "Chesuncook" and "The Allegash and East Branch," would come later. In the years between the publication of *A Week on the Concord and Merrimack Rivers* and *Walden*, Thoreau began his more systematic ventures into science, conceiving of his phenology project and *Wild Fruits*; he also started gathering his Indian Notebooks and reconceived the Journal not as raw material for other projects but as a way to embed himself in the Concord environment. This shift, I suggest, is not a turn from transcendentalism toward science, nor toward an abandoned Indian book, nor toward a parochial interest in the merely local, but instead an effort to better understand the wellspring of each. And the best place to see these strands intersect is in the magnum opus of Thoreau's late career, the Journal.

Thoreau's "indigenous project" is particularly evident in a pair of journal entries from March 1858—a year after his final trip to Maine and the time when he submitted "Chesuncook" to the *Atlantic Monthly*. On March 5, Thoreau recounts a lecture he attended by "a Chippeway Indian, a Doctor Mung-somebody,—assisted by a Penobscot, who said nothing." This was the Mississagua lecturer and performer Maungwudaus, or George Henry, a contemporary of George Copway who traveled throughout Europe and North America from the 1840s to the 1860s with a varied troupe of companions. The Penobscot, Thoreau was surprised to find, was Joe Polis's brother, either Newell or Piel Pole Polis—perhaps the one Joe had inquired about while guiding Thoreau in Maine the summer before, who had been absent for over a year.[14] Thoreau records a good amount of ethnographic material from Maungwudaus, who shared some Ojibwe artifacts, offered a theory of his tribe's connection to the Jews, and spoke with the "bow-arrow tang." He is more struck with Polis, who shares some language notes and then inspires a remarkable passage by Thoreau:

> Our scientific names convey a (very) partial information only—they suggest certain thoughts only—It does not occur to me that there are other names for most of these objects, given by a people who stood between me & them—who had better senses than our race. . . . How much more conversant was the Indian with any wild animal or plant than we are—and in his language is implied all that intimacy, as much as ours is expressed in our language—How many words in our language about a moose—or birch bark! And the like. The Indian stood nearer to wild nature than we. . . . It was a new light when my guide gave me Indian names for things, for which I had only scientific ones before. In proportion as I understood the language I saw them from a new point of view.

> A dictionary of the Ind. Language reveals an other & wholly new life to us. . . . It reveals to me a life within a life—or rather a life without a life—as it were threading the woods between our towns still, & yet we can never tread in its trail. The Indian's earthly life was as far off from us as heaven is. (JM 25:106–8)

Language, for Thoreau, blossoms here first into epistemology—a medium for understanding the world with a vividness and intricacy that Western science cannot hope to match—and then into ontology, a way of being in the world. Language is rooted in practical knowledge, Thoreau notes later in the journal entry, and when rooted in Native technologies, words "bring you to the ground" (JM 25:106–8). Thoreau had just been revising "Chesuncook" (which he sent off the same day he wrote this journal entry) and doubtless had reviewed the manuscript that would become "The Allegash and East Branch" before deciding not to publish it, for fear of giving offense to Joe Polis—a decision his brother's appearance no doubt affirmed. The lecture clearly reminded Thoreau how much the Penobscot world was woven of words and how tightly those words held a people and their land together. The English may have settled New England, but the Polises demonstrate that there is "life within a life—or rather life without a life—as it were threading the woods between our towns still." This phrase captures the ambiguous status of Native peoples in New England, at once within and without the settler colonial world, not entirely present, but not vanished either, living a marginal life "still," tethered to the land by their language in a bond their white neighbors can barely imagine. It comes near to describing the kind of nested sovereignty that Audra Simpson argues is a key feature of Native life, of coexisting and nonoverlapping communities, allegiances, and worldviews and that Joe Polis himself had allowed Thoreau to glimpse at the end of their voyage.[15]

Thoreau, at one point, mused about learning to speak Penobscot, and he was invariably eager to gather word lists and try out Native terms when the opportunity arose. Yet he never seems to have seriously tried to learn a Native language, though some of his white contemporaries did. A later journal in that same month suggests why. The entry from March 20, 1858, is typical of his later entries, a long account of an excursion through the local landscape punctuated with observations of local plants and animals. The village world is present, but it recedes to a comparative afterthought as Thoreau and his companion, Ellery Channing, "thread the way through woods between towns" and grow attuned to their environment. Once they do, a Native trace appears: "I had noticed from the Cliff by Lee's Road," he writes, "an elevated sandy point above Pole Brook which I said must be Indian ground—& walking there, I found a piece of a soap-stone pot"—another relic for his collection, an indicator of Thoreau's uncanny ability to find evidence of the Indian past in his native ground. More strikingly, in the brook's sluiceway he finds "another kind of Ind. Pot": a wicker eelpot or fish creel. Thoreau sketches and describes it in detail—a four-foot-long cone with a smaller funnel set inside it, with a door in the narrow end for removing any fish caught within. It was as effective as it was elegant. Inside were "8 or 10 pickerel . . . and 1 good-sized perch." Thoreau's response is curious. "It was pleasant to find that any were practicing such cunning art in the outskirts. I am not sure whether this invention is Indian—or derived from our own ancestors—Creel appears to be an old English word—But I have no doubt that the Ind. Used something very like this" (JM 25:128–29). He had heard of such traps being found before, though he doesn't know who made this one. Nor does he seem too eager to find out whether it was built and tended by one of the Natives who made their way through New England, setting up camp on the outskirts of town, and who frequently appear in Thoreau's journals, or by one of the white or Black people who lived in marginal spaces like Walden Woods, hunting, trapping, fishing, and foraging to supplement meager incomes. His interest here is less in the actual person who made the creel than in a certain kind of knowledge it embodies.

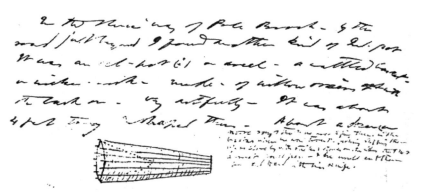

FIGURE 1: Wicker creel from Thoreau's Journal, JM 25:129. Reprinted with permission from the Morgan Library & Museum, MA, 1302.35. Purchased by Pierpont Morgan with the Wakeman Collection, 1909.

Native people had long used creels like this, a method of fishing supremely attuned to the environment. The thought inspires a striking lament: "How much more we might have learned of the Aborigines if they had not been so reserved—Suppose they had generally become the laboring class among the whites—that my father had been a farmer & had an Indian for his hired man—how many aboriginal ways we children should have learned from them!" (JM 25:129). This passage is jarring and gets to the heart of Thoreau's Indian problem. It is, on the one hand, as pure an expression of settler colonialism as we find in Thoreau. He seems to lament not that Indians vanished but that they did so a bit too quickly, before he and his kind could break through their reserve and fully appropriate their culture. Kim TallBear notes that settlers often seek to absorb some measure of Indigenous identity while denying accountability for dispossession—a tension at the heart of much of Thoreau's writing, though here he is unusually forthright in embracing his colonial legacy. Kevin Bruyneel uses the term "necro-Indigeneity" to describe the dynamic of settler memorials to a Native past—the more firmly the Native dead are buried, the more Indigeneity is available to settlers. If the fragment of the soapstone pot affirms Native absence, then the creel, likely fashioned by settler hands, anchors a kind of settler "indigeneity."

Yet the passage is marked by complicated crosscurrents. For one, it is deeply respectful of Indigenous knowledge. Thoreau emphasizes his stance in this exchange not as cold ethnographic curiosity about a savage precursor race, as so many of his contemporaries approached Native culture, but as a child learning from an elder—a role that complicates the class dynamic in the brief fantasy. Settler farmers often hired Native labor, often as part of indentures that were not far removed from slavery, as William Apess recounts his own childhood.[16] But Thoreau is not interested so much in Native labor as he is in Native culture—the technologies and knowledge that weave a people into their land. Such admiration for "aboriginal ways" was rare in his world. His desire to use this knowledge to deepen his claim to Musketaquid land was even rarer. Yet his inability to move from respect for Native culture to political action on behalf of those who still shared his land was common.

Instead of trying to find who made this wicker creel and how it fit into her or his efforts to make a living on the edge of Concord, Thoreau turns the creel into a symbol that further complicates this idyll of settler colonialism. "It was very pleasant to meet this kind of textile—or basket in our walk," he notes, "to know that some had leisure for other things than farming & town meeting—& that they felt the spring influence in their way. That man was not fitting for the State prison when he was weaving that creel. He was meditating a small poem in his way. It was equal to a successful stanza whose subject was spring" (JM 25:129–30). Not many higher categories of praise exist in Thoreau's lexicon than this. The person who wove this creel was living a life outside of the quiet desperation of the town, fully attuned to the details and rhythms of the environment around Concord, one that followed, in Thoreau's word, *aboriginal* ways. The language for such a trap was less important than the practice of using it. The act of weaving the trap is what establishes a relation between the weaver and the world, here in this marginal space between villages. The directionality of the previous passage—from language to lived relation, from epistemology to ontology, is here reversed. The creel is an exercise, then, in the phenomenology of place. The ambiguity about the creel, and the person who wove it, is crucial. It allows both the settler and the Native to occupy that place and enables Thoreau, who has woven his own basket of words from this scene, to claim his part in the bounty of spring.

This journal passage offers a useful handle on Thoreau's Indian problem. His was emphatically an exploration of place, and he increasingly saw the people who had lived in this region for untold generations not as objects of antiquarian curiosity but as custodians of an Indigenous way of knowing. European settlers lacked this. In the journal entry from May 5, 1859, he notes, "The wilderness in the eyes of our forefathers—was a vast and howling place or *space*" (JM 29:76). What these settlers needed was not a quasi-legal claim to this new land but an understanding of it. It was this epistemology, rather than the people who carried it, that was the focus of Thoreau's interest in Native peoples. Such a deep knowledge of the Concord landscape, one fully attuned to every aspect of the environment, brought with it a kind of native ontology. Careful attention to the specific materialities of place allowed the observer to see the face of God—in a sandbank by a railroad cut, in the earth's eye that was Walden Pond, or in the spirits at the edge of Spaulding's Farm at the end of "Walking." Or when looking over a familiar landscape and seeing an ancient Indian campsite alongside a newly fashioned wicker creel. Here is the pleasure of seeing a landscape shimmer into life, where time and place dissolve into an endless present.

Such a view, of course, carries with it a certain kind of ethics, and recent work on Thoreau and virtue ethics by Philip Cafaro, among others, has begun to make the connection between Thoreau's deep commitment to place and his ethical stance, weaving them together under the broader heading of *flourishing*.[17] As Thoreau became more aware of the extent of the vast environmental mesh, he became aware, too, of how human institutions—from slavery to capitalism to religion—tangled its threads. Humans were, as Thoreau increasingly realized, fully integrated into this web, and with his growing awareness came an increasing accountability to speak out when the well-being of any part of the web was choked off.

Why, then, did Thoreau not speak out against Native dispossession as he did against slavery? There are a number of reasons, I suggest—though they don't let Thoreau off the hook. They do, I hope, offer some guidance for how we approach Thoreau's Indian problem and for how scholars dealing with Indigenous issues should work with Native people. First, Thoreau. His Indian problem, I suggest, stems from his "indigenous" project. It was, for one, a project that turned away from government policy and reform politics. Indian policy, directed largely by a federal government Thoreau famously renounced, was something he steered clear of. Further, Thoreau's effort to develop his sense of *being* by enmeshing himself in the dynamics of place was a version of "playing Indian," of using elements of Native history and culture to cement his own claim to Native land—at times, this certainly aligns with the broader dynamics of settler colonialism. Yet for every instance where Thoreau plays Indian as a way of celebrating a naturalized cultural succession, there are others where Thoreau learns respectfully from Native peoples whose deep understanding of place he increasingly admires. His pattern was always to seek out sources that brought him closest to Native cultures that were fully intact and deeply embedded in place. His lack of interest in searching for Native peoples in Massachusetts stems from his belief—a misguided one, to be sure—that most of their traditional knowledge had been lost. Further still, Thoreau's goal was not to bring Native peoples into nineteenth-century American society but to use their cultural difference as a way to counter what he saw as its stultifying and damaging norms. He was thus open to meaningful encounters, especially with his Penobscot guides—moments that jolted him out of his European American complacency. The cruel fact that Native people were driven out of Concord during Metacom's Rebellion was not lost on Thoreau. His most transformative encounters were, consequently, rare and not situated in the landscape he knew best. Yet he was eager to make the most of the traces that remained, not simply hunting relics as trophies but using every artifact as a component in reconstructing a worldview that would better root him to his home ground. This is a far cry from the savagism that pervaded his world, which based its claim to Native land on the irredeemable backwardness of its Indigenous inhabitants. Most of his contemporaries had no interest in Native cultures, and even those who took an antiquarian or nostalgic interest in the people their ancestors had dispossessed felt they had nothing to learn from them beyond a few evocative place-names and stock figures from history. Thoreau sought to use Native knowledge for the benefit of his settler society, but his goal was to undermine the basic political, economic, spiritual, and environmental tenets of nineteenth-century American society. And, finally, it is important to keep in mind that while Thoreau was deeply interested in Native Americans, they were never his primary interest, even in the years when he gathered the Indian Notebooks. His great project, particularly after *Walden*, was tracing the intricate tapestry of the world around him. Native people played a part, but they were not the goal. This is not a judgment, and indeed, given that most Indian experts in the nineteenth century were agents of U.S. colonialism, it may be a mark of virtue that Thoreau closed his Indian Notebooks rather than writing a summa of the savagist notions they contained.

Thoreau's vision of a future in which an ecosystem and its people can fully thrive is powerful, but it didn't offer much help to the Native people caught in the cruel machinery of U.S. colonialism. This is the downside of his indigenous project. Its intense focus on the local landscape occluded the suffering of people outside its purview. More insidiously, Thoreau's self-appointed role as the custodian of "Indian wisdom" in Concord clearly compromised his ability to partner with Native communities—to see them fully as people adapting, as he did, to a changing world, and to imagine how his effort to learn from Native culture might, in turn, align with or undercut their efforts to preserve what remained of their political and cultural sovereignty. Thoreau worked to include African Americans and Irish Americans as a part of his renewed settler society, but it was difficult for him to imagine Native Americans as fellow citizens of his ideal state. As scholars, we need to acknowledge both the power of Thoreau's vision and its limits. And we need to engage fully, as Thoreau did only tentatively, with Native scholars, activists, citizens, and neighbors, listening carefully to their voices and taking part in ongoing conversations about how to rebuild community on terms that are just to everyone. Thoreau's writings, insightful and problematic as they are, can help foster this conversation—but they can't be the last word.

Fortunately for Thoreau studies, it is now possible to learn from a burgeoning scholarship about Native American culture and history in the nineteenth century and today, including by Native scholars. Much of this material comes from scholars working in early American studies, recovering long-overlooked voices and connecting the struggles of Native communities to survive and adapt in the face of settler colonialism in the contact era to revitalization efforts underway in Native communities today. Robert Warrior (Osage), Kristina Bross, Hilary Wyss, Joanna Brooks, Betty Donohue (Cherokee), and Bernd Peyer have focused new attention on the range of Native writers in the colonial era, often Christian Indians navigating the treacherous cross-cultural currents of this period and often using a range of literacies that preserved a Native voice outside the strict limits imposed by the rules of print distribution in this era.[18] A number of anthropologists have sought to recover the richness of oral literatures that have long structured and enriched Native cultures, gathering current versions of ageless stories from contemporary communities and retranslating or retranscribing traditions buried in colonial archives. Such work by Dennis Tedlock and Brian Swann, along with myriad collaborators, have helped make visible the incredible richness of the oral literatures indigenous to North America and have allowed us to reconstruct the world that informed some of the Native people Thoreau encountered. Native anthropologists, especially Margaret Bruchac (Abenaki), have helped recover the rich material literacy of the early Native Northeast, showing how wampum belts in particular help trace the intricate relations among Native and settler communities.[19] William Apess, whose writings were largely unknown before Barry O'Connell's collection appeared in 1992, now has two excellent biographies (by Philip Gura and Drew Lopenzina). Joseph Nicolar's account of Penobscot traditions and history, *Life and Traditions of the Red Man*, went out of print soon after it was first published in 1892; Annette Kolodny's new edition published in 2006 brought it the wide attention it deserves. A recent landmark collection has gathered writing long cherished by New England tribes but little known outside of them. Siobhan Senier's *Dawnland Voices* (2014) is a reminder that these tribes, far from having vanished, continue to build a rich literary tradition deeply rooted in tribal cultures.[20]

This follows a broader movement in Native American studies to focus less on the dynamic of the frontier, borderlands, or contact zone and more on how distinct Native communities worked to maintain their tribal integrity and use literature as one of many tools to preserve their sovereignty. Robert Warrior's *The People and the Word* (2005) is one key text in this movement that he, Jace Weaver (Cherokee), and Craig Womack (Creek/Cherokee) have termed "American Indian literary nationalism." Lisa Brooks's (Abenaki) work has focused in particular on Native New England from the colonial era through the nineteenth century, recovering the rich cultural networks that wove different tribal communities together and the many ways Native communities resisted colonial pressure by weaving themselves into the land. Jean O'Brien's (Ojibwe) *Firsting and Lasting* (2010) focuses on dismantling the myths of settler colonialism rooted in New England local history as a prelude to showcasing the tenacious survival of Native communities in New England.[21] These scholarly works are part of a larger revitalization movement of Native communities across North America that operates on many fronts—from reclaiming land through lawsuits to enforce long-ignored treaties (as with the Penobscot) to using casino revenue to fund cultural preservation (as with the Mohegans and Pequot) to efforts to reconstruct and reintroduce languages whose last fluent speakers died a century and half ago. The Wôpanâak Language Reclamation Project among the Wampanoag is the most dramatic of these, but far from the only one.[22] Native peoples have also led environmental preservation efforts from the nineteenth century to the present. Some of these efforts are local in focus but national and international in their impact, such as the Dakota Access Pipeline protests in North Dakota and the Stop Line 3 protests in Minnesota; others are more focused on key tribal territories and remain limited in the scope of their media attention, though often immeasurable in their impact on a tribal community. The Penobscot campaign for dam removal in their watershed, for example, has helped restore anadromous and diadromous fish runs and brought back a keystone of their culture, part of a broader movement of Penobscot revitalization traced by tribal members like James Francis and Darren Ranco. Siobhan Senier's *Sovereignty and Sustainability: Indigenous Literary Stewardship in New England* (2020) offers a fine-grained focus on how tribal literary production and environmental action have gone hand in hand in helping strengthen Native communities.[23]

Although the writings of Thoreau have long been touchstones for political protest and environmental stewardship for European Americans, it is not surprising that Native writers draw their inspiration from other sources. Native scholars who mention Thoreau tend to note his interest in Native peoples and his embeddedness in various Romantic stereotypes of the "Indian." The Penobscot value Thoreau's writings about the Maine Woods primarily for their detailed accounts of two revered tribal leaders, Joe Attean and Joe Polis; the Wampanoag, returning Thoreau's own indifference to Mashpee, find his writings on Cape Cod largely irrelevant to their efforts to revitalize Wampanoag culture and retell their story of survival and resurgence.[24] My book is not meant to offer Thoreau as a model or resource to Native people, nor is it a volume that fits within a Native American and Indigenous Studies (NAIS) framework—such a project would need to decenter Thoreau and foreground instead Native writers and communities as they fought to maintain their cultural and political sovereignty in a settler colonial world. Indeed, a key question for me in this book is why Thoreau did *not* seek to ally himself with Native communities when he had the opportunity. This is at once a simple and a complex question that I will return to frequently, though perhaps without arriving at a satisfactory answer. My aim here is not to apologize for Thoreau but to better understand the nature of his lifelong interest in Native people, to explore how his Indian projects shaped his other interests—in religion, in social reform, in proto-environmentalism. Indeed, the wealth of recent NAIS scholarship and activism rooted in Native communities sharpens this question, allowing us to see Thoreau's mid-nineteenth-century efforts to understand the Indian as part of a larger arc of settler colonialism and Native resistance reaching from the contact era to the present. Any reader hoping to find a Thoreau who emerges as a hero of Native American resistance will be disappointed. The growing field of settler colonial studies—led by Patrick Wolfe, Mark Rifkin, Jodi Byrd, Jean O'Brien, Kevin Bruyneel, and many others—helps illuminate much of the logic that shapes Thoreau's work.[25] These scholars show how many fields central in Thoreau's writing—ethnography, the natural sciences, history, and literature—were part of a larger ideological effort to erase and replace Native culture as ruthlessly as the machinery of conquest removed Native peoples from the American frontier. Thoreau's writing on Indians certainly played a part in this project. Yet as many of these writers also note, this ideology was never whole and complete—it was always already rife with contradictions and disjunctions that threatened to undo it. Thoreau's Indian project, I suggest, was neither wholly for nor wholly against this settler colonial effort—it was within it, and if his writings helped advance some of its goals, they also contested some of its key premises.

In this perspective, a few key themes emerge: The centrality of land to questions of identity and status. The relationship between human communities and the more-than-human world. The shifting definitions and boundaries of racial and ethnic identity in the United States. Competing versions of history, myth, and spirituality that intertwine and push against one another as cultures mingle and come in conflict. What it means to get a living in a settler colonial and, increasingly, global capitalist world. How to claim and complicate a political voice in the face of an unjust system. And what happens when we see Native Americans not as the passive objects of Thoreau's study but as people working to navigate the treacherous cultural currents of nineteenth-century America and, perhaps, wondering how this inquisitive writer might serve their cause.

Joshua Bellin and Richard Schneider, as noted above, have traced Thoreau's connection to the ideologies of Manifest Destiny and savagism, a problem that grows sharper and more nuanced in conversation with scholars focused on Native writers and issues. Studies focusing on Thoreau's engagement with nineteenth-century politics have tended to center on the abolitionist movement. Elise Lemire's effort in *Black Walden* (2009) to recover the stories of Concord's African American residents as a context for Thoreau's growing interest in abolition is an important model for this project, which seeks to place some key Native voices alongside Thoreau's work, though there is a fundamental difference. African Americans were able to build a fragile community on the edges of Concord in the wake of slavery to which Thoreau bore witness; Native people had long been driven from Musketaquid, and Thoreau saw only their traces. Recent detailed histories of political activism in Concord, including Sandra Harbert Petrulionis's *To Set This World Right* (2006) and Robert Gross's *The Transcendentalists and Their World* (2021), show how much the work of someone like Thoreau was shaped by fine-grained social forces, as neighbors and families fought over issues of justice, belonging, and citizenship.[26] Native American issues sometimes caught the attention of Concord activists (the most effective of whom were women), especially during the Cherokee removal crisis, but abolition increasingly became the overriding issue of town debates. In this Thoreau was consistent with other reformers in his community. A number of works have woven together Thoreau's political activism with his deepening interest in the natural world, showing that what Rebecca Solnit has called the "two Thoreaus" are different facets of Thoreau's larger project. Lance Newman's *Our Common Dwelling* (2005) exemplifies one approach to this problem, tracing Thoreau's incipient eco-socialism in the context of labor theory and efforts to develop alternatives to an emerging capitalist world. Another line of argument was established by Philip Cafaro in his study of virtue ethics in Thoreau—a stance oriented not around individual rights and duties but dedicated to the broad flourishing of every member of a community.[27]

Another major thread in Thoreau scholarship has shown how wide that community was for Thoreau, encompassing not just the range of human subjects but the myriad members of the more-than-human world. Drawing on the work of New Materialist theorists like Bruno Latour, Jane Bennett, and Timothy Morton, critics such as Laura Dassow Walls, Rochelle Johnson, Kristen Case, James Finley, and Branka Arsić have explored how Thoreau's deepening interest in science developed alongside an ontology that was less transcendental than immanent. The result was a kind of pantheism that saw the world of spirit not as faintly shadowed in nature but infused within it, erasing the distinctions between the human and more-than-human world and seeing every aspect of the natural world, from pencil-makers living on the shore of a quiet country pond to the waters of Walden itself, as part of a living, interdependent web of being.[28] As Alda Balthrop-Lewis and Lydia Willsky-Ciollo have argued, this approach to nature is a significant revision of transcendental spirituality, one that carries some powerful implications for understanding Thoreau's ethics and politics.[29] And while this new ontology drew on many sources, it took shape during the years Thoreau pored over his Indian Notebooks and returned again and again in his Journal and his travels to Native themes and Native people. They had, I argue, a profound impact on his work, by turns direct and oblique, admiring and disparaging, often marked by savagism and at others deeply human. Indians were, for Thoreau, both ghosts and guides, and for good and ill, they shaped his work from beginning to end.

I begin this book by situating Thoreau's early work in the twin movements of New England local history and "playing Indian." In one of his first Journal entries, Thoreau rhapsodizes about Tahattawan, the last leader of the Musketaquid, then stoops to find an arrowhead. It's a dramatic example of what Philip Deloria's "playing Indian," by which settlers lay claim to Native land by performing Native roles. This concept offers insight into Thoreau's early development as a writer, from the "Indian wisdom" of the "Natural History of Massachusetts" to his excursion essays. These works are also embedded within the local history movement in the early nineteenth century, a process by which settler historians engaged in the "firsting and lasting" of Native peoples. Both of these contexts help shape Thoreau's first book, *A Week on the Concord and Merrimack Rivers*—an excursion narrative that weaves together a deep exploration of a local landscape with the legacy of colonialism, textured throughout with Thoreau's grief at his brother's loss. These elements come together most fully as Thoreau retells one of the darkest stories from the contact era: the captivity and escape of Hannah Dustan. Thoreau's vitalist perspective emerged from this work of mourning; it was also indelibly marked by the Native American ghosts of Musketaquid.

I then turn to the Indian Notebooks—ten volumes of commonplace books Thoreau gathered from 1847 to 1860. They are a massive subterranean presence at the heart of Thoreau's writing life. They are difficult to access, and hence their impact on Thoreau's thinking has been difficult to measure, but they inform all his major work. They demonstrate, for one, Thoreau's steady interest in Native Americans, particularly in the 1850s; they also capture his expansive reading, with extensive passages from every source on Native Americans that he could obtain, from the accounts of early explorers and missionaries to government reports to several works by Native writers themselves. Many of these sources were key building blocks of savagist ideology, eager to demonstrate Anglo-Saxon superiority to Native American peoples, but others offered more nuanced and sympathetic accounts of Native culture. While scholars in more recent years have tended to pull elements from the Indian Notebooks to buttress a particular thesis, a fuller account of them, correlated with Thoreau's other writing projects, shows that the Indian Notebooks are a key point of reference as Thoreau developed his ideas about economics, politics, science, spirituality, and the environment.

My study then turns to the key works of the middle part of Thoreau's career as a writer, "Walking" and *Walden*. Thoreau began gathering his Indian Notebooks shortly after leaving Walden Pond, and the years between beginning his first Indian Notebook in 1847 and the publication of *Walden* in 1854 saw the evolution of *Walden* from an experiment in economic simplicity to something much broader—an effort to weave together the human and more-than-human world into an organic whole, founded on a deep, ethical commitment to living in place. Much of this shift is visible in the keystone essay "Walking," which Thoreau wrote in 1851 and delivered as lectures throughout the remainder of his life. The essay's meditation on westward expansion has been read by some as an embrace of settler colonialism. I argue that a careful reading in connection with the Indian Notebooks and his Journal suggests that the essay formulates a theory of what it means to live deeply in place, one that is certainly open to science and progress but also deeply indebted to Thoreau's reading about Native cultures. Both "Walking" and *Walden* celebrate a world in which humans are fully enmeshed with the wild—with nature.

The new ontology that Thoreau began developing in "Walking" and *Walden* owed a deep debt to Native cultures, carrying with it a clear ethics. Whereas Thoreau willingly went to jail rather than pay taxes that supported slavery, he was virtually silent on the brutal policies of dispossession, forced acculturation, and genocidal war that characterized United States–Native relations in this era. Although he chastised complacent citizens in "Slavery in Massachusetts," Thoreau ignored a compelling example of Native American resistance in his state. The Mashpee Wampanoag had, in the 1830s, won a rare victory for self-determination within Massachusetts and, by the 1850s, were building a community that was adapting to market capitalism while preserving a communal land base and a traditional cultural orientation. Thoreau should have been fascinated, but instead he passed within a few miles of Mashpee at least twice on his journeys through Cape Cod without stopping. Why did Thoreau overlook a thriving Native community in his own state? The Indian Notebooks offer one clue: Thoreau was focused on Native culture before the contact era. As a result, he ignored a community and, in William Apess, a writer, both of which were powerfully resonant with Thoreau's work in theorizing an individual's relation to an unjust political system and, more broadly, his effort to offer a more organic, environmental, and just alternative to nineteenth-century capitalism.

The next chapter turns from Cape Cod to Maine. I compare Thoreau's three essays recounting his trips to Maine, gathered posthumously as *The Maine Woods*, to the Penobscot writer Joseph Nicolar's *Life and Traditions of the Red Man*, printed at the end of the nineteenth century. Thoreau's Maine writings capture his evolving understanding of Native Americans, emerging alongside his increasing engagement with science and social activism. I argue that the manner in which *The Maine Woods* captures the intersection of these three themes unsettles normative European American attitudes toward the land. This process becomes particularly apparent when Thoreau's text is considered next to Nicolar's. *Life and Traditions of the Red Man* synthesizes a wide range of Penobscot traditions into a coherent written text adapted to issues facing the Penobscot community at the end of the nineteenth century. Placing these texts side by side illustrates some of the common features of Thoreau's and Nicolar's efforts to reconceptualize their relationship to the land, as well as the significant gaps between them.

Finally, I explore works that remained unfinished at Thoreau's death in 1862. Some scholars have suggested that had Thoreau lived past his forty-third year, he would have authored his Indian book; others argue that by the late 1850s, Thoreau's Indian project had evolved into the more scientific works that occupied his last years—*Wild Fruits*, the *Dispersion of Seeds*, and the Kalendar project. Thoreau never returned to Maine after his 1857 trip, and his trip to Minnesota in 1860, undertaken in poor health, included only a short tourist excursion to a Dakota gathering. Native peoples were, however, very much on his mind in his last years and final days on his deathbed. This last chapter will consider what role Native culture played in Thoreau's final writings, as well as how Thoreau was linked to Indians after his death by both his early biographers and in popular reception. Such a survey reveals a good deal about both Thoreau and the settler colonial world we still share.

CHAPTER 1

Ghosts of Musketaquid
Playing Indian, Local History, and A Week on the Concord and Merrimack Rivers

> *Musketoquid is one of their noted habitations.*
> —William Wood, *New England's Prospect*

> *Thy mother doth complain, and implores thy aid against this thievish people, who have newly intruded on our land. If this be suffered, I shall not rest quiet in my everlasting habitations.*
> —Washington Irving, "Traits of Indian Character," attributed by Irving to Chickatawbut

Thoreau was born on Native land. This was (and is) true for everyone born in what is, for now, the United States, though most of us have become quite good at ignoring it. Thoreau did not, returning again and again to the Native presence that was everywhere in his town, if one looked, from the stone artifacts that emerged every spring in the newly plowed fields to the wandering groups of Native people who occasionally passed through, camping on the banks of the Concord River or cutting black ash in the swamps for baskets. Thoreau wasn't alone in thinking about what it meant to be part of a thriving American town that had been, two hundred years before, a tentative frontier settlement and, for centuries before that, the home of the Musketaquid people. The early nineteenth century saw an explosion of interest in local history as New England towns observed their bicentennials, celebrating their relative antiquity and honoring their fading living connection to the Revolutionary era. Concord was a leader in this movement. In 1835, Ralph Waldo Emerson delivered the keynote address during the town's bicentennial, and Lemuel Shattuck published his landmark

History of the Town of Concord. Jean O'Brien, in her exhaustive account of nineteenth-century local histories, *Firsting and Lasting* (2010), notes that such accounts were ambivalent about the area's Indigenous peoples. Most noted with mixed measures of sympathy or smugness the "inevitable" decline in Native populations through disease, alcohol, or warfare, thus making room for a new people and a new history. Some looked back on the Native world the English colonists found with a measure of Romantic nostalgia; some very few drew parallels between the dispossession of Native peoples in New England a century or more before and the contemporary removal of the Cherokee. Even these individuals framed the vanishing of New England Indians as an entirely natural and just succession.

As Thoreau grew up, dividing his time between the village center and the wild edges of Concord, he remained mindful of the people who had walked the land before him. Thoreau's attitudes toward Native peoples in his youth and early adulthood, though varied, fall mainly into a Romantic, nostalgic mode. They serve as primitive foils to the ills of civilized society in a college essay; as role-playing amusement in a letter to his brother, John; and in references to artifacts he finds amid the Concord landscape and musings over historical figures. Yet as the early Journal account of his apostrophe to the Musketaquid leader Tahattawan and his finding an arrowhead suggests, Native people figured powerfully in Thoreau's sense of who, and where, he was. Both Emerson and Shattuck offer details of Tahattawan's biography, his relationship to other tribal leaders in the region, and his efforts to navigate this new colonial world. Neither, however, speaks of him as Thoreau does in *A Week on the Concord and Merrimack Rivers*, when, approaching Lowell, he refers to Tahattawan as "our Concord sachem" who came "to catch fish at the falls" (*Week* 80). The phrase nicely captures Thoreau's ambivalence. Is "our Concord sachem" nothing more than a mascot, an emblem of local pride asserted against this upstart mill town, signaling Concord's priority among Middlesex County towns by brandishing the person who sold the land for this first inland English settlement? Or is Thoreau acknowledging, even if playfully, his allegiance to a person so as to signify a deeper connection to this landscape than any mere paper title could assert? Tahattawan and his people had long since been dispossessed, but he still held some kind of power over Thoreau, something that made it hard to turn the page on New England's Indian past. Thoreau was not alone in being haunted by New England's Native past—in seeing Indian ghosts. But he saw them more clearly than most.

Seeing Indian ghosts, of course, does not free Thoreau from the strictures of settler colonialism—indeed, such a habit is very much part of its fabric. On the one hand, seeing Indian ghosts made it that much harder to see the Native peoples who were very much alive in nineteenth-century New England. As O'Brien traces at length, the obsession with New England's past during this era was an integral part of a broader dynamic of American colonialism, a systematic effort to naturalize a brutal legacy of dispossession that was very much ongoing. But what emerges in Thoreau's work in the early part of his writing life—up to and including his writing of *A Week on the Concord and Merrimack Rivers*—doesn't fit easily into the categories of "firsting and lasting" that O'Brien traces everywhere in this period, including in local histories like those by Emerson and Shattuck. Indeed, I argue that Thoreau's work, deeply indebted as it is to the local histories of the era, works to unsettle colonial history even as it affirms an American national teleology in two ways. First, Thoreau's focus on the natural world offers a different frame of reference from other settler histories, driven as they are by a narrative of progress centered on the human use value of the environment, with increasingly productive economies of exploitation. *A Week* and its predecessor texts gesture toward a holistic vision of humans and their environment that draws partly on his reading in geology and other sciences and partly on what he calls, in "Natural History of Massachusetts," "a more perfect Indian wisdom" (*Exc* 28). Second, Thoreau's primary goal in *A Week* is not some version of triumphalist history but the work of mourning his brother, John—a project that brings to Thoreau's account of the land and people of New England an array of powerful subconscious forces that resist any tidy social—or personal—closure. Thoreau, in writing *A Week*, summons his brother from the past, and he doesn't come alone. The boat the brothers rowed along the Concord and Merrimack Rivers was called, after all, the *Musketaquid*.

Musketaquid and Concord

Concord's Native history reaches back to the end of the last ice age—lithics found in the area include every era from the archaic hunters who followed megafauna across what was then tundra to just before contact with Europeans. Musketaquid was a well-known village located at the edge of three larger tribal territories: the Massachusetts to the east, the Nipmucs to the southwest, and the Pawtuckets to the north. While Musketaquid was part of the Massachusett federation—Squaw Sachem, the leader of the Massachusetts in 1636, signed the deed for the land that became Concord along with Tahattawan—the village had strong ties to its neighboring Native communities.[1] By the time Simon Willard arrived to set up a trading post at their village, at the confluence of the Sudbury, Assabet, and Concord Rivers, the Musketaquid had long been part of the trading networks that brought beaver and other furs to European ships in exchange for muskets, metal cookware, beads, and other manufactured goods. Brian Donahue, in *The Great Meadow* (2004), documents the richness of the land and the sophisticated agricultural practices that sustained a population of about a thousand for centuries. The area known as the Great Fields, a mix of sandy soil and loam close to the Concord River, was easily worked with hand tools, and the spring migration of fish, which were harvested and planted in the fields, supplemented the fertility of the soil beyond what was maintained in the Three Sisters combination of corn, squash, and nitrogen-fixing beans. Every spring, the Musketaquid people set fire to the undergrowth in the forests to foster the growth of berries, to improve the habitat for deer, as well as to make hunting easier. One sandy stretch of river just upstream from the confluence with the Assabet was particularly rich in mussels, and a thick shell midden nearby (a favorite source of artifacts for Thoreau) bore witness to what must have been a long tradition of regular feasts. Nearby, in what are now Acton and Carlisle, was an important ceremonial center, with serpent-shaped stone structures and memorial cairns in profusion. The people of Musketaquid had thrived for many centuries in a landscape of lush woods, meadows, and fields, all carefully managed to ensure that the natural world thrived alongside them. They combined their rituals of subsistence with larger ceremonies that gathered people from across the region and joined them in culture and trade. That landscape was vastly different from the cleared fields, widely scattered farms, and thriving manufacturing village of Thoreau's time, yet signs of this long past were everywhere, and Thoreau gradually learned to see them.[2]

In Thoreau's time, few European Americans cared to look beyond the broad outlines of what they considered "savage" life. Most nineteenth-century accounts of Indian history noted the devastating epidemics that spread through the New England tribes, wiping out some villages and prompting others to combine their dwindled populations. Fewer commented on the conflicts among Native peoples that were fueled by a number of colonial forces: the disruption of power balances that followed the epidemics, the rivalry for furs and trading posts, and the political maneuverings of English, Dutch, and French agents who spurred these rivalries to advance their own imperial interests. The Musketaquid, along with their neighbors along the frontier of English settlement, struggled to adapt to this new and rapidly changing world. After Tahattawan moved his people to Nashobah, the village was reorganized as a Praying Village, one of a dozen or so Christian Indian communities in Massachusetts. Few of these villages survived Metacom's Rebellion. Caught between their relatives fighting against the English and increasingly hostile settlers, some Praying Indians joined the English army, others took up arms with Metacom, and most searched for a place to ride out the war. The Nashobah were driven from their village in Littleton to Concord, where they were given refuge by the lawyer John Hoar; soon, however, they were seized by a group of militia and forced to join other Christian Indians on Deer Island in Boston Harbor—America's first concentration camp.

Only a handful of Nashobah Indians returned after their internment on Deer Island, and one brutal episode illustrates why. In August 1676, as the war was winding down, a group of six Nashoba women and children were given permission to leave Watertown, where they were housed, to pick berries at Hurtleberry Hill, on the edge of Concord. They were met by a group of colonial soldiers on patrol, who saw their pass and exchanged bread and cheese for berries. After they parted, four of the soldiers circled back and killed all six women and children, stealing their coats and hiding the bodies. One of the murderers was Daniel Hoar, the son of John Hoar, who had tried to protect the Nashobah earlier in the war. Two of the murderers were hanged; Daniel Hoar was pardoned. (One of his descendants was Edward Hoar, Thoreau's frequent travel companion.) The Nashobah who survived the war and returned to their village kept their small community going for another generation, but by the early eighteenth century, any who might claim Musketaquid ancestry had joined their Natick or Nipmuc relatives living quietly on the margins of Massachusetts society or joined Abenaki groups in far northern New England and Canada.[3] By the time Thoreau started gathering lithics from Concord's fields, there had been no viable Native community in or near Concord for over a hundred years. Native people still passed through town on a regular basis, and there may have been a few individuals in town who quietly acknowledged some measure of Native ancestry, but the people of Musketaquid had left.[4]

Local histories, however, were just getting started, and it is worth tracing some of their common features to better gauge Thoreau's efforts to come to terms with the ghosts of Musketaquid. Jean O'Brien reviewed hundreds of these histories from across New England written between 1800 and 1880. English settlers, as imagined by their nineteenth-century historians, fashioned modern American society against the backdrop of "uncivilized" Natives who, despite their long and complex history, remained "forever ancient." In the words of one historian, "They made no history."[5] Once the first English settlers arrived, it remained only to note the passing of the last Indian in a given town—often, an old man or woman whose children were named without irony. By a racial logic exactly the inverse of that applied to African Americans, Native individuals with any mixed racial heritage were deemed no longer Indian. Once this process of "lasting" was accomplished, the historians could begin, in O'Brien's words, "'firsting,' transforming English settlers into natives." This replacement narrative was at the heart of these local histories—a version of the genocidal logic that Patrick Wolfe deftly summarizes: "Settler colonialism destroys to replace." Many cheered on the process as a divinely ordained succession of an inferior race by a superior one. Some scoffed at those who claimed something priceless was lost in this march of progress; these were "sentimentalists [who] feel a wigwam by a waterfall was a far more romantic sight than a five-story cotton mill." One historian, Lucius Barber, registered a blistering critique of the brutality and hypocrisy of the English and American colonial project of Manifest Destiny, but even he ultimately toed the ideological line: "We may mourn over their decay and final disappearance, but who would wish them back?"[6]

These ideas were likely on the minds of the town leaders who invited the relatively unknown scion of Concord, a former minister who had just moved back to town and taken up a career as a lecturer, to give the keynote address at the town's bicentennial in 1835. Emerson's discourse largely follows the settler script, celebrating the hardy and honest group of Englishmen who journeyed from their homeland to a raw frontier. He gives more attention than most to their predecessors. "What was their reception at Musketaquid?" he asks. "This was an old village of the Massachusetts Indians. Tahattawan, the Sachem, and Waban, his son-in-law, lived near Nashawtuck, now Lee's Hill. Their tribe, once numerous, the epidemic had reduced. Here they planted, hunted and fished. The moose was still trotting in the country, and of his sinews they made their bowstring. Of the pith elder, which grows beside the river, they made their arrow. Of the Indian hemp they spun their nets and lines for summer angling." They were, in his account, a strong, noble, and kind people, and Puritan settlers named their town, in part, to commemorate their "peaceful compact with the Indians."[7]

There's no evidence that Thoreau was in the audience when Emerson gave this address. He would likely have approved of Emerson's sympathetic portrait and appreciated the deep connection he sketched between the Musketaquid people and their landscape. This was not a common feature of other local histories of the era, which typically dismissed the rich tapestry of Native culture as mere savagery. He might have been struck as well by Emerson's indictment of the English habit of Indian-hating: "The Indian seemed to inspire such a feeling as the wild beast inspires in the people near his den," he notes, before relating the "disgraceful outrage" of driving out the Nashobah families who had sought the protection in Concord during Metacom's Rebellion. Yet Emerson, too, accepted the results. "After Philip's death, their strength was irrevocably broken . . . a few vagrant families, that are now pensioners on the bounty of Massachusetts, are all that is left of the twenty tribes." After a mournful few lines of poetry, he picks up the proper thread: "I turn gladly to the progress of our civil history," he says, his "our" and "history" making it clear that New England's Native peoples are included in neither.[8]

We do know that Thoreau read Lemuel Shattuck's *History of the Town of Concord*, published later in that year—his father proudly bought a copy, and Henry cited it frequently.[9] He would have read there about the "Great Fields, extending from Great Meadows on the north to the Boston Road on the south . . . containing large quantities of open land, which bore some resemblance to the western prairies. These plains were annually burnt or dug over, for the purposes of hunting or the rude culture of corn." Thoreau was born here, in a farmhouse on Virginia Road on the edge of the Great Fields, where the descendants of those first English settlers continued to plant their own corn. From Shattuck, too, Thoreau learned the meaning of "Musketaquid"—"Grass-ground River," a term applied to both the sluggish river and the wide meadows surrounding it, as well as to the people whose lives had long been shaped by, and shaped in turn, these lands and waters. Shattuck carefully notes the names of the Natives who signed the deed transferring the six square miles of Concord to the group of English settlers: "Wibbacowett, Squaw Sachem, Tahattawants, and Natanquatick, alias Old Man, Carte, alias Goodman." The two years between the arrival of the settlers and the formalizing of the deed were, in

Shattuck's account, a period of cultural exchange. The first settlers dug what he calls "wigwams" against the glacial ridge along what would become the main street in town and planted their corn in the Great Fields in mounds fertilized by alewives caught at the fishing weir that would become the Mill Dam, where John Thoreau Sr. and his younger son would later perfect the art of crafting pencils.[10] But this moment was brief, and Shattuck was far more interested in the effort to Christianize Native peoples than he was by the limited efforts of the English to learn from those who knew the land so well. Nor did he care to devote much time to culture: "Their manners, customs and character form a subject for a general rather than a town history," he wrote. Concord, despite the peaceful relations with the Musketaquid, was strictly an English community. Shattuck devoted several pages to Metacom's Rebellion, with a nuanced account of the conflicted loyalties of the Praying Indians and an outraged description of the seizure and exile of the Nashobah Indians; ultimately, however, like Emerson, he moved on to his main subject: "The events just detailed reduced the number of Indians and prepared the way for the more safe and peaceable settlement of remote towns."[11]

Playing Indian and Indian Wisdom

Thoreau's two main sources of Concord history were fully embedded within settler colonial ideology. How closely did Thoreau follow suit? I would like to turn now to how his early writings—"A Walk to Wachusett," "Natural History of Massachusetts," and especially *A Week on the Concord and Merrimack Rivers*—engage with this broader movement of local history. What emerges from this view, I argue, is not a Thoreau free from savagism. In these works and in comments throughout his writing life, he echoes ideas about Native people as anti-modern; dismisses those who are adapting, even thriving, in nineteenth-century America; and accepts instead the inevitability of their replacement by European settlers. But Thoreau gives powerful voice to some quite different ideas as well, ones that value Native culture and wisdom, critique the whole project of modernity, and imagine another way for the settler world to inhabit the landscape they had so recently claimed. O'Brien notes that local histories engaged in the process of "seizing indigeneity in New England as their birthright."[12] Thoreau does this as well, but in ways that offer some radical revision of the terms "birthright," "New England" and "indigeneity." In these early works, a reader will look in vain for any meaningful engagement with Native people or any principled objection to Native dispossession. Indeed, these writings are better seen as part of a larger effort by European Americans to establish cultural sovereignty over this colonized land by crafting their own origin stories. As Jace Weaver argues, stories were key to establishing settler indigeneity, with literature forming "national canons . . . rooted in the soil of a new place." This process, though relentless, was messy—Patrick Wolf notes that "settlers generally had a lot to say," but as Jodi Byrd observes, the stories they told were full of contradictions and complications that never fully cohered into a uniform discourse. These settler stories are "a cacophony of contradictory hegemonic and horizontal struggles," and focusing on this dissonance enables us to see how Thoreau's early writings are at once a part of settler discourse and help break down its logic.[13]

Thoreau's interest in Indians began early. The arrowhead he found after his apostrophe to Tahattawan in an early Journal entry was clearly not his first encounter with a stone tool, and as Emerson notes in his introduction to "Natural History of Massachusetts," Thoreau had a wide reputation in town for an interest in Native people that went back to his boyhood wanderings. At Harvard, one of his final college essays proclaims, "The savage may be, and often is, a sage. The Indian is more of a man than the inhabitant of a city. He lives as a man—he thinks as a man—he dies as man."[14] This vein of Romantic savagism had been seen in American literature at least since Benjamin Franklin, who, in his "Remarks concerning the Savages of North America" (1783), used his sympathetic portrait of Native culture to satirize the corruption of European American society. Washington Irving, in his *Sketchbook* (1819), offered King Philip as a model American hero, and this pattern informs Emerson's brief portrait of Tahattawan. More central to Thoreau's understanding of Concord's Native people was his relationship with John. Laura Dassow Walls notes that "playing Indian . . . fostered a deep bond between them," citing a letter in which Thoreau adopts Tahattawan's persona and describing John's gift to the family, while teaching in Taunton, of a box of Native relics.[15] Such Indian play, as Philip Deloria has argued, might help European Americans develop a more sympathetic attitude toward Native culture and could, on occasion, foster some fruitful relationships with Native people, but the primary effect of such role-playing was to deepen settler claims to colonized territory and to members of their own community. The artifacts in John's box offered no connection to the Wampanoag community still living in the Taunton area; instead, by digging them up and shipping them to Concord, they became dead relics, mute artifacts of past that served not to preserve Native culture but instead as trophies of dispossession—an example of what Kevin Bruyneel calls "necro-Indigeneity."[16]

Yet something else is at work in their play. Walls also describes a memorial the brothers erected on Fairhaven Hill in December 1836: "A Son of Nature, Tahattawan, Sachimaupan, The Last of the Indians, has hunted, and in this stream he has fished. This crag shall be his cenotaph. Oh Indian! Where have your people gone?" The inscription, written in Latin, ends with a quote from Psalm 2 written in the Wampanoag language: "Ask of me, and I shall give thee the heathen for thine inheritance, and the uttermost parts of the earth for thy possession."[17] The epitaph is striking for several reasons. The date, barely a year after Concord's bicentennial, suggests that the Thoreau brothers wrote it as a response to the two landmark histories anchoring that event. While it follows their settler colonial rhetoric on the surface—Tahattawan is, after all, the Last of the Indians—the epigraph also unsettles the ideology of English succession. For one, Thoreau uses not the past tense in the epigraph—"he hunted, he fished"—but the present perfect, "he has hunted," suggesting a continuing Native presence. For another, as Walls notes, "cenotaph" means "empty tomb"—a common feature in ancient Greece as a war memorial, but with a different resonance in Christianity. Tahattawan, as Thoreau well knew, adopted Christianity, and he or his successors would likely have owned a copy of the Eliot Bible translated into Wampanoag, the *Up-Biblum God* (1663); Thoreau copied from the same edition the passage from Psalms. And finally, that passage, which seems to underscore the divinely ordained succession of Christian settlers over their heathen predecessors, suggests that the Christian Tahattawan, too, is divinely ordained. The ironies woven into the statement unsettle the smug narratives of local history. The setting of the inscription, too, complicates its message. Written not in a book or spoken to a crowd of townspeople gathered in church but rooted in the landscape, the message suggests that the status of people is determined not by written or spoken discourse but by their connection to the land itself. The question at the heart of the inscription—"Where have your people gone?"—hints at an answer. Those who fish and hunt on this land, those who speak with Tahattawan's voice, in short, John and Henry Thoreau, can claim to be the heirs of Tahattawan. This is, of course, an appropriation of indigeneity that was an integral part of the settler colonial playbook. But is an entirely different sort of claim than the rhetoric of "firsting" described by O'Brien. The Thoreau brothers are not tracing descent from the initial English settlers to build a community on land from which the Natives had miraculously vanished. They are, instead, through Latin inscriptions and quotes from a missionary Bible, trying to establish a kind of continuity with the Musketaquid people whose lives—whose wisdom—had been deeply embedded in this landscape. The fact remains, of course, that the Thoreau brothers here try to establish a connection not to Native people still living in Massachusetts and New England but to the ghosts of those long driven from the land they claim as home. What exactly this meant would occupy the rest of Henry Thoreau's life.

Two of Thoreau's early essays begin to work out this question. In "A Walk to Wachusett" (1843), he recounts a journey taken with Richard Fuller to the mountain that had long helped define the western horizon of his favorite Concord vistas. The journey also retraced a defining episode of Metacom's Rebellion, the captivity of Mary Rowlandson. Lancaster, the home of Rowlandson and the center point of Thoreau's journey to Wachusett, was founded on the territory of the Nashaway tribe on terms less harmonious than those of Concord. The Nashaway sachem Monoco led the raid on Lancaster, and part of Thoreau's journey followed Monoco's journey with a group of captives that included Rowlandson on their "removes" within Nipmuc territory. Several months later, John Hoar and Tom Doublet, a Nashobah, would pay Rowlandson's ransom at Redemption Rock near Wachusett. As Thoreau gazes over the Nashua valley, with Lancaster a tidy village among verdant meadows and fields, he drifts into history: "This, it will be remembered, was the scene of Mrs. Rowlandson's capture, and other events in the Indian wars, but from this July afternoon, and under that mild exterior, those times seem as remote as the irruption of the Goths. They were the dark ages of New England. . . . We do not imagine the sun shining on hill and valley during Philip's war, nor on the war paths of Paugus, or Standish, or Church, or Lovell, with serene summer weather, but a dim twilight or night did those events transpire in. They must have fought in the shade of their own dusky deeds" (*Exc* 44). Of note here is the passage's spareness. Rowlandson's narrative was immensely popular in its time and long was a prime exhibit of the brutality of Indian warfare— her family attacked, she and her children dragged off beyond the burning town into the wilderness in the heart of winter. Thoreau omits such details entirely. More striking still, Thoreau departs from the usual settler colonial narrative that cast precontact America as the dark ages against which European modernity established itself. Here, instead, the dark ages encompass both sides of the Indian wars—Paugus, Standish, Church, and Philip—all working in the "shade of their own dusky deeds." Rather than claim one line of ancestry or another, Thoreau casts them both in the shadows, seeing his own sunlit world as a place apart. Perhaps even more notable is how little space Thoreau gives to this keystone event in New England history. Mostly, he writes about the landscape, the interplay of brooks, streams, fields, woods, and mountains, the human world nestled among its folds and taking its shape according to the lay of the land. Human geography, rather than colonial history, takes center stage.

This emphasis is even more pronounced in "Natural History of Massachusetts" (1842), written just after John's death from lockjaw. Neither that devasting personal loss nor the devastation of colonial conquest are mentioned in the essay, but both absences shape the essay throughout. As Emerson had hoped when he suggested the topic to his bereaved friend, handing him a parcel of scientific surveys just published by the state legislature, the essay allowed Thoreau to imaginatively retrace the countless excursions he had made with his brother through the landscape of Musketaquid, to re-channel his grief so that it ran through the circuits of the natural world and so became reinfused with life. And although the dry accounting of the state's animal and vegetable resources had little to say about Native people, Thoreau's reimmersion in the landscape summoned them everywhere. The crow, for example, is not the one found in an avian inventory but a totem of indigenous New England: "I have seen it suggested somewhere that the crow was brought to this country by the white man, but I shall so soon believe that the white man planted these pines and hemlocks. He is no spaniel to follow our steps, but rather flits around the clearings like the dusky spirit of the Indian, reminding me oftener of Philip and Powhatan than of Winthrop and Smith. He is a relic of the dark ages" (*Exc* 12). A relic, that is, not in the sense of a dead remnant of a vanished age, like the box of lithics sent by John, but as living embodiment of spiritual power, a sign that those "dark ages" have not vanished at all. If the beaver has been hunted to extinction, the muskrat continues to thrive on the banks of what the Natives called the "Musketaquid, or Prairie River," and white trappers have picked up where the Native trappers left off. What emerges from Thoreau's account is not a sense of the economic value of the fur trade or the innovations in trapping techniques of the settlers but of the tangled web of the environment that draws humans, whatever their race, into the natural world—begins, in short, to naturalize them. Follow the warp and weft of the natural world, Thoreau suggests, and you will find the Native and, to a degree, become "native" yourself. The essay builds to a view of the world shaped not by the dry catalogs of the books he was nominally reviewing but one forged "by direct intercourse and sympathy. It is with science as with ethics,—we cannot know truth by contrivance and method; the Baconian is as false as any other, and with all the helps of machinery and the arts, the most scientific will still be the healthiest and friendliest man, and possess a more perfect Indian wisdom" (*Exc* 28). Thus Thoreau sets as his agenda natural history shaped by a colonial past. He seeks an understanding of nature from the perspective of the Native or, inversely, a history of New England with nature at its center. At the beginning of his career, at the end of his first truly Thoreauvian essay, Thoreau calls for a holistic approach to understanding the world around him, one that draws on both emotion and data, intuition and science, one learned from a direct engagement with the natural world that summons in its processes a perspective that Thoreau describes as "Indian wisdom."

With that phrase he summons a different history from the one being written in books across New England. The logic of settler histories—including Emerson's and Shattuck's—asserts that Indians have no history. Thoreau does not dispute this, but he does change the terms of the discourse. If Indian history is unavailable, even unimaginable, to someone embedded within a settler society, Indian wisdom, a way of being that takes its cues from Native culture and lifeways, an epistemology rooted in the landscape itself, is available to Thoreau. Without a strong tie to living Native communities, of course, Thoreau's use of Indian wisdom is yet another colonial appropriation, an act of cultural theft. But it can also help dismantle some of the key elements of settler colonial ideology. These early essays—"A Walk to Wachusett" and "Natural History of Massachusetts"—introduce the two key themes that would shape Thoreau's first major work, *A Week on the Concord and Merrimack Rivers*—a book that combines New England and natural history under the broad heading of "Indian wisdom."

Reweaving Musketaquid

What does it mean for Thoreau—for us—to draw on Indian wisdom to rethink our connection to a colonized landscape? One answer, I suggest, is that any insight gained from this effort is necessarily imperfect, marked by the omissions and unpredictability of an uneven cultural exchange. Settler society was shaped not just by its interactions with Native peoples but also by contact with the New England environment, and this zone of contact—its relations with the more-than-human world—is similarly marked by crossed signals, lethal misunderstandings, and sudden insight.[18] Place these two fields together—environmental and cultural contact—and the universe grows dizzying. Points of ecocultural contact were common—indeed, ubiquitous—in the long and ongoing history of European colonization. Musketaquid, or Concord, was one of these sites, and Thoreau's work enables us to glimpse how the process of ecocultural contact played out in both the early decades of settlement and the long wake of colonial conflict, at a moment when an emerging scientific epistemology was also transforming European American understanding of the natural world. In "Natural History," Thoreau reframed a European discursive field into an ecocultural one, insisting that science incorporate the human world that was everywhere interwoven with the natural one and adopt a cross-cultural framework as well.

A number of scholars have traced Thoreau's complicated relationship to this emerging scientific discourse. Jane Bennett, Laura Dassow Walls, Rochelle Johnson, Kristen Case, and James Finley, to name a few, have explored Thoreau's shift from the transcendental idealism of Emerson toward an ontology rooted the materiality of the world, writing accounts that draw on Object-Oriented Ontology and the New Materialism to show that Thoreau, in the face of an emerging scientific orthodoxy, helped map out a more embodied, decentered sense of being-in-the-world that offers a fruitful model for our world today.[19] This is, I suggest, part of what Thoreau means by "Indian wisdom." Branka Arsić's study *Bird Relics: Grief and Vitalism in Thoreau* (2016) is an important touchstone in this body of work. Her focus on mourning as the driving force of Thoreau's rethinking of materiality—his effort to deal with the loss of his brother by channeling his grief through the mesh of the natural world—offers an example of how Thoreau tempers science with sympathy. Native peoples played a role in this process, though Arsić draws more heavily on Hindu and classical Greek philosophy in tracing Thoreau's radical rethinking of European ontology.

For Arsić, the Huron Feast of the Dead, recorded in the Indian Notebooks, was more influential in shaping Thoreau's approach to mourning than his grappling with the ghosts of colonialism on his own native ground.[20]

Other readings of *A Week* frame the book as a counterweight to triumphalist New England history. Linck Johnson suggests that for Thoreau, the destruction of Native peoples was part and parcel of the loss of a "wilderness paradise"; for Robert Sayre, the violence of colonialism marked the banishment of New Englanders from Nature.[21] For some critics, Thoreau's early turn to science, especially geology, reinforced the ideology of cultural succession—Richard Schneider, in particular, argues that this framework allowed Thoreau, despite his sympathy for Native people, to naturalize Indian vanishing. Other critics, however, position Thoreau in opposition to the ideology of cultural succession. Joan Burbick's account of *A Week* in *Thoreau's Alternative History* (1987) suggests that his focus on the natural world offers a different ground for American identity and chronology, and more recent studies by Brian Gazaille and Mark Luccarelli elaborate on this theme, using the sweep of deep time or the depiction of landscape as a palimpsest to unsettle the settler narrative. Such an effort to make the past present, of course, is bound to summon the ghosts who lingered in the wake of dispossession and violence. Whether this haunting follows the pattern of what Renée Bergland has called the "national uncanny"—merely a symptom of colonial guilt—or marks an effort to come to terms with the legacy of settler colonialism demands a closer look at Thoreau's unruly book.[22]

Whatever *A Week* ultimately enfolds, the opening of the book frames it as a response to the local history movement. In the epigraph to "The Concord River," lines from Emerson's "Musketaquid" neatly encapsulate the narrative of English succession—"our river" may still be mindful of "sannup and of squaw." But the settlers in their pine houses, "supplanters of the tribe," are here to stay, and in the opening lines of the introductory chapter, Thoreau seems to agree: "The Musketaquid, or Grass-ground River, though probably as old as the Nile or Euphrates, did not have a place in civilized history" until the English arrived in 1635, replacing the "extinct race" whose departure is a given, and considering that the settlement "appears to have commenced in the spirit of peace and harmony," their departure appears to have been as natural as the rise and fall of the river's waters (*Week* 5).

Yet as quickly as Thoreau establishes the pattern of settler history, he begins to complicate it. The epigraphs that precede the opening chapter—from Ovid's *Metamorphosis* and from his own poetry, including his haunting invocation of his brother—speak not to history or the founding of nations but to a timelessness beyond history. Thoreau quotes Lemuel Shattuck in the first paragraph for his description of the river's course, which flows outside human history. "It will be the Grass-ground River as long as the grass grows and the water runs here," while the English name of Concord is entirely contingent. Humans come and go; the river "is still perennial." The wealth of natural detail in the opening overwhelms human history. "Many waves are there agitated by the wind, keeping nature fresh, the spray blowing in your face, reeds and rushes waving, ducks by the hundred . . . gulls wheeling overhead, muskrats swimming for dear life, wet and cold, with no fire to warm them that you know of . . . such healthy natural tumult as proves the last day is not at hand." The thrust here is to defy the ordered teleology of the settlement narrative: "As yesterday and the historical ages are past, as the work of today is present, so some flitting perspectives, and demi-experiences of the life that is in nature are in time veritably future, or rather outside to time, perennial, young, divine, in the wind and rain which never die" (*Week* 6–8).

Living within this perennially renewed landscape is a purposefully ambiguous race of humans. The Native inhabitants of Musketaquid are clearly extinct, but the people of the river meadows Thoreau describes are not exactly the English settlers who feature in Emerson's and Shattuck's history. They are, instead, naturalized men whose lives flow into the unsettled edges of the "Grass-ground River." "It is worth the while," Thoreau notes, "to make a voyage up this stream and see how much country there is in the rear of us; great hills, and a hundred brooks, and farm-houses, and barns, and haystacks, you never saw before, and men everywhere, Sudbury men, that is Southborough men, and Wayland, and Nine-Acre-Corner men, and Bound Rock." These place-names gradually shift from English towns to geographic features rooted in the land, and the men themselves follow suit. "You shall see rude and sturdy, experienced and wise men, keeping their castles, or teaming up their summer's wood, or chopping alone in the woods, men fuller of talk and rare adventure in the sun and wind and rain, than a chestnut is of meat" (*Week* 7–8). These are, in short, neither Concord nor Sudbury men but Musketaquid men, whose lives spring from the earth on which they dwell. They are made not from the narrative of "firsting and lasting" but from the river and land, where the grass grows and the water runs—natives who are part and parcel of the river, "a huge volume of matter, ceaselessly rolling through the plains and valleys of the substantial earth with the moccasoned [*sic*] tread of an Indian warrior" (*Week* 11). Thoreau offers both an alternative history and an alternative ontology: a shared human and more-than-human origin in this ceaseless flow of matter. Arsić suggests that Thoreau's thinking in *A Week* draws on his reading of Plotinus, whose "central hypothesis is that all matter contemplates. . . . The very motion of nature that makes beings is contemplation."[23] Yet while this view of animate, thinking matter may have roots in Ancient Greece, it travels through Concord with a "moccasoned tread," embodying the Indian wisdom of the land's Native people. Those who live in harmony with this ceaseless flow of matter carry not New England history but, to use Thoreau's term from later in *A Week*, a "mythus"—"a superhuman intelligence [that] uses the unconscious thoughts and dreams of men as its hieroglyphics to address men unborn" (*Week* 61). Matter and mythus, then, make up the hieroglyphics that Thoreau teaches us to read.

The river people Thoreau highlights are not, of course, members of the Musketaquid tribe, and if Thoreau is aware of the irony in anchoring this indigenized settler identity in a phrase that was a common motif in treaties between English and American settlers and Native nations—"as long as the grass grows and the water flows"—he makes no direct comment on it. The opening of *A Week* is, after all, a replacement narrative, a way for a settler society to lay claim to indigeneity. The "Grass-ground River" may last as long as the grass grows and the water runs, but Musketaquid people do not. In Thoreau's logic here, what matters is a shift in settler focus from seeing the land not as a backdrop and resource for European American expansion but as the very ground for identity itself. Nature, in this view, is the ultimate reality, one that shapes more ephemeral categories like "Concord" or "New England" or "America"—or, for that matter, "Indian." *Nature* matters for Thoreau, not politics or history or national identity. This stance frees Thoreau to offer a radical critique of the American settler project but also limits his ability to engage with its brutal legacy. In *A Week*, he can imagine a different European American society; he cannot imagine how Native American communities might thrive in this world.

Yet Thoreau is not blind to the rich world Native people built along the banks of the Concord and Merrimack Rivers. Indeed, his methodology for describing this world enables him to see the New England landscape and its Native heritage in ways that have proven central to contemporary Native historians. Lisa Brooks, in *The Common Pot* (2008), argues for a historiography that centers on the land itself, seeing past the settler divisions of town, state, and property to better capture the way Native cultures were woven into the natural fabric of the land, shaped by watersheds and communal resources and routes of trade from which sprang the ceremonies and stories that held the people (human and more-than-human) together in a web of interdependence.[24] Thoreau's focus in *A Week* is not on a temporal narrative of settlement but instead on the human geography of the watershed, through which he shapes his own story according to the contours of earth and water, rather than an ideology of Western progress.[25] This choice also shifts from a temporal stance of succession to one of recurrence, the perennial cycles of flowing water and shifting seasons, in which past, present, and future blur. In this framework, Native people are not fixed to a past secured by an archive of relics but part of the ongoing cycle of nature—not dead artifacts, nor even ghosts, exactly, but part of the immaterial texture of the land.[26] While Thoreau does not have the resources to trace the rich interrelationships between Native communities that make Brooks's history of Metacom's Rebellion, *Our Beloved Kin* (2018), such a revelation, *A Week* does offer a glimpse of Native peoples who live along the banks of these rivers, rather than simply appearing on stage as a prelude to the main act of English settlement.[27]

Thus the Musketaquid tribe emerges in this book not merely as signatories on a land deed but also as close allies of the Pawtucket, who in turn have strong ties to the Penacook further up the Merrimack. Tahattawan, Wanalancet, and Passaconaway may serve as the hinge in the turn from Native to English habitation, but they are also people who travel up and down the same rivers as Thoreau, engaging in fishing, hunting, trading, ceremony, courtship, diplomacy, and war. This story, told from a boat whose oars drip the same water that was cut by Native paddles, makes them present. Rowing past Nashua, Thoreau retells an account of a Penacook-Mohawk skirmish near Souhegan—154 years later, "we went unalarmed on our way without 'brecking' our 'conow' and reading the New England Gazetteer, seeing no signs of 'Mohogs' on the banks" (*Week* 221). The moment is a reminder of the complex political dynamics of the frontier, where Abenaki people tried to strike a balance between newly aggressive Native rivals like the Mohawks and the relentless English newcomers. Life in this zone was largely invisible to English colonists, and it rarely featured in the settler histories of the nineteenth century. For Thoreau, traveling in a handmade boat following the contours of the watershed, this Native past becomes visible.

Visible, too, is the great green world of New England before the arrival of the English, where the forests teemed with beaver, bear, deer, and muskrat and the rivers brought fish in their uncountable numbers to feed gatherings of Native peoples at the falls and fertilize their cornfields along the upland streams. This world was a distant trace in 1839, when New England was approaching the peak of its deforestation; Thoreau would need to travel to the Maine Woods to see this Great Northern Forest more intact, and as he gathered his Indian Notebooks in the years after publishing *A Week*, he became increasingly aware that the precolonial environment was not a virgin landscape but one carefully managed to create the flourishing world that awed the first European visitors. What he saw instead was its inverse: cleared fields and denuded mountains on the horizon, canals and locks along the waterways, and deserts where overgrazing had turned lush woods and meadows into sandy wasteland. But even here, Native people had left their mark in the traces of campsites old and new. If the Thoreau brothers thrilled to find evidence of an ancient fire circle near one of their stopping points, they were equally pleased to learn, as Henry recounted in "Thursday," that they had set up their tent at the same spot a Penobscot group had camped a few summers before (*Week* 299).

Indeed, how to characterize this New England landscape becomes a theme in "Sunday," after the brothers make their way past the site of the Old North Bridge and its newly raised memorial to the Concord Fight on to the fields and farmhouses downstream. What emerges from Thoreau's description is not the ubiquitous celebration of a fertile American landscape but something a bit more ambiguous:

> Some spring the white man came, built him a house, and made a clearing here. . . . He rudely bridged the stream, and drove his team afield into the river meadows, cut the wild grass, and laid bare the homes of the beaver, otter and muskrat, and with the whetting of his scythe scared off the deer and bear. He set up a mill, and fields of English grain sprang in the virgin soil. And with his grain he scattered the seeds of the dandelion and the wild trefoil over the meadows, mingling his English flowers with the wild native ones. The bristling burdock, the sweet-scented catnip, and the humble yarrow planted themselves along his woodland road, they too seeking "freedom to worship God" in their way. And thus

he plants a town. The white man's mullein soon reigned in Indian cornfields, and sweet-scented English grasses clothed the new soil. Where, then, could the Red Man set his foot? The honey-bee hummed through the Massachusetts woods, and sipped the wild-flowers round the Indian's wigwam, perchance unnoticed, when, with prophetic warning, it stung the Red child's hand, forerunner of that industrious tribe that was to come and pluck the wild-flower of his race up by the root. (*Week* 52–53)

This is a striking narrative of replacement. It is as relentless as any of the local history narratives filling the shelves of New England parlors and libraries, framed with an air of natural inevitability that undergirded the ideology of "firsting and lasting." Yet Thoreau frames this succession in markedly different terms—plants become the leading players in this drama, with apple and pine, burdock and wild meadow flowers standing in for English settler and Native American, the only human violence a bee sting, and the brutal process of dispossession smoothed by its analogy to the plucking of a wildflower by the root.

Thoreau decenters the Puritan founders of English towns celebrated in typical histories, generalizing instead to the slow, plodding, relentless work of the less-celebrated farmers who did the work of transforming the land, "building a house that endures, a framed house. He buys the Indian's moccasins and baskets, then buys his burying grounds, and at length forgets where he is buried and ploughs up his bones." This is not a succession endorsed by the march of Christianity or of a vaguely framed Anglo-Saxon progress; indeed, Thoreau is less interested in how New England carries the torch of progress than he is in how the English—these "New West Saxons"—become, after their name among the Red Men, Yankees. This is more than a human drama, and Thoreau injects a note of ambivalence into what is conventionally a narrative of triumph. "Everyone finds by his own experience, as well as in history, that the era in which men cultivate the apple, and the amenities of the garden, is essentially different from that of the hunter and forest life, and neither can displace the other without loss. . . . There is in my nature, methinks, a singular yearning toward all wildness" (*Week* 54). This early iteration of Thoreau's great theme will become the key principle at the heart of "Walking" and *Walden*. This first expression occurs in the context of settler history, framed to counter the narrative of progress and meant to inspire the descendants of those first English settlers to be more like the people they displaced. It is also important to note that this is not a critique of the brutality of that displacement. Nor is it a call to offer some tardy measure of justice to the descendants of these dispossessed people who still remained on the margins of New England or struggled to survive on the bloody edge of the American frontier. Nor does Thoreau wish readers to learn from the accumulated wisdom of the Native people who tended the green world, whose knowledge might restore the denuded rivers and woods to their former flourishing state—that would come later.

But Thoreau insists there is something to be learned from Native people: "The young pines growing up in the cornfields year to year are to me a refreshing fact. We talk of civilizing the Indian, but that is not the name for his improvement. By the wary independence and aloofness of his dim forest life he preserves his intercourse with his native gods, and is admitted from time to time to a rare and peculiar society with Nature" (*Week* 55). Thoreau is not so much advocating for the status of Native culture as he is undercutting the smug certainties of European civilization by drawing on a familiar Romantic trope. He goes further still at the end of this long meditation: "If we could listen but for an instant to the chant of the Indian muse, we should understand why he will not exchange his savageness for civilization. Nations are not whimsical. Steel and blankets are strong temptations, but the Indian does well to continue Indian" (*Week* 56). Thoreau has come some distance from his habit of playing Indian along the banks of the Concord River. Though the passage still relies on the logic of an essential racial difference and is fully within the logic of the noble savage, Thoreau offers a rare expression of respect for the distinctiveness of Native culture, an insistence that it is neither lesser nor bound to vanish, and a plea that European Americans learn respectfully from it.

This passage doesn't appear in the first draft of *A Week*, and Thoreau may have written it to replace one that hews far more closely to the savagist line. In that omitted passage, Thoreau writes, "The Indian has vanished as completely as if trodden into the earth; absolutely forgotten but by a few persevering poets . . . For Indian deeds there must be an Indian memory; the white man remembers only his own."[28] In this deleted passage, the Indian is emphatically in the past tense, irrevocably vanished and mute as the stone artifacts exposed by the plow. Thoreau replaces it with a passage that puts the Indian world in present tense, in conversation with contemporary New England, its wisdom still vital, deeply embedded in the fabric of the land itself, audible in the call of the owl from the forest and palpable in the flow of matter that is the river itself, moving with "moccasoned tread" through the settler colonial world. There is even a hint that the Indian will continue Indian, survive alongside the vast and violent project of the United States, making it into something different from what it typically imagines itself to be, and better. This gesture is important but very tentative—Thoreau can't yet imagine an Indian nation that embraces both steel and blankets and remains Indian. Native people are valued not for themselves but for their difference from European Americans and the example they offer of life in closer communion with the wild.

Thoreau's focus, ultimately, is not on the indigenous grasses and flowers of the river meadows but on the English plants that sink their roots into this new soil—in botanical terms, plants that naturalize. Robert Sayre notes that the people most celebrated in *A Week* are not the traditional heroes of colonial history—the town fathers and military leaders whose actions anchored the colonial project—but those who were most transformed by their life in the woods and among Native peoples, those figures who, like the real Daniel Boone or James Fenimore Cooper's fictional Natty Bumppo, weave Native and European threads into an American identity. Thoreau admires the courage of those who live or work on the frontier—"We have need to be as sturdy pioneers still as Miles Standish, or Church, or Lovewell"—but more for their abstract bravery than their actual deeds (*Week* 120). Thoreau's account of the eighteenth-century Indian Wars in New England celebrates not Captain John Lovewell, who brought his English military tactics to the frontier and blundered into a bloody ambush that cost him and half his men their lives, but instead his lieutenant, Josiah Farwell, who understood the nature of warfare on the frontier far better than his captain. Wounded and left behind in Lovewell's Fight in western Maine, Farwell led a group of survivors toward the Maine coast, helping them forage for food. His companions made their way to Berwick and Saco, but Farwell "left his bones in the wilderness. His name still reminds us of twilight days and forest scouts on Indian trails, with an uneasy scalp;—an indispensable hero to New England" (*Week* 168).

Yet Thoreau's true heroes left an even fainter mark on history. One of these is the fisher he describes in "Saturday": "A straight old man he was and took his way in silence through the meadows, having passed the period of communication with his fellows; his old experienced coat, hanging long and straight and brown as the yellow-pine bark, glittering with so much smothered sunlight, if you stood near enough, no work of art but naturalized enough" (*Week* 24). This is one of those nameless men mentioned in "The Concord River," who knit the towns together and are out in all types of weather accruing the kind of wisdom that rarely makes its way into books, let alone town histories. They are, in a word, *naturalized*. "His fishing was not a sport, nor solely a means of subsistence, but a sort of solemn sacrament and withdrawal from the world, as the aged read their Bibles" (*Week* 25). Subsistence as sacrament—this nameless old man, this ghost of Musketaquid, has seized on a thread of wisdom that Thoreau will trace throughout the rest of his life.

If this wisdom doesn't make it into Shattuck's or Emerson's histories of Concord, others learned it. Rowing past Billerica, Thoreau muses over others who made their living from the river. "One would like to know more of that race, now extinct, whose seines lie rotting in the garrets of their children," Thoreau writes, playfully summoning the ghosts of the Musketaquid people before shifting our attention to those settlers who, like the English fisher, made their living directly from the waters. He notes that "Salmon, Shad and Alewives were formerly abundant here, and taken by Indians in their weirs, who taught this method to the whites," who in turn "fed their townsmen creditably. . . . Dim visions we still get of miraculous draughts of fishes, and heaps unaccountable by the riverside" (*Week* 34). Here is a glimpse of an alternative New England history, where both Natives and settlers could live comfortably on the abundance of the rivers, both groups becoming the people of Musketaquid. New Englanders had the chance, Thoreau suggests, to become naturalized, to sink their roots into the meadows fed by the Grass-ground River. And yet these settlers, like the Native people who taught them to harvest fish and, perhaps, the ceremonies such a harvest required, are now extinct. The reason is hinted at—these townsmen stopped trying to feed their fellow New Englanders "creditably"—and so fishing became not an act of sacramental subsistence but part of an extractive economy, using the same colonial logic that built the dams in Billerica and Lowell and "put an end to their migrations hitherward" (*Week* 34). Thoreau would, a decade later, survey the Concord River on behalf of the farmers who claimed their meadows were ruined by the Billerica Dam. Thoreau's conclusions—that the rapid cutting of the farmers' own woodlots and the careless construction of bridges were at least as responsible for the flooded meadows as the dam itself—suggested that neither market farmers nor cotton mill owners were innocent in the destruction of the river's health.[29] "Who hears the fishes when they cry?" asks Thoreau, later in the passage (*Week* 37). The ghosts of Musketaquid, perhaps, but not the people who drove them from the river. But Thoreau finds hope in a longer view. "Perhaps, after a few thousands of years, if the fishes will be patient, and pass their summers elsewhere, meanwhile, nature will have leveled the Billerica dam, and Lowell's factories, and the Grass-ground River run clear again, to be explored by new migratory shoals, even as far as the Hopkinton Pond and Westborough Swamp" (*Week* 34). Thoreau does not make clear whether the descendants of the English colonists will be there to greet them, having finally learned the lessons of their homeland, or will be swept away with the dams and factories.

What is clear is that Thoreau has left behind the parameters of local history, with its tidy narratives of ordained racial succession. He mocks the parade of "great men" in the New Hampshire villages they row by, summarizing the pantheon of founding fathers in a two-page laundry list. Indeed, Thoreau abandons the practice of history altogether. Even if, for a moment, Manchester and Lowell rise on the sites of Native villages, if "the murmur of unchronicled nations has died away along these shores," these cities are still "on the trail of the Indian" (*Week* 249). This gesture toward deep time, the *longue durée*, is inspired in part by Thoreau's reading of Charles Lyell—the slow churn of rock and water Thoreau traces in the glacial potholes at Amoskeag laughs to scorn the proud history of small New England towns that measure spans in mere centuries. Thoreau's turn from history to presence also marks his affinity with traditional Native oral literatures—works that Thoreau would better come to know, if not fully grasp, as he filled his Indian Notebooks. Leslie Marmon Silko describes how the remains of human settlement in Pueblo communities, from trash to human bones, are not lifeless artifacts but living matter in the process of becoming something else. Native history, in Peter Nabokov's phrase, privileges "topography over chronology." Arsić argues that in Thoreau's work, "linear temporality is demoted in favor of different temporal moments that are simultaneously embodied and visible."[30] Thoreau turns to the sacred literatures of the Hindus and Greeks in *A Week* to serve much the same function, and if he does not know the stories told and retold along the Concord and Merrimack Rivers before the Puritans arrived with their own stories, Thoreau is attentive to their source—the cycles and rhythms of the natural world.

This effort to see natural succession through the lens of mythic presence shapes Thoreau's most powerful meditations on New England's Native peoples. Along the Merrimack near Bedford, Thoreau notes the presence of an Indian graveyard eroding into the river. "The land still bears this scar here, and time is slowly crumbling the bones of a race. Yet, without fail, every spring, since they first fished and hunted here, the brown thrasher has heralded the morning from a birch or alder spray, and the undying race of reed-birds still rustle through the withering grass. But these bones rustle not. These mouldering elements are slowly preparing for another metamorphosis, to serve new masters, and what was the Indian's will ere long be the white man's sinew" (*Week* 237). This is, of course, a succession narrative. It is different in that it runs through the currents of the natural world rather than enacting an Anglo-Saxon teleology. While Thoreau takes for granted the replacement of Indian with white, the passage radically decenters the story of European settlement. This is no savagist account of a superior race supplanting an inferior one; instead, the new settlers along the Merrimack are simply new conduits for the matter that flows through the ecosystem, a new stopping place for the atoms and minerals that make up the watershed. As Arsić notes, this naturalizing of grief is Thoreau's core strategy in mourning his brother and the linchpin of Thoreau's emerging materialist ontology. It was, she writes, a "radically anti-teleological understanding of life," one defined by the premise that "no living form is more accomplished than any other, and life therefore doesn't unfold hierarchically and progressively but, more democratically, moves simultaneously in different directions."[31] Native and white may swap places along the river, but the "undying race of reed-birds" rustles through the grass still.

If this contemplation of Native bones is a more complex moment of Indian play, then the metamorphosis at work here applies both to John's remains transforming into the sinews of this book as it does to the transubstantiation of Indian bones to white flesh. And as the passage flickers back and forth between frames of reference (personal mourning, racial succession), it undercuts any neat racial hierarchy. Neither Indian nor white, after all, controls this process—the elements will serve old or new masters indifferently. Worth noting is that this grave site is not being plundered for trophies but being treated according to best current standards of respectful management of Native graves. The bones are allowed to erode into the river, to resume their part in the natural cycles that are at the heart of Native spiritual practice. As Arsić notes in reference to the Huron Feast of the Dead, "Bones were considered not just vehicles hosting souls but were indeed indistinguishable from souls." Found here, woven into the natural world rather than locked away in stone crypts, the bones, and the Native souls they embody, are as alive as the birds perched on the wild and naturalized plants rising above the riverbank. They are anything but vanished.[32] Thoreau is thinking of the dead—of John and of the people who followed the course of these rivers year in and year out. His words, like the river itself, work a metamorphosis.

This process is most vivid in Thoreau's retelling of Hannah Dustan's captivity and escape, a story that had long been framed as a legend from a distant frontier history and the one moment in *A Week* where the trauma and grief of a colonial past breaks through the delicate texture of narrative and merges with Thoreau's own loss. How does Thoreau manage this? By weaving a story of cultural contact at its most brutal into a living present rooted in the mesh of the material world. Dustan's story seems an odd choice to anchor a book that weaves together John's loss and New England's Native past. It is as shocking as any in the long history of conflict that lay beneath the quiet surface of towns like Concord. It began in Haverhill, where Dustan and her family lived during King William's War. A group of Abenaki raided the town in 1697; having recently given birth, Dustan was captured while her husband fled with their seven other children. Her infant was killed, dashed against a tree, and Dustan and her nurse, Mary Neff, were taken north, where they would likely have been ransomed or, perhaps, adopted into a Native community. Dustan feared she would be forced to run the gauntlet and killed, so some days later, having been transferred to another group of Native people, she and a captive English boy took their captors' tomahawks and killed ten of them in their sleep—men, women, and children. After scalping their victims, the three escaped captives canoed south to the English settlements, where they received a large bounty for the scalps.[33] The story was well-known; Thoreau's is one of a half-dozen versions from the nineteenth century. John Greenleaf Whitter and Nathaniel Hawthorne both retell it, and it appeared in a popular schoolbook by Peter Parley. Her story was deemed highly appropriate for children, an example, as Hawthorne writes, of when "our great-great-grandmothers, were taken captive." Most nineteenth-century accounts recoil from Dustan's violence—Hawthorne, though mindful of the impact of her murdered babe, describes Dustan as a "bloody hag" with "ghastly visage" who better deserved to die in a swamp with her girdle of scalps than to return home and claim a bounty. Thoreau's main source is Benjamin Mirick, who, early in his *History of Haverhill* (1832), renounces any effort to portray the Abenaki as noble savages. "Nothing could justify their treacherous conduct—no plea can be urged on their behalf sufficient to palliate their diabolical cruelties." Mirick is more matter-of-fact about the "terrible vengeance" Dustan took against her captors. After weighing the morality of her actions, Mirick concludes that "a wife in such a situation would not be apt to critically analyze the morality of the deed."[34]

The episode was often treated as something from the dark ages of early settlement, an indicator of the vast gulf between the days of Indian warfare and the modern present. Yet in retelling Dustan's story, Thoreau is able, as Johnson notes, "to make the past present."[35] Thoreau has little interest in the war itself—the diplomatic and military maneuverings that shaped the events he describes are entirely absent from his account—but a great deal of interest in bringing the raw trauma of colonial violence into nineteenth-century New England. Thoreau summons not the ghosts of the murdered Abenakis but Dustan herself, floating down the same river as the Thoreau brothers when their own journey turns toward Concord, their native ground. Thoreau sets the scene both the day after Dustan and her companions slew their captors and at the moment of writing, jarring the reader out of an historical perspective that safely consigns this troubling story to the past: "Early this morning this deed was performed, and now, perchance, these tired women and this boy, their clothes stained with blood, and their minds racked with alternate resolution and fear, are making a hasty meal of parched corn and moose-meat while their canoe is gliding under these pine roots whose stumps are still standing on the bank. They are thinking of the dead" (*Week* 322). With the pine roots and the ghost trees that once filled the air over their stumps, Thoreau draws the currents of their trauma into the web of the natural world, framing these events in the timeless return of spring in the North Woods:

> Every withered leaf which the winter has left seems to know their story, and in this rustling to repeat it and betray them. . . . The stolen birch forgets its master and does them good service, and the swollen current bears them swiftly along with little need of the paddle, except to steer and keep them warm by exercise. For ice is floating in the river; the spring is

opening; the muskrat and the beaver are driven out of their holes by the flood; deer gaze at them from the bank; a few forest birds, perchance, fly across the river to the northernmost shore; the fish-hawk sails and screams overhead, and the geese fly over with a startling clamor; but they do not observe these things, or they speedily forget them. Sometimes they pass an Indian grave surrounded by its paling on the bank, or the frame of a wigwam, with a few coals left behind, or the withered stalks still rustling in the Indian's cornfield on the interval. (*Week* 322–23)

In "A Walk to Wachusett," Thoreau consigned the colonial violence of Mary Rowlandson's story to a dim, dark past; here, Abenaki blood is barely dry on these travelers' clothes. This is a complicated shift, marked by the unruly chronotope of trauma. Colonial violence here escapes the confines of history to haunt the present and, in this moment, merges uneasily with Thoreau's grief.

In Henry's imagining, he and John together witness this specter of the Indian wars glide past their campsite, as his long effort to summon his brother's ghost by retracing this journey through their New England home summons as well the monstrous violence that made this home possible. Yet the present tense of the passage soothes this trauma by weaving it into the ahistorical cycles of the natural world. Dustan's deed is subsumed into the perennial arrival of spring along the Merrimack. This green world, woven of such elements as breaking ice, muskrats and beavers, deer and fish hawks and geese, absorbs the presence of these colonials as seamlessly as the silent frame of an empty wigwam. There is brutal irony at work here. Thoreau's *present*-ing of Dustan's story, for one, echoes Native American storytelling practices. Margaret Bruchac, for example, in an account of Abenaki traditions of the Deerfield raid of 1704, quotes an elder, Lynn Murphy: "We know that antiquity exists, but we prefer to tell the old stories as if they happened yesterday. The immediacy . . . made the stories more believable. Europeans get all tied up in issues of linear history . . . it's really all about place, time and family."[36] And while Thoreau, in this shift to the present tense, makes both colonial and personal trauma more bearable, he does not summon the murdered and scalped bodies of the Abenaki men, women, and children. They remain, for him, unimaginable. Hannah Dustan's family gathers again around the apple tree against which her infant's brains were dashed, eating of a fruit that becomes a sacrament of mourning, a ceremony that weaves them into the land (*Week* 324). The Abenaki people simply vanish.

This is not a moment of haunting, exactly—Dustan and her companions are not ghosts but ancestors, figures from a well-remembered history that is, for Thoreau, very much alive, and although Thoreau briefly conjures a Native world along the Merrimack, he gives no voice to the murdered Abenaki family. Where most episodes of colonial haunting feature an accusatory or tragic Indian ghost, Thoreau's tone here is curiously neutral. He describes the Indian attack on Haverhill in oddly passive terms: Dustan "had been compelled to rise from her bed" and soon thereafter "had seen her infant's brains dashed against an apple-tree" (*Week* 321)—a moment of horrific violence that Thoreau conspicuously does not use to justify Dustan's killing of her captors. Instead, Thoreau diffuses the violence, portraying it as a ripple in the fabric of a landscape that encompasses competing groups of humans, but only as part of a system that stretches to include the wide reaches of the more-than-human world as well. Human blood has been spilt along the Merrimack, and ice is in the river, and the beaver and muskrat have been flooded out of their dens. This passage naturalizes racial succession—colonization becomes part of the natural order of things. But the present tense of Thoreau's passage also undercuts this colonial logic. History is not past, nor has the Native world vanished. As Thoreau pans above this scene of brutal colonial violence, what we see is the broad expanse of the natural world: "On either side, the primeval forest stretches away to Canada, or to the 'South Sea,' to the white man a drear and howling wilderness, but to the Indian a home, adapted to his nature, and cheerful as the smile of the Great Spirit" (*Week* 323). This glimpse of the American landscape as a primeval forest and cheerful home is not firmly anchored in the past but placed in an eternal present, and if Thoreau here echoes the opening line of Longfellow's *Evangeline* (1847)— "This is the forest primeval"—he seems more willing than his fellow New Englander to unsettle colonial norms. Thoreau finds in Dustan's story not a relic of the dark ages but an Indian wisdom that decenters the narrative of colonial succession and widens to include the two boatsmen who ponder the memory of a canoe voyage taken some hundred and forty years before.

Robert Sayre and Richard Schneider both argue that Dustan's act of violence, justified or not, carries a terrible price—an estrangement from nature that bears the bitter fruit of anger and revenge embodied in the apple tree.[37] But that isn't quite the tone of the passage, which is less of anger or triumph than of sober memory—the apple, after all, is for Thoreau not an emblem of the fall as much as a vehicle of belonging, a European seed that takes root in American soil, grows wild, and proffers a certain kind of naturalized wisdom. His writing doesn't restore the Abenaki world, but Thoreau clearly suggests that to be fully embedded in a place, one needs to begin to confront this past. The best way to do so, he suggests, is to immerse yourself not in dry and brittle archives of history but in the storied mesh of the landscape, where the flow of water through land mingles past and present. As they sail past their encounter with Hannah Dustan's ghost, Thoreau notes that "all things with us seemed to flow; the shore itself, and the distant cliffs, were dissolved by the undiluted air. The hardest material seemed to obey the same law as the most fluid, and so indeed in the long run it does. Trees were but rivers of sap and woody fibre, flowing from the atmosphere, and emptying into the earth by their trunks, as their roots flowed upward to the surface. And in the heavens were rivers of stars, and milky-ways, already beginning to gleam and ripple over our heads. There were rivers of rocks on the surface the earth, and rivers of ore in its bowels, and our thoughts flowed and circulated, and this portion of time was but the present hour" (*Week* 331). In tracing the Grass-ground River that shapes his home from the meadows of Musketaquid to the farthest reaches of the watershed high atop Agiocochook (Mount Washington), Thoreau encompasses the whole sweep of the ecosystem and its history, weaving together the disparate points of this rapidly changing world in both time and space. Dustan's apple—a European tree growing from American soil, an emblem of renewal and fertility rooted in violence—is less an emblem of cultural succession than the fruit of this contact, of mourning made present by the flow of matter through the natural world.

Thoreau returns to this motif in "Friday," when he describes Elisha's apple tree in Tyngsborough. The tree was named for "a friendly Indian" who was killed in the Indian wars and whose grave, long forgotten, was revealed when floodwaters caused the earth to settle around it. It had been lost again, "yet no doubt, Nature will know how to point it out in due time, if it be necessary, by methods yet more searching. Thus there is not only a crisis when the spirit ceases to inspire and expand the body, but there is a crisis when the body ceases to take up room as such in nature, marked by a fainter depression in the earth" (357). Nature, in short, forgets nothing—the crisis comes when humans do. Thoreau may not be able to bring Elisha back from the past, or any of his fellow natives who lived and died along the Concord and Merrimack Rivers, any more than he can bring John back from the grave, this faint depression in the earth. But he can remember the nail in Elisha's apple tree that marks the height of the great freshet, and he can remind his readers that the floods will come again. Thoreau's goal, in short, is to remember the dead and bring the living into harmony with the larger natural forces that shape all the lives that run their course along this watershed. To share the stories, in other words, that make the land and its people whole. This is Thoreau's version of settler history, and while it promises to radically remake his own society, it cannot imagine Native people living within this circle. He doesn't seek any Abenaki who might have stories about Hannah Dustan, and although he notes the Penobscot group who camped on the very same shore a few summers before, Thoreau is more comfortable imagining Native people who are safely in the past.

On his journey upstream, passing Amoskeag Falls, Thoreau recalls the Pennacook Sachem Passaconaway, whom Daniel Gookin reports meeting in 1674 when he was 120 years old. "He was reputed a wise man and a powwow, and restrained his people from going to war with the English," Thoreau writes, and then quotes, Gookin: "They believed 'that he could make water burn, rocks move, and trees dance, and metamorphose himself into a flaming man; that in winter he could raise a green leaf out of the ashes of a dry one, and produce a living snake from the skin of a dead one, and many similar miracles'" (*Week* 257). As a powwow, Passaconaway was both a spiritual and political leader, one whose primary role was to use his knowledge of the spiritual forces that shaped the natural world to maintain a balance among them. If his arts proved "unable to prevent [English] settlement," then he counseled peaceful accommodation—a stance his son Wanalancet followed during Metacom's Rebellion (*Week* 253). Thoreau was no political leader or diplomat, and he has little to say about Indian-white relations in Passaconaway's time or his own. But he has much to say about the spiritual forces that shape his world. In the second draft of *A Week*, he suggests that Passaconaway was "a sort of transcendentalist in his day," which suggests in turn that Thoreau was a sort of powwow in his own.[38] It is not clear why Thoreau omitted the remark from the final version—he may have understood that his book was already pushing too far past New England orthodoxies—but it is clear that Thoreau saw some affinities with his countryman. He, too, summoned the ghosts of

Musketaquid, and he, too, sought to restore a kind of balance to a world that was already, at this dawn of industrial capitalism, threatening to spin out of control. And if there were no graves or monuments along "their native river" to mark the passing of Passaconaway or Wanalancet, Thoreau would weave their stories into his book.

But if Thoreau sought to claim, in some manner, Passaconaway's role as a keeper of story and spirit along the Concord and Merrimack, he did not claim the other part of a powwow's role: as a political and social leader of the people. This is the paradox of Thoreau's attitude toward Native peoples in his early essays and *A Week*. On the one hand, he rejects the celebratory ideology of "firsting and lasting," of Indian vanishing and Anglo-Saxon supremacy—a key feature of savagism and the settler colonial world that very much included Thoreau's Concord. Instead, he adopted some of the same discursive practices Native peoples used to build their ties to one another and to their land—a geographic imagination tied to the natural features of the environment rather than to abstract political boundaries; a sensibility that saw the human and more-than-human world as intricately connected and very much equal, rather than hierarchical; a sense of time that was mythological and circular, rather than historical and teleological. And yet he accepted the succession of races in New England, smoothing the brutal process of colonization and dispossession under the broad sweep of Nature's ceaseless churn. Further, he showed little interest in the Native peoples still living in New England, preferring the ghosts of Musketaquid he could summon along the shore to their living descendants and relatives struggling to keep their communities together in nineteenth-century New England. It may have been easier to see John among these ghosts, a kind of playing Indian that kept his brother's spirit visible among the waterways, meadows, and woodlands they both loved. But it meant the only Indians he saw were ghosts.

CHAPTER 2

Savagism and Its Discontents
The Indian Notebooks

Men lived and died in America, though they were copper-colored, before the white man came.

What a vast difference between a savage and a civilized people.
—Henry Thoreau, Indian Notebooks (7:112, 115)

In reading through Thoreau's Indian Notebooks, I came across something unexpected as I neared the end of the final volume. In the middle of a long extract about the Greenland Inuit was a three-page essay by Thoreau critiquing people's tendency to judge a thing's importance by its size. A "small potato is a little thing—a big one a great thing . . . a hippopotamus is a great thing—a dove a little thing . . . a great big cheese which it took so many oxen to draw is a great thing—a snow flake a little thing" (IN 12:320).[1] The great husk is celebrated, the kernel of truth dismissed. For journalists and politicians, "great things are not great but gross—they are some pumpkins. Their little things are not little but fine—they are some huckleberries" (IN 12:323). My initial excitement—Was this a long-overlooked piece of original writing by Thoreau, quietly inserted into the last volume of the Indian Notebooks by himself or one of the people who held the volumes before they arrived at the Morgan Library a century ago?—was soon dispelled. The passage is a draft of the opening of "Huckleberries," part of the *Wild Fruits* manuscript, and Elizabeth Witherell includes it in the final volume of the online Journal (JM 33:110–13).[2]

Yet its insertion in the final volume of the Indian Notebooks, if not marked by authorial intent, is fitting. The mini-essay speaks of our difficulty in judging the import of what is before us, of distinguishing between husk and kernel, and Thoreau's final analogy—comparing the grossness of pumpkins and the fineness of huckleberries—resonates powerfully with the Indian Notebooks themselves. They are, after all, lengthy: some three thousand pages of manuscript in eleven volumes gathered over at least as many years. Whether they are gross or fine is a matter of long debate. Are they an abandoned book project and a dead end, soaked with savagism and permeated with the mustiness of a lifeless archive far removed from Native peoples themselves? Or do they hold some kernel of truth that infused the best of Thoreau's work in the years he labored over what appears to be a fruitless task? Are the Indian Notebooks some pumpkins or some huckleberries?

Thoreau's Indian Notebooks remain one of the great critical puzzles of his career. They might be termed the dark matter of Thoreau studies—a vast mass of words whose impact on the more visible universe of Thoreau's writing is hard to measure but impossible to ignore. Robert Sayre, in his *Thoreau and the American Indians* (1977), makes the case that Thoreau did not so much abandon his proposed Indian book—the presumed goal of these notes—as reimagine it. In Sayre's words, if the Indian Notebooks didn't lead to a distinct Indian book, "then the thousands of pages of notes on Indians must be construed more broadly as self-education and preparation for what he *did* write."[3] In this chapter I take up that question and argue that the best way to understand the Notebooks is to see them as Thoreau's effort to learn from the people who had lived in North America from time immemorial how best to live in the Concord of the mid-nineteenth century. The Indian Notebooks are, in short, Thoreau's effort to become more native to the land he called home, to learn from the traditional ecological knowledge of Native peoples and adapt it to a territory from which they had been driven. If that project sounds at once deeply hopeful and profoundly problematic, it is both. Its problems cannot be dismissed, nor do I believe its problems spoil the whole of Thoreau's project. Both the problems and the promise of Thoreau's Indian Notebooks bring the whole of Thoreau's work into sharper focus, and they have much to say to our current moment.

Indian Extracts

Let me begin with a few words about the manuscripts themselves. Written on the covers of the Notebook texts is "Extracts Relating to the Indians" (likely penned by Harrison Blake when he inherited the manuscripts from

Sophia Thoreau); they are numbered from 2 to 12.[4] There is some debate about whether an additional notebook, numbered 1, containing material associated with *A Yankee in Canada*, is the first in this series, though most recent scholars see this as a separate project. Sayre raises the possibility of a missing first Indian Notebook, one that was either cut up by Thoreau and used in the drafting of *A Week on the Concord and Merrimack Rivers* and *Walden* or simply lost in the era between Thoreau's death and the arrival of the remaining manuscripts at the Morgan Library.[5] The notebooks are not widely available.[6] The two most comprehensive accounts of the notebooks, by Robert Sayre and Suzanne Rose, exclude the Canada notebook, since it contains material about French settlement with only incidental notes about Native peoples, and begin the numbering with 2, which matches scattered references to the Indian Notebooks in Thoreau's Journal. The notebooks themselves are really commonplace books of material that Thoreau copied from books and articles he gathered from a number of libraries, though mainly Harvard's. There are a few scattered passages of Thoreau's original writing—a short, rough essay on Indians in Notebook 7, written in 1852, and briefer comments on some of the notes he copied, often made when he returned to earlier passages in light of new reading. They comprise something of a personal library culled from a huge range of material—hundreds of sources from the earliest European explorations of North America to the most recent government reports and memoirs, with a focus on Native peoples from the northeastern United States and southeastern Canada but also including material from across the continent and around the world, including texts on early and prehistoric Europeans. Additionally, some items in Thoreau's personal library—namely, George Copway's *Traditional History and Characteristic Sketches of the Ojibway Nation* (1850), which Thoreau heavily annotated—might best be seen as part of the Indian Notebooks.[7]

What to call them presents some problems. "Extracts Relating to the Indians" is a bit cumbersome, and some scholars, including Sayre and Joshua Bellin, refer to these extracts as Thoreau's Indian Books; Thoreau himself used the term "Indian book" at least once in his Journal (June 23, 1853). To call them "books" brings to mind the long-established theory, first argued by Franklin Sanborn, that Thoreau had planned to gather the material into a comprehensive book about Indians before tuberculosis took him from this task.[8] Calling the manuscripts "books," however, suggests a coherent project that the extracts don't really support. Calling them the

"Indian Notebooks," as William Howarth, Richard F. Fleck, and Rose do, better describes the nature of the manuscripts as a collection of material that has a consistent theme—Native Americans—and was meant to inform Thoreau's original writing projects rather than serve as a draft of a distinct book. The term doesn't quite convey their nature as commonplace books—they consist almost entirely of passages copied verbatim from other texts, rather than notes in Thoreau's own words—but it better indicates their status as the fruits of Thoreau's work over more than a decade in systematically gathering and recording information about Native Americans. Their best analog in the Thoreau archive is the collection of natural history notebooks that similarly inform a number of his writing projects without serving as the primary source for any one of them.

The Indian Notebooks vary considerably, as befitting a research project whose scope and purpose certainly evolved over the dozen or so years Thoreau pursued it. They can be dated with some precision based on Thoreau's borrowing records from various libraries and gathered by Robert Sattelmeyer in *Thoreau's Reading* (1988).[9] Sayre and Rose differ about some details but largely agree about the dates of the books. Thoreau began gradually, filling the first volume we have, 82 manuscript pages, between 1847 and 1850; the pace picked up slowly from 1850 (63 pages) to 1852, when he filled at least two notebooks totaling more than 300 pages; then more quickly in the mid-1850s. Thoreau filled a 500-page notebook between 1852 and 1855, then a 437-page notebook in 1855. His pace then settled, with roughly 200 pages per year between 1856 and the final entry in 1861. If he had been planning to write a book about Native Americans, as Sanborn argued, then, as Sayre suggests, Thoreau most likely seriously considered it around 1855, after the publication of *Walden*, when his pace of research was at its highest. If the Indian Notebooks were, after that point, no longer seen as the raw material for a new book, then they clearly served some other purpose. To get a better sense of what that purpose might have been, I now turn to the notebooks themselves.

What's in them? Well, just about everything, which makes them at once hard to summarize (Rose's summaries of the first five notebooks run up to twenty pages each) and easy to cherry-pick. There is a tendency to find what you're looking for. Do they contain a stirring defense of the humanity and dignity of Native peoples? Yes. Are they a comprehensive record of the savagism and virulent racism that shaped the rise of ethnology and anthropology in the United States? Yes. Do they portray Native

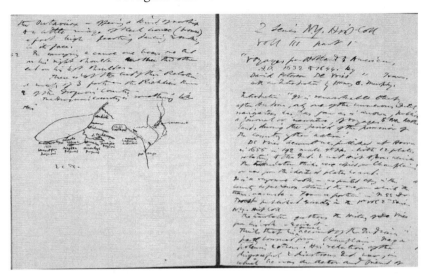

FIGURE 2: Page from the Indian Notebooks, IN 11:7–8, MA 605. Reprinted with permission from the Morgan Library & Museum, New York, NY. Purchased by Pierpont Morgan with the Wakeman Collection, 1909.

peoples as sophisticated and admirable, undercutting notions of European cultural supremacy? Offer vivid images of savage squalor? Yes and yes. If one approaches them looking for an archive of powerful Native American myths, a sustained exploration of how language shapes our perception of reality, or a deep meditation on rituals of grief and mourning, you will find them. And more: Detailed instructions on how to build canoes from birchbark, tree trunks, or buffalo hides. Recipes galore, especially for the myriad ways Native peoples prepared corn. A surprising range of sexual norms. Descriptions of stone tools and earthworks. Brutally intimate descriptions of torture. Military tactics. Ceremonies, prayers, and shamans. Clothing to beat the heat and keep out the bitter arctic wind. Hunting and fishing techniques for every North American ecosystem and for some in South America and Australia. Fun and games and funerary rites. Lots and lots of plants. These topics come in no particular order but are scattered throughout the Indian Notebooks as they appear in the various texts Thoreau took in hand. I will make some careful generalizations in due course, but I want to stress, first, that any firm conclusions about Thoreau's attitudes toward these texts can only be tentative and are bound to be contradicted, and so they must be made with caution. He does include occasional comments on texts, though these should be seen as tentative rather than conclusive. The essays and subject lists that appear in his own voice never moved to a finished piece of writing. It is possible to make some judgments about what was on Thoreau's mind as he copied these extracts by noting what he included (which is easy) and by comparing them with what he left out (which decidedly is not, though I will do so at times). The key point is that the Indian Notebooks are not a product that represents Thoreau's settled views on Native people but an inclusive and evolving process of understanding that continued to the end of his life. That said, I will hazard a list of some of the key themes and subjects that run through the Indian Notebooks before returning to what I believe are the two key questions about how this great mass of words shapes our broader understanding of Thoreau's work and legacy: How do the Indian Notebooks help us measure his relationship to Native people? And how do they inform the environmental projects that shaped his writing after *Walden*?

Native New England

The first key theme in the Indian Notebooks is Native New England. It is the main focus of the first notebook we have, and if the theory that a missing earlier notebook went into *A Week* is accurate, this New England focus shaped the project from the very beginning. Thoreau began with the sources near at hand, mainly from the modest Concord library, and in just about every subsequent notebook, he filled gaps with works by early explorers, missionaries, the first English settlers, local histories, other archives as they became available, and even a few Native writers themselves. Thoreau's focus in these sources was not the history of European settlement, though he relied heavily on accounts by early explorers and settlers, but the world they supplanted—the great green world, teeming with plants and animals and lovingly inhabited—tended, really—by people who were not noble savages but intelligent, resourceful, and very much human.

The first of the Indian Notebooks we have, dated by Sayre to 1847–50, offers a good example of what caught Thoreau's interest. The notebook draws mainly on town histories and the collections of the Massachusetts Historical Society, which published a wide range of sources on early New England history in the late eighteenth and early nineteenth centuries. Thoreau copied extracts from Bartholomew Gosnold's and George Weymouth's voyages along the New England coast in the early 1600s. They offer a portrait of a thickly inhabited and fertile land. "The coast," Gosnold notes, and Thoreau copied, "was full of people that ran along the shore. . . . They roasted crabs, red herrings and ground nuts. Some of the last big as hens eggs, 40 on a string" (IN 2:4–5). This first notebook includes accounts of Penobscot canoe making and other political and cultural information. From several town histories, Thoreau copied such items as the Native custom in the early colonial period of planting elm trees before ministers' houses and the political geography of Native communities, often centered on key fishing spots. *Mourt's Relation* and Roger Williams's *Key to the Language of America* offer deeper insights into Wampanoag and Narragansett cultures from the earliest English settlers, with the former centering on food, wampum, houses, and early diplomatic contacts and the latter on a broader ethnography, including farming techniques and major wild plants, especially the abundant strawberries in burned-over woodlands. Williams wrote, and Thoreau copied, "Of strawberries—one of the chiefest doctors in England was wont to say that God could have made, but God never did make, a better berry. In some parts where the natives have planted, I have many times sees as many as would fill a good ship, within a few miles compass. The Ind. bruise them in the mortar, and mix them with meal, and make a strawberry bread" (IN 2:63–64). Thoreau copied hunting and fishing techniques, as well as a rich overview of Narragansett religion, with its thirty-seven gods, a rather open-minded account of their sexual mores, and descriptions of games and ceremonies. He also copied Williams's comment that "for the temper of their brain," the Narragansett are "not made inferior to the Europeans," and they are generally more healthy and more honest. He copied, too, their origin story: "They say themselves that they have sprung and grown up in that very place, like the very trees of the wilderness" (IN 2:52). What emerges from Thoreau's extracts is a portrait of Native communities deeply rooted in place, carefully attuned to their environment, and living in plenty through a highly refined economy of hunting, fishing, farming, and gathering. Native New England, in this portrait, is a world woven together in a web of ceremony, language, and belief that yields a society that was not without conflict, either among its own members or with its neighbors, but needed little from the European arrivals.

This portrait is limned by his sources rather than crafted by Thoreau himself, of course—the Pilgrims were desperate to earn the good will and support of the Wampanoag people into whose territory they had strayed, and Williams was eager to distinguish his treatment of his Narraganset neighbors from the Puritan attitudes that prevailed just to the north. Thoreau also finds two sources written by Native writers: Henry Aupaumut's "History of the Muh-he-con-nuk Indians" (ca. 1790) and Samson Occom's "Account of the Montauk Indians" (1761), in the Massachusetts Historical Society collections. It's worth noting that Thoreau completely ignores a long account of the Mohegan tribe in the late eighteenth century that precedes Aupaumut's history; he instead copies from Aupaumut a detailed account of how Mahican farmers (mainly women) cleared fields by girdling and then burning trees and how the men managed the wild game of the region by hunting sparingly in different seasons. "They were not to kill more than necessary, for there was none to barter with them that would have tempted them to waste animals—consequently game was never diminished" (IN 2:47). From Occom, Thoreau copied different ways of arranging marriages, as well as their many gods: "They had gods etc. as S. west—north and south—'there was a god of corn, another over their beans, another over their pumpkins and squashes, etc. There was one god over their wigwams, another over their fire, another over the seas, another of the winds, one of the day and another of the night; and there were four gods over the four parts of the year, etc. etc.' But there was also one great good God and one great evil one" (IN 2:49). From other sources, Thoreau gathered a range of other information about hunting; technologies for making canoes, wampum, hoes, bows, and wigwams; political structures and the customs that helped mediate conflict; and the animals and plants that shared these environments. The notebook includes a Maushop legend from Cape Cod as well as an account of memory cairns in Mashpee and elsewhere that helped weave Wampanoag culture and history into the landscape. According to the eighteenth-century Puritan missionary in Mashpee, Gideon Hawley, there were "everywhere heaps of stones and sticks, gradually accumulated. His guide would look about for a stone at such places to cast in the heap. . . . The heap is 'an altar, the heap an oblation'" (IN 2:76). What Thoreau transcribed into his notebooks, Native peoples wrote on the land itself.

Some key aspects of Native New England culture would come into focus in later Indian Notebooks, particularly as he read the works of Daniel Gookin and John Josselyn: the richness of this teeming world, where "sturgeon were so numerous it is hazardous for canoes" (IN 4:70); the extensive use of fire to shape the landscape, burning the undergrowth to provide for better hunting and gathering; the myriad ways Native peoples harvested plants and animals to meet their needs, as well as the ceremonies and stories that helped shape these relationships. And from other local histories, he would record practices that English settlers learned from their Native predecessors—recipes, hunting and fishing techniques—as well as accounts of English captives who remained with their adoptive Native families, returning to visit their English relatives but happy in their Native world. Although Thoreau's interests quickly took him far beyond the borders of New England, he clearly saw the Native peoples of this region as a distinct topic. There were comparatively few materials about the Musketaquid people who had long inhabited his area, but Thoreau was attentive to the ecological and cultural shifts of colonial Concord. Thoreau quotes Thomas Shepherd's 1648 account of an agreement of local sachems to adopt more English manners—take only one wife, stop the habit of picking and eating lice, abandon their mourning practices of painting their faces and howling, no longer require women to isolate while menstruating (IN 8:301). He also copied Edward Johnson's account of the first settlers, who dug simple houses into a hillside, planted alewives with their corn, "which they plant in hills five foot asunder," and traded with Natives for venison and raccoon. Their cattle, forced to feed "on such wild fother [fodder] as was never cut before," died in droves, "also wolves caught their swine." The settlers "were compelled to eat Indian bread . . . They had pomkins & squashes of divers kinds" (IN 8:303–4). Thoreau was able to glimpse Musketaquid/Concord as a place of transformation, and if the English settlers were able to survive this earlier experiment in living simply, close to the land, and ultimately to create a New England world from the woods and wetlands along the Grass-ground River, the Indian Notebooks enabled him to better see its Native traces. And since Johnson offered only a few tantalizing details, Thoreau methodically combed through sources about nearby communities, from Maine to Western Massachusetts to Cape Cod to Rhode Island. He was eager to learn about his New England home.

Witnessing Genocide

A second theme running throughout the Indian Notebooks was a corollary of the first—the toll of colonization on Native peoples. As he pieced together the world of Native New England, Thoreau watched that world dissolve, often through the actions of the very writers he copied. Thoreau was keenly aware that Indians had not, as some of his sources phrased it, simply melted away. He recorded time and again the impact of the diseases that ripped through Native populations as Europeans arrived, first in Virginia and New England and Quebec, and then across the west, including the epidemics of smallpox and other diseases that tore through the Plains and West Coast communities in his own era. Many of his sources—early explorers, colonists, and missionaries—were stunned by the devastation caused by these diseases, and many also noted the toll taken on Native communities by alcohol and the allure of the marketplace, which led to overhunting and famine. Thoreau noted these throughout his extracts, often including the voices of Native peoples themselves. One Huron assessment was recorded by a Jesuit missionary, Julien Perrault, in 1635: "It is not these drinks that take away our life, but your writings, for since you have described our country, our rivers and our land & woods, we all die, which did not happen before you came" (IN 7:84). The Jesuits themselves had a sense of their role in this devastation. Charles Lalemont noted with grim resignation in 1640 that "where we were most welcome, where we baptized the most people, it was there in fact that they most died" (IN 8:135). And yet they kept coming—and, as Thoreau's Notebooks show, they kept writing.

Other colonists weren't content to let disease work unaided. In Notebook 4, Thoreau copied an account of the brutal extermination of the Beothuk people of Newfoundland: "From the first, they were deadly foes . . . the rifle and the bayonet soon broke their spirit. Abandoning the coasts and hunting grounds of their fathers, they fled into the dreary forests of the interior. Sometimes in the long winter nights, they crept from their wild fastnesses, and visited some lonely house with terrible vengeance. The settlers, in return, hunted them down like wolves, and in the course of years, their life of misery reduced their numbers, and weakened their frames so much, that they never ventured to appear. It was known that some few still lingered, but they were almost forgotten" (IN 4:4–5). Thoreau was certainly familiar with the cycle of wars that wrested control of the American landscape from Native peoples—episodes in this struggle played a major role in *A Week on the Concord and Merrimack Rivers*, and references to Metacom (or King Philip) occur throughout the Indian Notebooks, including a letter from Metacom to colonial authorities that Thoreau examined in Plymouth. The Indian Notebooks also contain many accounts of war among different Native communities, some of which clearly predated European contact but many more of which were part of the political and economic chaos that followed colonization, as tribes jockeyed for access to weapons and the hunting grounds that provided the furs and, thus, funds to buy European goods, including the guns that fueled this cycle of warfare. The palisaded villages, war parties, strings of scalps, and captives either adopted into new homes or tortured to death all mark a colonial landscape that extended far beyond the frontier of settlement. Notebook 8 closes with a string of speeches by Native leaders protesting various acts of colonization. Thoreau copied a speech by the Onondaga chief Grangula to the leader of a French expedition to Iroquoia in 1684, which summarized intertribal conflicts spurred by the fur trade: "We knocked the Twihtwies and Chictaglicks on the head, because they had cut down the tree of peace, which were the limits of our country. They have hunted beavers on our land: They have acted contrary to the laws of all Indians; for they left none of the beavers alive, they killed both male and female. . . . We have done less than either the English or French, that have usurped the lands of so many Indian nations, and chased them from their own country. This belt preserves my words" (IN 8:484–85).

Thoreau also copied the speech of the Onondaga chief Canassatego in 1742: "We know our lands are now become more valuable; the white people think we do not know their value; but we are sensible that the land is everlasting, and the few goods we receive for it are soon worn out and gone" (IN 8:490). As Thoreau clearly notes, Native peoples did not "vanish" quietly or without resistance. They were both eloquent and blunt in naming the acts of treachery and violence that drove them from their lands.

Yet these wars and their aftermath are never the object of Thoreau's research. He ignores accounts of Native war chiefs and the brutal aftermaths of European victories in the same way he ignores accounts of Native communities that survived (and even, on occasion, flourished) in the wake of colonization. Thoreau would eagerly visit Native people who traveled through the Concord area (often Penobscot families engaged in seasonal travel and trade), sought out several Wampanoag people in the company of Daniel Ricketson, and returned repeatedly to Maine in the hope of learning from Penobscot guides what he couldn't learn from books. Yet the books he sought out were ones that would take him as close to the original point of contact as possible. They helped him peer beyond the event horizon of colonization.

The Algonquian World

As the Indian Notebooks develop, it becomes clear that Thoreau was trying to build a full portrait of Native culture in the American Northeast as it existed apart from colonization. If the sources from New England proved limited, the next best thing was to broaden his reach to include closely related groups. His early reading suggested that New England Native languages and cultures along the Atlantic coast from Canada to Virginia and inland to the Great Lakes and south to the Ohio were closely related (the Iroquois were, Thoreau learned early on, an exception). Thus Thoreau settled on the project he identified when approached by the American Association for the Advancement of Science in 1853: "The Manners & Customs of the Indians of the Algonquian Group previous to contact with the civilized man" (*Corr* 310). This was the third great theme of the Indian Notebooks. By expanding his range, Thoreau opened up a vast array of sources. The Jesuit Relations were the great trove. These long accounts were written in the early seventeenth century by various Jesuit missionaries to Native tribes in Canada and sent to their superiors in France; they were newly published and available at the Harvard library. If the Hurons, Montagnais (Innu), and Ojibwe, living in a more frigid, boreal environment than the New England tribes, were not exact analogues of the Abenaki, Nipmuc, and Wampanoag peoples, the richly detailed reports of the missionaries, who spent years living in these communities in the very earliest stages of colonization, made up for the difference. The Delaware, or Lenape, were closer still to their New England relatives culturally and politically, and Thoreau mined both early Dutch sources and the long accounts of the Delaware by the Moravian Church missionary John Heckewelder, who lived with them during their eighteenth-century migrations to lands just beyond the English frontier. What appears as somewhat scattered cultural observations gleaned from New England sources in the early notebooks become, as the pages in the later notebooks fill up, a comprehensive ethnography of Algonquian culture. This broad theme might be broken into any number of categories; a long list that Thoreau wrote in 1858 includes thirty-five headings, ranging from "First Aspects of Land & People" to "Manners" to "Food &c" to "Superstitions and Religion." It's not clear whether this list was meant to try out possible chapter titles for a book, as Sayre argues, or simply a way of cross-referencing his own voluminous notes, as Bellin suggests.[10] It does, however, indicate the incredible range of Thoreau's research on Algonquian culture.

Thoreau gathered a great deal of material on Native cultures that were not Algonquian—this might be termed the fourth major topic of the Indian Notebooks, a version of comparative Indigenous studies that included the members of the Haudenosaunee Confederacy, Siouan peoples to west, Innuit people to the north, and the tribes of the American Southeast. The Indian Notebooks also include shorter notes on global Indigenous peoples from South America, Australia, Africa, Asia, and (dipping into prehistory) Europe. Yet as expansive as the range of Thoreau's inquiry was, the Notebooks keep circling back to Algonquian peoples, and I would suggest that this material is meant primarily to contextualize the information he gleaned about Algonquian cultures.

This research might be more conveniently gathered into a handful of general areas. One is Indigenous technologies: the many techniques Algonquian people had developed to gather resources from their environment and put them to use. These include strategies for hunting and fishing as well as the knowledge needed to move about a broad territory, from tracking animals to finding directions to building canoes, along with descriptions of the many tools that made these activities possible. Another focus is on the domestic arts: building wigwams, arranging villages, clearing fields for planting, and growing the main crops that recur across the region and beyond, such as corn, beans, and squash. Also in this area might fall the making of clothing and the various recipes for preparing and preserving food. Recipes for corn abound—for stews, porridges, cakes, and the parched corn that was the staple of travel. These areas are highly relegated by gender, and Thoreau notes the varying attitudes toward these gender roles among his sources. Some of the writers he copies protest that women were treated as little more than slaves, forced to do the bulk of heavy labor while men played at hunting, often to make the case of Indian cultural inferiority. Most of his sources recognize that men's and women's roles were equally vital, highly taxing in different ways, and respected in their difference.

Another category might be termed "culture," ranging from the gender and sexual mores that shaped people's social roles to the customs and rituals that governed everyday life to the broader traditional knowledge and spiritual beliefs that structured their understanding of the world. Thoreau's interest in sexual norms is surprising, given his general reticence on the topic. Although sources and tribal contexts varied, the Indian Notebooks generally capture a freer attitude toward sex outside of marriage, the common custom of polygamy, the widespread knowledge of how to induce abortion, and the general respect given to the marriage bond among his sources.

Thoreau was also eager to record Native traditions, gathered in his earliest sources and from the growing corpus assembled by Henry Rowe Schoolcraft in his early studies of Native cultures. These stories fueled Thoreau's interest in Algonquian religion, from sacred origin myths (including a half dozen earth-diver creation myths) to ceremonies of welcome, initiation, thanksgiving, and mourning, and to beliefs about gods and spirits and the nature of the soul. The range of sources for these details indicates that Algonquian religion was intensely collective—people engaged with the spiritual powers of the world and marked their milestones not as individuals but as communities, most often as a village but frequently as a larger tribal community. The Huron Feast of the Dead, in which villages gathered together at intervals of a decade or so to ritually mourn and sanctify the carefully preserved remains of those who died in the intervening years, serves as a good example of Algonquian ceremony—in Indian Notebooks 6 and 7, Thoreau devotes some twenty pages to copying an account from the Jesuit Relations in 1636, fascinated by the way in which individual grief is woven into a broad tribal network of renewal. Thoreau copied the skeptical accounts of powwows written by Jesuit, Puritan, and Moravian missionaries. Traditional Indigenous spiritual leaders managed the ceremonial life of tribal communities, and they were, after all, the key points of resistance to the Christian proselytizing that was a key element of colonization. Yet Thoreau included enough details about their ceremonies and beliefs to give a sense of their role in the spiritual world of Algonquian peoples.

Traditional Ecological Knowledge

It is not clear from reading the Indian Notebooks whether Thoreau grasped how central powwows, or shamans, were to managing Algonquian relationships to their environment—certainly, few of his sources did. But Thoreau was highly attuned to the manner in which Indigenous culture mediated Native people's interaction with their environment, from their stories to their rituals to their recipes to their intimate knowledge of the more-than-human world. The Indian Notebooks are full of careful descriptions of plants and animals, with an understandable bias toward larger fauna they hunted and the principal food plants they farmed and gathered. Thoreau learned about moose, bear, deer, and beaver; sturgeon, salmon, trout, and whitefish; and pumpkins and huckleberries, along with a dizzying array of other plants used for food, medicine, and a range of crafts, as well as the innumerable technologies that Native peoples used to turn plants, hides, and stone into the material of their daily lives. And it was this knowledge—not of plants, animals, or people in and of themselves but how Native peoples wove themselves into the rich tapestry of their environment—that may have been the central goal of the Indian Notebooks.

Thoreau was not alone in drawing on Indigenous knowledge to advance a scientific understanding of the American environment, though most other scientists collected or shot their own specimens and drew their own conclusions, preferring to put a firm boundary between their emerging scientific knowledge and the traditional knowledge of Native peoples. The Indian Notebooks, of course, include material from a number of scientific expeditions of this sort, many of which used Native guides and many more of which offered the kind of ethnographic analysis of tribal communities useful to a colonial power. Thoreau's interest in the Indian Notebooks, on the other hand, appears to be neither scientific knowledge abstracted from tribal contexts nor the kind of colonial knowledge needed to pry Native peoples away from their land. Instead, the Indian Notebooks suggest a sustained interest in the nexus of plants, animals, and people in a given environment. More particularly, Thoreau returned again and again to how Native peoples understood and managed their relationship to the more-than-human world. Not simply ecology, but human ecology; not just the names and traits of individual species and systems, but the epistemology that shaped this knowledge and, more broadly, the ontology that governed the relationship among the many parts of this living world. In short, Thoreau was after a complex of beliefs that we now term "traditional ecological knowledge," which Fikret Berkes defines as "a cumulative body of knowledge, practice and belief, evolving by adaptive processes and handed down through generations by cultural transmission, about the relationship of living beings (including humans) in their environment." Other kinds of traditional knowledge about other domains of human culture exist, of course, and Thoreau's notebooks include plenty of material that is not directly concerned with the environment. Traditional ecological knowledge is connected to these other domains, but its focus on a given people and landscape gives it a certain coherence. This knowledge is also distinct from the paradigm of Western science. Traditional ecological knowledge certainly encompasses the naming and classification characteristic of Western science, but it also extends to the practices and beliefs of a people who engage with these plants and animals.[11]

Thus traditional ecological knowledge, and Thoreau's voluminous notes, include not only a physical description of beavers and a detailed understanding of their habits but also hunting methods, techniques for processing hides, prices for fur, recipes for cooking beaver tail, and the oral traditions about beaver that portray the animal as a fellow person to be treated with respect. From Schoolcraft, he copied an Osage tradition of the first man, who was taught by the Great Spirit how to hunt, make fire, and cook his food: "Finally, he married a beaver by whom he had many children & they have formed the Osage people. Hence the Osage do not kill the beaver" (IN 6:97). From the Jesuit Relation of 1640, he copied an account of a Montagnais (Innu) shaman tracing the source of a malady by burning beaver bones (IN 10:187); from a story in *Harper's Magazine* in 1855, an account of using beaver teeth as a woodworking tool (IN 10:255); from the narrative of Jean Bernard Bossu, who traveled the Mississippi and Ohio in the mid-1700s, recipes for beaver feet and tails (IN 12:158). Beaver may have been hunted to extinction along the Concord River even as the first English settlers dug and framed their frontier homes, but Thoreau, through his vast reading, came to know them.

The rich texture of these complexities has made it difficult to summarize the Indian Notebooks. Efforts to identify one main focus have tended to seize on one aspect or another: language, myth, science, ethnography, or savagism. What is more difficult to see is the weave these distinct strands of inquiry make and why Thoreau took up this long task. I will return to these questions below, but I turn first to two other recurrent themes in the Indian Notebooks: theories of Native American origins and racial classification that permeated nineteenth-century ethnography. Thoreau's use of this material offers some important insights into his relationship to the settler colonial world and the tide of dispossession and genocide that gathered force as he patiently filled book after book.

Notes on Savagism

The topics of Native origins and racial categorization are scattered throughout the Indian Notebooks, and they are at the heart of the savagist ideology that was the softer cultural wing of the brutal politics of nineteenth-century American colonization. Most frequent are speculations about Native American origins and history. The notebooks capture a vigorous debate of the era: Did Native Americans originate in the New World as a separate creation, as a number of Native traditions suggested? Did they migrate from central Asia, as their physical characteristics and cultural practices seemed to suggest? Or did they blend a number of immigrant strains from both Asia and premodern Europe, as some theorized? Was the existing distribution of tribes and territories the result of long habitation, or was Indian prehistory marked by successive waves of migration and conquest? The Indian Notebooks offer carefully chosen arguments for these theories but no sense of where Thoreau settled on this issue. His habit of skipping over the outdated or outlandish theories suggests that he was comfortable with the growing consensus of a long-ago migration from Asia, something hinted at in some of the Algonquian traditions he records. His striking dismissal of Tuscarora writer David Cusick's work, *Sketches of the Ancient History of the Six Nations*, which Thoreau read about in Ephraim Squires's work in 1850 and then read in full in 1857, may reflect his hope that Cusick's history would address these questions. His initial response is one of disappointed condescension: "Almost entirely fabulous and puerile," he writes in a rare comment, "only valuable in showing [in imperfect English] how an Indian writes history [and perhaps for some dim and on the whole interesting suggestions and traditions]" (IN 10:109; brackets in original). The bracketed comments—later emendations—suggest that Thoreau may have turned to Cusick for a Native perspective on origins and migrations and found instead sacred traditions that had a very different value from what he initially sought.

If Thoreau wasn't quite sure what to do with the rich Haudenosaunee heritage that Cusick so carefully assembled, he was more comfortable with another Native account of tribal history, George Copway's *Traditional History and Characteristic Sketches of the Ojibway Nation*, which he purchased rather than copy into the Indian Notebooks. Copway doesn't offer an account of the original peopling of the Americas, beginning instead with the more recent cultural memory of a migration from the East to the tribe's then-current home in the vicinity of Lake Huron; most of his book instead describes the flora and fauna of the region and the tribe's many techniques for making a good living. This was right in line with Thoreau's interests, and he marked up the book heavily. In addition to his many annotations of Ojibwe history and ecological knowledge, Thoreau's annotations highlight his interest in birchbark writing and oral traditions. He omitted material about missionary efforts in the community and Copway's strong pleas for more-just political treatment.[12] Neither the distant origins of Native peoples nor their current conditions were at the heart of Thoreau's note-taking. Most striking about Thoreau's notes on Native origins is the general attitude of detached curiosity. Other than his comment about Cusick and his omission of theories that were no longer plausible, Thoreau copied contemporary beliefs at modest length and without emendation. And yet in settler colonial ideology, these questions had high stakes. William Cullen Bryant, in his poem "The Prairies" (1834), argues that the current inhabitants of the land just beyond the frontier were barbarians who had conquered a civilized race of Mound Builders, a stance that helped to justify European conquest. For Louis Agassiz, the theory of separate creation undergirded the "scientific" racism he shared with people like Samuel Morton and Josiah Nott.[13]

A theory of Asian origins for Native peoples was more consistent with the Darwinian view of a single human origin that Thoreau eagerly adopted toward the end of his life—and that he fully understood undercut racist arguments for slavery.[14] That said, the theory of Asian origins presented no bar to the savagism of people like Henry Rowe Schoolcraft and Lewis Henry Morgan.

Indeed, Thoreau copied extensively from the works of the key architects of nineteenth-century savagism. The elements of this ideology are well known.[15] It begins with a belief in the innate difference between the European and Indian races, assumes the superiority of the former, and concludes with the inevitable vanishing of the latter when the two races come into contact. Savagism may have come in different varieties—the relentless Indian hating that drove the most brutal violence on the frontier or the softer idealization of Native peoples that relegated them to a noble savage status inevitably corrupted by modernity. Both versions, though, took as a given the naturalness of Native decline, and both had a difficult time imagining that Native communities could learn to adapt and thrive in a modern American society on their terms. But the most popular liberal stance among white supporters was to send missionaries and teachers to Native communities in an effort, as Richard Pratt would later say, to "kill the Indian to save the man."[16]

Thoreau's views have been a matter of long debate among readers of the Indian Notebooks. Early accounts, from Sanborn to Henry Salt to Albert Kaiser, saw Thoreau as a "friend of the Native" in what was essentially the primitivist mode of savagism. Richard Fleck and, to some degree, Suzanne Rose, argue that the notebooks offer, on the whole, a strong case against the darkest elements of savagism, gathering evidence from the Indian Notebooks that highlights the injustice of colonization and captures the richness of the Native world. Far from limning the scientific inevitability of racial succession, the notebooks capture a culture that was anything but primitive and has much to offer European Americans—particularly, for Fleck and Rose, a rich heritage of myth that Thoreau draws on in his own effort to remake American culture. Such a view, which sees Thoreau mining vanished Indian communities for cultural treasures that would benefit a settler society, doesn't exactly escape the orbit of primitivism, and to the extent that it ignores the ongoing political struggles of Native communities, it partakes of the savagism that is at the core of settler colonialism. Robert Sayre recognizes how thoroughly embedded the Indian Notebooks are within the larger project of savagism, even as the sheer wealth and range of information they contain belie the savagist stereotype of Native people as a primitive, static, hunter race.[17]

For Sayre, Thoreau's deep reading about Native people and his never-resolved struggle in the Journal to come to terms with what this meant for someone living in Concord in the mid-nineteenth century took him, as a chapter title suggests, "beyond savagism." Joshua Bellin is not so sure—in his reading of the Indian Notebooks, Bellin sees Thoreau as settling increasingly into the orbit of savagism, falling into Lewis Henry Morgan's stance on the essential sameness of Native cultures, seeing the many notes on Indian origins as a sign of racial distinction, and noting the pull of the vast compendiums of Schoolcraft, "the dean of racial difference," on the later Indian Notebooks. "Taken as a whole," Bellin argues, "the Indian Books prove Thoreau to be far more the antiquarian than the advocate."[18]

It is certainly true that the Indian Notebooks are anything but the research of an advocate. I would argue, however, that the notebooks do not fit as easily within savagist ideology as Bellin suggests and that their purpose was decidedly not antiquarian. On the first point, Thoreau copied everything he could find on his subject, from the most virulent racists, like Morton and Nott, to the strongest advocates for the equality and humanity of Native people, like Williams and Heckewelder—including a number of Native writers themselves. Thoreau includes notes from Morton about the relative size of crania—"On comparing 5 Iroquois heads, I find that they give an average internal capacity of 88 cubic inches, which is within 2 inches of the Caucasian mean" (IN 6:46)—but also much more information about the intelligence and variety of Native peoples. From a Jesuit missionary, he records this praise of oratory in Notebook 2: "I believe if I should commit to writing what this Indian said to us extemporaneously and without preparation you would be convinced without difficulty, that the most able

Europeans, after much meditation and study, would scarcely compose a discourse more solid and better turned" (IN 2:24–5). From William Bartram, in Notebook 4, he copied an incident in which a Georgia Indian chief disputed the measurements of an English surveyor: "The surveyor replied that the little instrument (pointing to the compass) told him so. The Indian answered, he knew better, and that the wicked little instrument was a liar." The surveyor proved to be incorrect, and they agreed that "the compass was to be discarded" (IN 4:101–2). This ambivalence continues through his final notebook, which includes both praise of Indian intelligence, especially in their oratory, and an account by Josiah Nott about the comparative primitiveness of Native languages. Thoreau doesn't keep score, but on balance, the picture of Native people that emerges is far from that of a simple, primitive, and unchanging stereotype. The broad generalizations of people like Morton are balanced by accounts of those who spent long stretches of time living with Native people and are content to see them as individuals: "The circle of faces [around a fire] presented the same variety as to expression, intelligence, etc. as would be exhibited by an equal number of civilized men," wrote Thaddeus Culbertson in an account of traveling among the Lakota in 1850 copied by Thoreau (IN 6:15). The Indian Notebooks are a better record of the ambivalence in European American accounts of Native peoples than they are of any one position. Thoreau copied, for example, Lewis Cass's attack on pro-Native writers like John Heckewelder and John Tanner (IN 12:37) as well as long extracts from Heckewelder (Notebook 9) and Tanner (Notebook 8) themselves.

This ambivalence was not just a feature of the different sides in the debate but also often within these writers themselves. Schoolcraft is a good example. His politics were invariably aligned with U.S. Indian policy, yet he more often captured his tangled frontier alliances in his work. This is, after all, the man who sent maple sugar made by his Ojibwe wife's family to Andrew Jackson's White House.[19] Schoolcraft's politics were not necessarily of a piece with his multifarious publications, which included the first real recognition by a white writer of the vast oral heritage of Native peoples—the value of which Thoreau quickly grasped. Schoolcraft's many publications, moreover, included verbatim reports of a wide range of informants, from Indian agents to Native culture keepers to older accounts by the range of people who moved into Native territory for a host of reasons and wrote from various perspectives. Like Thoreau's Indian Notebooks themselves, these writings are a better record of the diversity of views about Native Americans than they are a manifestation of a unified ideological stance.

Other authors more narrowly capture the ambivalence of writing about Native peoples in an age of savagism. Lewis Henry Morgan, whom Thoreau read carefully, wrote an incredibly detailed and textured account of the Iroquois, richly informed by extensive research and his own connections within the Seneca community; he fully represents the way Iroquoians migrated and adapted to new conditions, maintaining their status as an independent people long after the arrival of Europeans, thanks in part to a rich culture and sophisticated political system. Despite this, Morgan accepts the essential sameness of Native cultures and the inevitability of Indian vanishing, developing a model of cultural succession that he often refutes in his writing. Thoreau died before Morgan fully developed his model of cultural succession, and he did not include in his notebooks Morgan's remarks in *League of the Ho-dé-no-sau-nee, or Iroquois* (1851) about Indian vanishing. His notes on Morgan end with this passage: "About 4000 Iroquois now in N. Y. At the present moment their decline has not only been arrested, but they were actually increasing in numbers, and improving their social conditions" (8:401).[20] If the savagism of these writers filled the pages of the Indian Notebooks, their contradictions did as well.

More important, Thoreau did not seem to share the goals of these architects of savagism. Schoolcraft and the many Indian agents, leaders of military expeditions, and writers of scientific surveys were authoring material in the service of the U.S. government, actively feeding the many-headed hydra of colonization. Samuel Morton and Josiah Nott worked tirelessly to establish a scientific basis for the racism at the heart of white nationalism. Ephraim Squier and Lewis Henry Morgan are better suited to Bellin's category of antiquarianism—preserving the precontact heritage of the United States in folio pages and museum exhibits and thereby consigning surviving members of the Native communities they described to the status of anomalous relics, soon to vanish. Thoreau did none of these things. That he seriously considered writing a book about Indians seems likely; what is certain is that he didn't, even though, in the aftermath of *Walden*, he had plenty of time to move forward with such a project.

Beyond an Indian Book

Why did Thoreau keep filling notebooks as he revised *Walden* and as he pursued other writing projects in its wake? Sayre suggests that Thoreau himself may not have been sure of the answer. The Indian Notebooks perhaps began as source material for *A Week* and *Walden* and then as the possible source for a separate work. The abbreviated essay in Notebook 7 and the list of what may have been chapter headings in Notebook 11 suggest that Thoreau could have been mulling over the possibility of writing a book about Indians up to his last illness, drawing on his essays about the Maine Woods and his journey to Minnesota. But such an idea seems to have remained very much on the back burner. Thoreau never turned this material into a lecture, his usual first step in working up a new project, and the original manuscripts he left unpublished, "Wild Fruits" and "The Dispersion of Seeds," as well as the systematic phenology he gathered in the late 1850s as part of his Kalendar, clearly indicate that this comprehensive ecology of Concord was the great broken task that Emerson hinted at in his eulogy.[21] The Indian Notebooks, I argue, played a key role in that project, which I will return to below. But as Sayre and Howarth suggest, the Indian Notebooks perhaps evolved into more of a practice than a product—that the discipline of gathering, reading, copying, and reviewing material about Native Americans became, to some degree, its own end.[22] They may have played a role that was less like the natural history notebooks and more like the Journal, which in the early 1850s shifted from serving mainly as source material for lectures and essays to its own project, a meditative discipline for honing Thoreau's ability to see the world around him—the written counterpart to his daily walks around the Concord landscape. Writing about what he saw helped him see it more clearly, offering a less direct but more powerful inspiration to essays that increasingly provided a contrarian vision of the United States at midcentury.

The Indian Notebooks, then, served as another means for Thoreau to leave behind the village, to immerse himself in a written world that was as wild and renewing as the swamps and forested edges of Concord. He makes this exact analogy in a Journal entry from March 16, 1852: "While we are clearing the forests in our westward progress, we are accumulating a forest of books in our rear, as wild and unexplored as any of nature's primitive wildernesses. . . . When I look into Purchas's Pilgrims, it affected me like looking into an impassable swamp, ten feet deep with sphagnum, where the monarchs of the forest, covered with mosses and stretched along the ground, were making haste to become peat. . . . Decayed literature makes the richest of all soils" (*PJ* 4:62). The accumulated pages of notes, gathered from yellowing books on library shelves, are the muck Thoreau celebrates in "Walking," the source of fertility, of new life, that the tired fields of Musketaquid so desperately needed. More literally, Thoreau immersed himself in the Jesuit Relations for the same reason he immersed himself in Beck Stow's swamp—to see the world from a different perspective and be jolted out of village complacencies and national ideologies alike. To see the world from the perspective of a birchbark canoe threading the upper reaches of the St. Lawrence in the 1630s, to settle in with people who farmed, fished, hunted, and gathered different foods from those served at Concord tables, in houses built from saplings and bark, whose stories told of a woman who fell from the sky or warned of the depredations of a neighboring tribe, was to see Concord through different eyes and to open up new insights.

One reason Thoreau kept adding page after page to the Indian Notebooks, then, was for the *frisson* of difference—that sense of distance and recognition that drove his long exploration of ancient Hindu and Chinese sacred literature and fueled his voracious appetite for travel literature from around the globe. In the vast literature of Native culture he explored, Thoreau found echoes of some of the beliefs and practices at the core of his life. The philosophy of simplicity at the heart of *Walden*—the effort to pare life down to its essentials, to discard the accumulating dross of early capitalist consumerism and start over with the basics of food, clothing, and shelter—was everywhere in the Indian Notebooks, as early explorers and missionaries documented how people in the New World had found very different solutions to these universal human problems. The vision of political simplicity that animates "Resistance to Civil Government"—of a community that didn't interpose a web of law and political expediency between citizen and citizen, of a government that governs not at all but instead allows individuals to measure out their own mutual obligations and restraints—was depicted again and again in the notebooks. Thoreau noted how Native communities kept order without the friction of government apparatus and how Native peoples treated the lands and waters that sustained them not as private but as shared resources. In Notebook 3, Thoreau copied Charlevoix's observations of the Algonquins: "Independence among them is not destructive of subordination. Scarcely any 'criminal justice' among them—their greatest fault—because they appropriate so little property" (IN 3:6–7). In Notebook 10, Thoreau quotes Peter Loskeil, who writes, "The Delaware have no regular political constitution. . . . This they call liberty, and there is nothing they value more" (IN 10:1). In 1849, if Thoreau looked in vain for a state that could treat the individual with respect, he gathered example after example in his Indian Notebooks in the 1850s.

And in the many accounts of Native American spiritual beliefs, Thoreau saw a version of his transcendental ontology, of a Nature where nothing was inorganic, at the center of which he could gaze into the Earth's eye of a humble pond he sanctified in ceremony and myth. The earliest Jesuit Relations noted the Algonquian belief that "not only men and animals but all other things are animated" (IN 6:160), and Thoreau must have felt a shudder of recognition as he read Heckewelder: "All animate nature, in whatever degree, is in their eyes a great whole from which they have not yet ventured to separate themselves" (IN 9:267). John Hunter may have been writing about the Osage in what follows: "Every Indian of any standing has his sacred place, such as a tree, rock, fountain, etc. to which he resorts for devotional exercises. . . . None is compelled to do this, but those who omit it are thought less of, and their conduct is ascribed to an indifference to holy things, and a want of solicitude for the general welfare" (IN 8:417). As Thoreau copied this into his notebook, he surely thought of himself, his sacred places on the edge of the village and his evolving effort to serve the general welfare of Concord and the world beyond.

It is important to keep in mind that while the Indian Notebooks were full of moments of recognition, passages that correspond with Thoreau's writing, they are always also marked by difference. Thoreau's cabin was not built of elm bark, and his bean field was no Three Sisters garden. If he saw, in the Huron Feast of the Dead, a ritual that spoke to his own grief, he nevertheless followed his loved ones from the Unitarian church to the village graveyard. And if he saw the living world through eyes that shared as much with the Algonquian powwow as with the Harvard scientist, he showed no more interest in counting the thirty-seven gods of the Narragansett than he did of the thousands of manifestations of Vishnu. What Thoreau recorded in the Indian Notebooks was more cultural analogy than appropriation. His were more the careful jottings of a fellow seeker than earnest copying of an acolyte or the systematic observations of a scientist.

Learning to Live in Place

This not to say that the Indian Notebooks weren't integral to Thoreau's own turn to science in the years following *Walden*—indeed, as I have been suggesting, they are crucial to understanding the ongoing and evolving studies of the ecology in and around Concord that increasingly occupied his later years. His response to the invitation to join the American Association for the Advancement of Science captures something of his own difficulty in articulating what exactly was taking shape in his Journal, notebooks, and manuscripts during this time. Not science, exactly—at least not the campaign of classification and resource identification that filled museums of the era with stuffed and mounted fauna, dried and pressed flora, and neatly boxed samples of minerals and ores. If Thoreau's interest was the "manners and customs of the Algonquian tribes prior to contact with civilized man," he did not try to categorize these people and parcel them out to museums. He was still "a mystic, a philosopher, and a Transcendentalist to boot" (*PJ* 5:469–70; *Corr* 2:151–53). By this he meant that he sought ideas not in things but in the living relationship between things. Thoreau did not wish to enlist the Native informants of early explorers and missionaries as collectors of field specimens, though he clearly recognized the immeasurable value of Native people's knowledge of the plants and animals of their homelands. Instead, his interest lay in the Native understanding of the immensely complicated web of relations that made up a landscape—an early impulse toward ecology, to be sure, but one that reached beyond the interactions of the nonhuman world to fully include humans within this web. What he sought, in a phrase, was traditional ecological knowledge. As Gregory Cajete has noted, this complex overlaps with science, though it is hardly the same thing. "Native science," as he terms it, is "born of a lived and storied participation with landscape and reality." It is a kind of "map of natural reality drawn from the experiences of thousands of human generations."[23] Unlike Western science, the ontology of Native science is based on an intelligence present in all things, and its understanding is embodied not in charts, tomes, and exhibits but in the symbolic culture expressed through "myth-dreams" conveyed in stories, ceremonies, and visions. It is also conveyed through the practice of living in place—in the patterns of gathering and preparing food, shelter, and clothing and in the lore that conveys and adapts this knowledge. And it is taught not by rote memorization but through careful mentoring, including exercises meant to open the senses and weave together spiritual and material domains. Cajete mentions "night-walking" as one such method used to still the conscious, categorizing mind and cultivate a more intuitive understanding of what Thoreau calls, after describing a night-walking experience of his own, "the infinite extent of our relations" (*W* 171).

This relationality was fostered through both spiritual practice and the medium of everyday life. Simon Ortiz writes that "Pueblo languages are the cultural foundation that secures every Pueblo Indian his or her place on the *haatse*, or land," an idea that Thoreau noted repeatedly in the Indian Notebooks and his other writings, though his European sources, focused on learning a language for missionizing purposes or categorizing different tribes, offered little help in pursuing this insight. What Thoreau did glean from his sources was a growing sense of how deeply integrated tribal communities were into the web of the landscape and particularly how that relationship was not one of systematic exploitation of resources but one of reciprocity. It is not clear how far Thoreau's understanding went. As with the Mahicans in Notebook 2, he seized early on accounts of how different Native communities managed game and gathered many examples of how Indigenous people used fire to clear the undergrowth and make better habitat for both game and for wild fruits. The myriad notes about different kinds of plants in different territories are not extracted and categorized but woven into Native practices—their use as food, medicines, or tools emerges as a greater interest than their botanical classification. Thoreau seems to have understood what Jeanette Armstrong, writing about the Nsyilxcen-speaking peoples of the Northwest, calls *tmix^w*—the life force of a place embodied in the "myriad relationships that make a place what it is" and how each village in a region uses its landscape like a single permagarden, moving up and down the watershed to gather resources and manage the ecosystem. Thoreau may not have fully grasped what Robin Wall Kimmerer calls the essence of traditional ecological knowledge: "If we respect a plant and use it well, it will flourish; if we disrespect it or ignore it, it will go away." But there is no doubt that Thoreau's own understanding was moving steadily in that direction.[24] In watching the dispersion of seeds and the growth of oak and pine seedlings, in speaking a word—many words—for trees and plants that his fellow Concordians were wont to ignore or exploit, in paying visits to individual trees and flowers to mark their health and record their blooms, Thoreau embodied the respectful attention and care toward the more-than-human members of his community at the heart of traditional ecological knowledge.

The decade-plus project of gathering the Indian Notebooks, then, was a way of helping him see his own world through the deeply experienced eyes of Concord's former inhabitants. This long practice also made him keenly aware of what he could not see—what had been lost in driving out the land's Indigenous people. This is a regular motif in the Journal—"How much more we might have learned of the aborigines if they had not been so reserved!" he laments in an entry from March 20, 1858 (JM 25:129)—and it is implied by the pattern of Thoreau's reading. Thoreau's work is, from beginning to end, shaped by the empty space once occupied by the Musketaquid people. He circles this void in ever-widening loops, hoping to fill in their knowledge of this place by turning to the Jesuit Relations, Schoolcraft's endless compilations, and other accounts of Native peoples near and far, current and past, as he chased down notes about plants, hunting techniques, traditional stories, recipes, and ceremonies that helped him reimagine, and reweave, the intricate pattern that connected Concord's original people with their place. He was aware, to the end, of what he did not know. His broken task—his effort to write a new book of Musketaquid that would restore the web of relationships among its human and more-than-human inhabitants—might be seen as a response to this absence. By looking at how other communities tended to their land, he sought to apply it to his own: to notice what was there, to celebrate the value and standing of every member of this more-than-human community, and to argue fiercely for an approach to the environment that saw it not as a resource to be privatized and exploited for personal gain but as a commons to be shared, nurtured, and valued. When seen through the prism of the Indian Notebooks, it becomes easier to consider his late works as part of an effort to transform science into something more fluid, relational, and respectful. More Indigenous.

This is not to say that Thoreau ever fully renounced savagism or escaped the settler colonial dynamic that shaped his world. Even as he copied account after account of Native communities and immersed himself in their traditions and practices, Thoreau remained a settler using traditional ecological knowledge to better root himself in stolen land, performing what Jace Weaver calls the "uneasy illusion of indigeneity" on the part of a settler culture. He may have done so admiringly, but he did so without devoting much attention to the political aftermath of this long theft. As Glen Sean Coulthardt notes, for Native people, traditional ecological knowledge is profoundly political, an anchor of sovereignty planted deep in the land and a powerful tool for decolonizing Native minds struggling to shake free from the influence of missionaries, traders, teachers, and scientists. Thoreau, in removing this knowledge from the communities who gave it life, made it fundamentally different, lesser, and colonial. In his long reading, Thoreau ignored passages or sources that spoke to the brutal policies of conquest and removal in his own day, he ignored accounts of how Native communities adapted and survived in the wake of colonization, and he made no effort to connect with the Nipmuc, Massachusett, and Wampanoag communities that remained in Massachusetts. This absence is both striking and structural. In considering the distinction between Thoreau's fierce opposition to slavery and his relative silence on Native dispossession and genocide, Sayre suggests that African Americans called on Thoreau's sense of duty, whereas Native people got deep into his very being. Thoreau failed to see this was part of colonialism—in Patrick Wolfe's terms, the structure that followed the event.[25]

And yet Thoreau was trying to use traditional ecological knowledge to help live more ethically in the world and to save an emerging capitalist America from the disaster he could see coming before almost anyone else. It is important to note that the Indian Notebooks were not the final word on Indians for Thoreau—indeed, they only barely count as Thoreau's words at all. He traveled to Maine, learning from Joseph Attean and Joe Polis in particular that Native communities were addressing some of the same issues that he was struggling with in Concord, which may have been the end of any imagined "Indian Book" drawn from the notebooks' pages. Rather than write a book about Indians, then, he began a book about Concord, where the seeds planted in his long gleanings might bear a different fruit. In Notebook 8, completed at the end of 1854, Thoreau copied from the Jesuit Relation of 1639 part of a letter by Paul Le Jeune about the spiritual beliefs of the Huron. "Some figure for themselves a paradise filled with bluets; these are little blue fruits whose grains are as big as the *plus de gros graines de raisin*. I have not seen any of them in France, they are of a pretty good taste. This is why the souls love them very much" (IN 8:444). Thoreau's Indian Notebooks enabled him to glimpse a heaven not of some pumpkins but filled with huckleberries. Our broken task is to build a world where Native and settler alike can live in a paradise of huckleberries. Thoreau couldn't imagine such a world; we must.

Appendix: Bibliographical Information about the Indian Notebooks

The Indian Notebooks are housed at the Morgan Library in New York City, and I am grateful to the Morgan for making available digitized copies of some of the notebooks, as well as the existing transcriptions made in the

1930s by graduate students at Columbia University under the supervision of Arthur Christy. Revised versions of the Morgan transcripts are held in the Columbia library as master's theses or in the Arthur Christy Papers, including the one transcript not held by the Morgan, for Notebook 11 (MA 605/Thoreau 53). I follow the work of Robert Sayre in ordering and dating the notebooks. The Indian Notebooks are titled "Extracts Relating to the Indians," and each has a number written in pencil on a sticker on the cover. It's not clear whether the numbers and titles were added by one of the owners of the collection after Thoreau's death (most likely H. G. O. Blake) or were written by Thoreau himself. These numbers begin with 2, and they do not correspond to their listing in the Morgan catalog, but they do correspond to references in Thoreau's Journal. George S. Hellman, the book dealer who arranged the sale to the Morgan, argues that the number 1 was erroneously applied to the notebook about Canada (MA 595/Thoreau 43), and so begins numbering the Indian Notebooks with MA 596/Thoreau 44. Sayre suggests there may have been a now lost earlier notebook, perhaps cannibalized by Thoreau himself in writing *A Week* and *Walden*, and that this was the number 1 in Thoreau's series. The dates are drawn from Sayre.[26]

MORGAN CATALOG	SAYRE NUMBER	DATE	PAGE TOTAL
MA 596/Thoreau 44	2	1847–50	82
MA 597/Thoreau 45	3	1850	63
MA 598/Thoreau 46	4	1850–51	121
MA 599/Thoreau 47	5	1851–52	126
MA 600/Thoreau 48	6	1852	166
MA 601/Thoreau 49	7	1852	167
MA 602/Thoreau 50	8	1852–55	507
MA 603/Thoreau 51	9	1855	437
MA 604/Thoreau 52	10	1856–58	667
MA 605/Thoreau 53	11	1858–59	203
MA 606/Thoreau 54	12	1859–61	352

CHAPTER 3

Becoming Native

Walden, "Walking," and the Poetry of Place

What kind of poets—what kind of events are those which transpired in America before it was known to the old world?
—Henry Thoreau, Indian Notebooks (7:115)

Ah beauteous tree! Ah happy sight!
That greets me on my native strand
And hails me with a friend's delight
To my own dear bright mother land.
—Jane Johnston Schoolcraft,
"To the Pine Tree"

In his late essay "Wild Apples," Thoreau offers a model for how to become native to a place: "Our wild apple is wild only like myself, perchance, who belong not to the aboriginal race, but have strayed into the woods" (*Exc* 270–71). It's a different wild fruit, however, that takes pride of place in *Walden*. In the chapter "House-Warming," Thoreau's discovery of groundnuts near the railroad bank helps transform Walden Woods into a place-world shaped by ecocultural contact. The plant appears in a litany of foraged foods: "In October," he writes, "I went a-graping to the river meadows, and loaded myself with clusters more precious for their beauty than their food." Cranberries, too, he admires, "small waxen gems, pendants of the meadow grass, pearly and red," whose harvest for the urban market he compares with that of tongues of bison raked from the prairie (*W* 238). Thoreau's materiality here takes shape in contradistinction to the market, which commodifies objects by isolating them from their contexts, dismembering things from all that gives them life. The aesthetic thrill Thoreau describes in harvesting a cluster of wild grapes or pausing to admire cranberries is not some ode to painterly sentiment but a reward for appreciating things in place, part of the rich network that meshes the human and the more-than-human world. Wild apples and chestnuts fill both his eye and his larder; in describing the latter, Thoreau launches into a brief explication of the phrase "a half bushel for winter," complete with a history of the best chestnut grounds in the region and how to follow the jays and squirrels to their hoards of sound nuts, the summer fragrance of a flowering tree, and the fate of many of those trees to lie beneath the newly laid rails.

Here is unalienated food, fully rooted in place, and it sets the stage for an even more remarkable one. "Digging one day for fish-worms, I discovered the groundnut (*Apios tuberosa*) on its string, the potatoes of the aborigines, a sort of fabulous fruit, which I had begun to doubt if I had ever dug and eaten in childhood, as I had been told, and not dreamed it" (*W* 239; italics in original). The passage is a late addition to the *Walden* manuscript, expanded from an October 12, 1852, journal entry that simply describes the digging of groundnuts near the railroad bank. In "House-Warming," it takes root among other native plants, and finding it is cast as a rediscovery, a new encounter with a plant he only partially remembers from his youth. He finds the tubers while looking for fishworms—an act of subsistence that pulls him deeper into the web of the environment. It is, in his words, a "fabulous fruit," one that suddenly connects the bright August flower with a tidbit of family lore and small thread of his reading.

The groundnut reknits the strands of family and history. Thoreau finds, too, that this act of foraging holds history at bay. Though "cultivation has well-nigh exterminated it," the passage suddenly executes a temporal about-face. "This tuber seemed like a faint promise of Nature to rear her own children and feed them simply here at a future period." Rather than looking back to a vanished, primitive past, Thoreau describes his present discovery ("this tuber") as a token of a future very different from the one typically imagined in mid-nineteenth-century letters. It may be true that "in these days of fatted cattle and waving grainfields, this humble root, which was once the *totem* of an Indian tribe, is quite forgotten," he notes (italics in original). "But let wild Nature once more reign here," he writes, and the English grain and even Indian corn will disappear and "the now almost exterminated ground-nut will perhaps revive and flourish in spite of frosts and wildness, prove itself indigenous, and resume its ancient importance and dignity as the diet of the hunter tribe.... When the reign of poetry commences here, its leaves and strings of nuts may be represented on our works of art" (*W* 239).

It's a remarkable passage, not so much a rejection of a scientific perspective as a supplement to it—he cites the old Latin name (*Apios tuberosa* is now named *Apios americana*) as a quick aside before letting the plant tell its story. That story tells of a wildness that flourishes outside the register of civilization and exists outside of a civilized chronology. Thoreau hints at how a people, like a plant, might prove themselves to be *indigenous*. It is one of a few places in *Walden* where the word appears, and it's striking that Thoreau applies it not to a vanished past but to a living present and an imagined future. And it is a moment mediated by Thoreau's deep interest in Native peoples. He references the story of the bringing of corn and reconstructs, as best he can, the hint of a story he doesn't know but can only deduce—some "Indian Ceres or Minerva must have been the inventor and bestower" of this plant (*W* 239). The earth speaks such a story to him, promising a better world to come. "When the reign of poetry commences here, its leaves and string of nuts may be represented on our works of art" (*W* 239). Left ambiguous is who will populate this new/old world. The "hunter tribe"? Nature's "own children"? For Thoreau, racial identity matters less than a people's ability to weave themselves into the land. One becomes native to a place not by studying Indians but by learning the poetry of the earth, by tasting of its wild fruits. By eating groundnuts.

In *Walden*, Thoreau learns to listen closely to what the woods have to tell him. Native people themselves have little to say. There is only one scant reference to the groundnut in the Indian Notebooks from this period before the above passage was added to the *Walden* manuscript in 1852. In Notebook 4, which Sayre dates to 1850–51, Thoreau copies John Josselyn's 1672 inventory of New England flora and fauna: "Earth-nuts, differing much from those of England, our sort of them bears a most beautiful flower" (IN 4:75). The reference could have done little more than jog Thoreau's memory of harvesting groundnuts in his childhood, which may have been accompanied by stories of their value as food for New England's Natives. In a journal composed shortly after July 16, 1850, Thoreau writes an early iteration of the *Walden* passage that has a quite different inflection. He ponders the legacy of Musketaquid's Natives. Among the descendants of "those who bought these fields of the Red men the wild men of the woods," a few have Native blood; a "solitary pure blooded Indian" will be seen boarding a train, and an "Indian squaw with her dog . . . and few children or none" will eke a living on the edge of some town, "for whom the berries condescend to grow," performing the last offices for her vanishing race (*PJ* 3:93).

Thoreau's account here is an evocative example of Jean O'Brien's "firsting and lasting"; Thoreau's example takes a botanical turn. "Not yet absorbed into the elements again–A daughter of the soil—one of the nobility of the land—the white man an imported weed burdock & mullein, which displace the groundnut" (*PJ* 3:93). In the context of her white neighbors, this Native woman is wholly marginalized; once Thoreau reimagines her in the context of her land and its wild fruits, her status grows, anchored by thin tendrils of this indigenous plant, soon to be displaced. At this moment, the groundnut is symbol rather than food, and if Thoreau yearns for the nobility of a vanishing indigenous past, there is no sense here of how to reclaim it. The groundnut is merely a fabulous fruit, associated with a people he glimpses only through the misty haze of savagism.

Yet something happens between the Native woman passage in the 1850 journal and the 1852 passage in *Walden* that enabled Thoreau to turn from a vanishing Indian presence to imagine an indigenous future. In between those dates lay hundreds of pages of the Indian Notebooks, particularly, in mid-1852, his excited discovery of the Jesuit Relations. The accounts he copied into his Indian Notebooks as he wrote the 1852 draft of *Walden* have a great deal to say about Native foodways—hunting and fishing are balanced by detailed descriptions of growing corn, squash, and beans, with a range of recipes. But nothing about harvesting groundnuts. Thoreau's vision of an indigenous future, I suggest, is partly based in his growing understanding of how Algonquian societies flourished in the region before contact, but it also springs from the earth itself. The groundnut is less interesting to him as a food source (though he does taste his find) than as a symbol—an emblem of a future quite different from the relentless capitalism settling over Massachusetts. His is a naturalization not of politics but of poetry—a kind of Indian wisdom more interested in place than in the specific people who had long inhabited it. Indeed, by focusing on the poetry of the land, he turns his back on the politics that left it empty of its Indigenous people and consigned their descendants to the margins of his world. Thoreau's groundnuts might be considered an example of what Kim TallBear calls the "absence/presence" of Indigenous people in settler narratives: the dynamic of summoning and claiming an indigenous identity while denying accountability for dispossession and genocide.[1]

The terms he uses to describe the Indian wisdom that he's after— "aboriginal," "indigenous," "native," "naturalized"—suggest the problems he faced in pursuing this knowledge while enmeshed within settler colonialism. Each term captures, to various degrees, Thoreau's desire to tie himself more tightly to the land and summons as well the presence of the Native people he and his society have displaced. These terms are haunted—the more so because Thoreau himself never fully makes peace with the stakes of his effort to claim Indian wisdom for himself. The word he eventually settles on—"wild"—embodies the ambivalence and overdetermined nature of his project, his effort to draw on a Native perspective to push against the constraints of a settler, capitalist ideology that he, in part, helped advance. "Wild" is a term full of anarchic, ecological energy, but it is, as we will see, a haunted term as well.

Such, I argue, is Thoreau's project in *Walden* and "Walking," the main texts in the middle of his career. It is a project ripe with hope and rife with problems. In *Braiding Sweetgrass* (2013), Robin Wall Kimmerer, the Potawatomie botanist, activist, and writer, has argued that the modern world desperately needs to become more indigenous: "For all of us, becoming indigenous to a place means living as if your children's future mattered, to take care of the land as if our lives, both material and spiritual, depended on it." She argues, too, that while indigeneity is a birthright, a way of being long woven into the traditional cultures of Native peoples, its lessons are available to newcomers to a given place. The work of America's more recent immigrants, she proposes, "may be to set aside the ways of the colonist and become indigenous to place." To do so, she suggests, settlers need to learn from the traditional knowledge of the people who have long learned to live in this place. Learn the names of the plants and animals. Watch and listen to the lessons they teach. Learn to live in harmony with them, drawing sustenance for your own kind from their abundance and doing your part to keep the land thriving, nurturing the web of reciprocity. And most important, tell and retell stories that keep this relationship, this ceremony of interdependence, alive and strong. For those struggling to learn these lessons for the first time as colonists or the children of colonists (for all human cultures were once indigenous, though many have forgotten these lessons), this means attending to what is broken in the land and acknowledging what has been lost. But these lessons can be learned again. "Being naturalized to place means to live as if this is the land that feeds you, as if these are the streams from which you drink, that build your body and fill your spirit. To become naturalized is to know that your ancestors lie in this ground. Here is where you give your gifts and meet your responsibilities."[2]

This, certainly, is one story of *Walden* and "Walking"—of Thoreau immersing himself in the knowledge of his Native predecessors and then turning to learn the lessons of his natal place, weaving the wisdom of the land into a story that offers a different path from the one that was fast turning Concord into a regional hub of a global capitalist system. In writing *Walden*, Thoreau plants a seed that promises to bear native fruit. If Thoreau might have mixed feelings about what Walden Pond has become in the century and a half since he left its shores, a small enclave in an extremely wealthy town, its woods and water always on the edge of being overrun by visitors, it nevertheless figures as a keystone in what Keith Basso and Lisa Brooks might call a *place-world*—a locus that conveys a powerful story about how a people should be in the world.[3] In American environmentalism, *Walden* and "Walking" are as close to Original Instructions as we have. Their roots in Native tradition and culture, and the complications of those roots, deserve to be better known.

Real problems exist with seeing these key works as Thoreau's effort to become indigenous to place. For one thing, he writes remarkably little about Native peoples in either text. There are references, to be sure, and I will trace some of these below to see how they fit into some of Thoreau's major themes. But the list is short: the groundnut passage above; a brief anecdote about a Native basket seller; a description of the Creek ceremony of first fruits, or Busk; a note of praise for the serviceability of a Penobscot tent as shelter; some comments about stone tools in the bean field; and an observation about aboriginal paths around Walden's shore. Indian, or corn, meal, which Thoreau proudly eats, is mentioned as often as Indian people, who serve primarily as an icon for his doctrine of simplicity rather than subjects for his contemplations. There is far more in *Walden* about India than there is about Indians and little direct borrowing from the vast Indian Notebooks whose accumulating pages quickened as Thoreau began his final revisions of *Walden*. Thoreau may have relished playing Indian with John and been celebrated by his friends for his Indian ways, but his sojourn at Walden Pond wasn't truly an example of playing Indian. He built a small version of a modern framed house, not a wigwam, and his bean field was a market garden rather than an effort to re-create a Three Sisters garden of corn, squash, and beans. Thoreau was trying to reinvent New England culture rather than revive traditional Algonquian lifeways. More significant, for all of his deep interest in Walden Woods and sustained meditation on its former inhabitants, Thoreau writes little about the history of the Musketaquid people and nothing of the clear accounting of their removal that is essential in coming to terms with the legacy of settler colonialism. In *After One Hundred Winters* (2021), Margaret D. Jacobs details the importance for settlers themselves to tell these stories—as Lemuel Shattuck and Ralph Waldo Emerson had in their histories of Concord.[4] Without such a commitment to facing the hard truth of living on Native land, there can be no real reconciliation, and such an effort was not among the many projects of *Walden* and "Walking." Nor is there any effort in either text to engage meaningfully with Native communities. Thoreau's trip to Katahdin took place during his second summer at Walden Pond, but he failed to secure a Penobscot guide. He describes, briefly, his night in jail for refusing to pay his poll tax and, thus, support an expansionist, proslavery war, but he fails to draw the connection between this principled act of civil disobedience and his own debt to the Native people whose absence he simply accepts as a given.

These are not incidental omissions if we see Thoreau's project in *Walden* and "Walking" as an effort to become naturalized to the woods, fields, and waters of Musketaquid, and they become more striking when we see these works against the backdrop of Thoreau's more systematic engagement with Native history in *A Week* and his increasing immersion in the Indian Notebooks. The Native absence in these works becomes, indeed, significant. This absence is, I suggest, embedded in the project itself. Thoreau's effort to become "native" made it more difficult for him to account for his status as a settler living on Indigenous land, more difficult for him to make common cause with the Native peoples who still managed to keep their communities together in Massachusetts and across New England at a time when they could have made good use of allies. Mark Rifkin has argued that *Walden* is characterized by "settler common sense," a complex of attitudes and feelings that don't directly address Native dispossession but are everywhere shaped by Indigenous absence; indeed, Thoreau's effort to critique an emergent American capitalism from an "Indian" stance depends on the absence of Native peoples themselves. Thoreau, in short, fell into the replacement trap: in trying to become native himself, Native people became what Thomas King has called "inconvenient."[5] Thoreau wrote, moreover, not for an audience of Native people but for his own community—his neighbors, first and foremost, who wondered what exactly he was up to living on the edge of town, and then more broadly for an American public struggling against the quiet desperation that threatened to eat away at the settler world they had so painstakingly, and brutally, created. These are real problems, and they are ones that would come to the fore again and again in Thoreau's later works. But they do not, I suggest, fully negate the value of what Thoreau was able to articulate in *Walden* and "Walking." His insights about what it means to live as if you were native to a place and his struggles to connect those insights to the Indigenous communities struggling to survive in a settler colonial world are, I hope, ones we can still learn from today.

Living on the Edge

An early passage in *Walden* captures the ambivalent, contradictory nature of critiquing the settler colonial world while living within it. In "Economy," Thoreau describes a "strolling Indian [who] went to the house of a well-known lawyer in my neighborhood to sell baskets" and was dismayed when he was refused. "'What!' exclaimed the Indian when he went out the gate. 'Do you mean to starve us?' . . . He had not discovered that it was necessary to make it worth the other's while to buy them, or at least to make him think it was so." This passage is usually read as a metaphor for Thoreau's personal struggle in the marketplace, particularly the economically disastrous publication of *A Week*: "I, too, had woven a basket of delicate texture, but I had not made it worth anyone's while to buy them," he writes, signifying his own Indian position outside the capitalist economy (*W* 19). Joshua Bellin notes that this symbolic conflation diminishes the very real economic hardship faced by Native people in New England, who faced both overt racism and systematic indentured servitude as they made a precarious living on New England's margins. This precarity was, after all, part of the settler colonial system, and it was manifest not just in government policy but in myriad individual interactions like the one Thoreau captures here. Neither Samuel Hoar, the lawyer of the incident, nor Thoreau himself may have intended to starve this man and his family, but they played their part, nonetheless. This is one lesson of Thoreau's effort to become more native.[6]

Yet the episode also conveys another lesson: that "neighbor" is an expansive term, one that reaches beyond the narrow confines of a settler colonial village to include people—both human and more-than-human— pushed to the edges of New England. The strolling Indian has entered

Thoreau's neighborhood, and if he failed at making a capitalist transaction, he managed to shift the terms of the encounter. He may have approached the lawyer not as a merchant of baskets but as a neighbor offering an item he had woven himself, drawn from the New England woods. Indeed, some years later, Thoreau helped an Indigenous group locate the black ash trees used in basketmaking in the Concord swamps he knew so well (JM 31:52, March 8, 1860). This basket-maker was, perhaps, proposing a transaction that owed more to what Kimmerer, drawing on the work of Lewis Hyde, describes as the culture of reciprocity, of ceremonial, symbolic, diplomatic exchange meant to reweave the bond between communities, rather than one dictated by the cash exchange of the marketplace.[7] Thus his exclamation—"What! Do you mean to starve us?—is not that of a neophyte capitalist but of a community leader whose neighborly gesture has been spurned. The basket-maker may be outside of the capitalist world of Concord, but he still articulates a powerful alternative to it that Thoreau, in weaving his own basket of words on the edge of town, gradually teases out.

For Thoreau, it was important that he turn his back on the main story of Concord, away from the leading citizens and the marks of progress that left the landscape stripped of trees and striped with railroads, and focus instead on the marginal edges of town where swamps eluded the axe; where the fox, muskrat, and otter still roamed; and where, as Thoreau observes in *Walden*, are "wild men, who instinctively follow other fashions and trust other authorities than their townsmen, and by their goings and comings stitch towns together in parts where else they would be ripped" (*W* 283). In moving to Walden Pond, Thoreau planted himself firmly on the margins, on land that had been deemed too poor for productive farming and left as woodlots and, occasionally, as a place where people not entirely welcome in the village could attempt to eke out a living. In "Walking," Thoreau enacted a similar journey on his daily walks, moving from the garret of his family home on Main Street to the wild margins of town, the wooded patches, swamps, and meadows where the fox, the otter, and the muskrat still flourished among the tangle of indigenous and naturalized plants. What he found on the margins of Concord was an edge community, a place where the world of a modernizing New England town blended with the older world of forest, marsh, and river.

The term "edge community" is a classic one in environmental studies. Coined by Frederic Clements in 1904 in a monograph about the botany of Nebraska, the term was popularized by Aldo Leopold in his 1933 textbook

Game Management—animals thrived, Leopold noted, in areas where two ecosystems intersected, as species suited to each joined those who specialized in such edge habitat. Edges can be rich, resilient places, though contemporary ecologists have cautioned that the edge effect is less suited to describing habitat fragmentation that comes with human development—not all edges are equal. More recently, a number of scholars from outside ecology have noted that edge effects can apply to both the human and more-than-human community. Nancy Turner, Ian Davidson-Hunt, and Michael O'Flaherty framed the concept in 2003 of a "cultural edge"—a zone where two or more cultures meet and exchange ecological knowledge in a manner that enriches both the human and ecological community. Other scholars, including Monica Mulrennan and Véronique Bussières, have picked up the term, tracing, by way of example, the interactions between the Inuit, Cree, and Anglo communities on James Bay, where each traded knowledge to help better manage a changing ecosystem. The concept of cultural edge, they argue, better captures the dynamism and multiple agencies of these encounters in ways that similar categories—such as the frontier, the borderlands, the contact zone, or the middle ground—can overlook. While cultural edges are certainly shaped by power differentials and larger historic and economic inequalities, this framework allows for a fuller acknowledgment of both human and more-than-human voice and agency. According to Mulrennan and Bussières, "Cultural edges take us beyond the middle ground to bring attention to the production of sites of contestation, dispossession, and resistance as well as sites of cooperation, assistance, and sharing, supporting greater consideration of local agency." William Cronon has turned to the concept in recent years, titling the blog for the University of Wisconsin Center for Culture, History, and Environment "Edge Effects" so as "to echo Leopold's insight that edges are places where very different kinds of creatures (and people) come together, mingle, and change."[8] This process of gathering, mingling, and changing is, I suggest, central to Thoreau's work in the years when he gradually turned his two-year experience of living at the edge of Concord into a work that sparked America's slow environmental revolution.

The edge community is hardly invisible in *Walden*: Thoreau may have lived alone on the shore of the pond, yet he devotes many pages to his visitors, and accounts as old as N. C. Wyeth's *Men of Concord* (1939) and as recent as Robert Gross's *The Transcendentalists and Their World* (2021) have traced Thoreau's deep connection with people who may have lived on the outskirts of the village but were deeply rooted in the landscape around it. Elise Lemire, in *Black Walden* (2009), explores in detail the largely African American women and men whose marginal lives are central to the "Former Inhabitants" chapter—Cato Ingraham, Zilpha, and Brister and Fenda Freeman—and she notes the grim toll that poverty and racism took on these formerly enslaved people who tried to build a new life as a free community in the decades after the Revolution. She notes that other edge communities in Concord—by the Great Field and along Old Marlborough Road—fared better, remaining a vital, if marginal, part of Concord through Thoreau's own life. Laura Dassow Walls has examined Thoreau's relationship to the Irish immigrants—Hugh Quoil, John Collier, and John Field in particular—whose lives briefly but powerfully intersected with his at Walden Pond. Though he does not tell the story of how the Musketaquid tribe was driven from their native ground, Thoreau is mindful of the long Indian presence in the Walden Woods, their stone tools tinkling against his hoe in the beanfield, their path still faintly visible around the pond. Thoreau wonders why "this small village, this germ of something more," failed, but it is worth noting that such marginal villages were common in nineteenth-century New England, where poorer folks from a variety of ethnic backgrounds scraped a fragile living on land that was not particularly desirable, and where people found a measure of freedom from the norms and hierarchies of village life.[9] And if we turn from *Walden* to the Journal, it might be more fair to say that this edge community did not quite fail after all.

Some members, such as the contrarian farmer George Minott and the trapper Ray Melvin, lived in houses in or near the village but spent their best hours in the woods and waters on the village outskirts; some, like African Americans Jennie Dugan and her family near Old Marlborough Road and the Garrison family by the Great Field, were carefully tending their farms and building a secure foothold; some, like the Riordans and other Irish immigrants who worked for the Thoreau family, followed paid labor where it took them, at times building strong ties to their employers, sometimes moving on, or occasionally, like the French Canadian woodchopper Alex Therien, sinking roots into Concord soil. Native people had not entirely vanished. Thoreau notes in his Journal that Penobscot families would occasionally visit to sell baskets and trade, individual Natives would pass through town going about their business, and among the white inhabitants of Concord, "you may still find a man with Indian blood in his veins" (*PJ* 3:93); he later recorded (on November 26, 1860) his mother's mention that one Lidy Bay, "an Indian woman (so considered)," used to live near the Caesar family by Great Field and sold baskets (JM 33:18). This was the community Thoreau found on the edges of Concord. "I wish my neighbors were wilder," he commented in 1851, and here on the outskirts of town, they were (*PJ* 3:201).

What Thoreau gains from this edge community is access to a different story from the one that shaped the village. Someone like Bill Wheeler, who hobbled about on "two clumps, having frozen his feet," may have been the most marginal of citizens, living in extreme indigence, sleeping in barns when he could and in the meadows when he couldn't, but Thoreau follows him far from the village center. "He seemed to belong to a different caste from other men, and reminded me of the Indian Pariah and martyr," reaching across the world to find the right analogy for this naturalized man of Concord. Wheeler scraped by doing odd jobs and living off the land; Thoreau describes coming across him in the Great Meadows: "One day . . . I saw in my walk a kind of shelter such as woodmen might use . . . made of meadow hay cast over a rude frame. Thrusting my head in at a hole, as I am wont to do in such cases, I found Bill Wheeler there curled up asleep, who, being suddenly wakened from a sound sleep, rubbed his eyes and inquired if I had found any game." Thoreau muses on this encounter, wondering if Wheeler "might be some mighty philosopher, greater than Socrates or Diogenes, simplifying life, returning to nature, having turned his back on towns. . . . Here was one . . . whose very vividness of perception, clear knowledge, and insight have made him dumb, leaving no common consciousness and ground of parlance with his kind,—or rather, his unlike kindred! Whose news plainly is not my news nor yours" (*PJ* 4:258–60). Elisha Dugan, too, though living an impoverished and marginalized life along Old Marlborough Road, offers a model of how to live a backwoods life in the middle of Middlesex County. In "Walking," Thoreau celebrates his life in verse:

> O man of wild habits,
> Partridges and rabbits,
> Who has no cares
> Only to set snares,
> Who liv'st all alone
> Closest to the bone
> Where life is sweetest
> Constantly eatest. (*Exc* 193)

What matters to Thoreau here is not Elisha's race (he was the son of the formerly enslaved African Americans Thomas and Jennie Dugan) or his status on the tax rolls of Concord (he had lost the family's land) but his ability to carve out a different life on the edge of the village, one with its own sweetness. What he most admires about Dugan is his *wildness*—Thoreau's increasingly preferred term for the process of naturalization at the heart of these works.

Wildness is what thrives in this edge community. Part of what Thoreau finds here is a deeper knowledge of an environment that is not simply a resource to be extracted but an incredibly complex weave of different threads. Thus Thoreau learns from these edge neighbors about the flowering of different plants, the habits of muskrats, and the migratory patterns of fish and birds. Thoreau's earliest efforts in phenology date from this era, after he left Walden Pond and began his more systematic walks from the family home on Concord's Main Street. His first charts of flowering plants appear in 1851 and 1852, but more striking in the Journal is that this knowledge first comes in a form quite different from spare tables of data that would define his Kalendar—not isolated bits of information but part of a web of subsistence. People who made their living from the wild fruits of Musketaquid saw things differently from the scientists of the day. As he describes in an early Journal, the fishnets he finds floating below the surface of the river "are no more intrusions than the cobweb in the sun. . . . I wonder how the blustering people of the town could have done this elvish work (*PJ* 1:329). "Science," Thoreau argues in 1851, "does not embody all men know, only what is for men of science. The woodman tells me how he caught a trout in a box trap, how he made his trough for maple sap of pine logs, and the spouts of sumach or white ash, which have a large pith. He can relate facts to human life" (*PJ* 3:174). "Wild" is, in this era, still interchangeable with "Indian" for Thoreau, and both are terms of high praise. One February day, during "our month of crusted snow"—quickly guessing (correctly) that this was an Indigenous name for the month: "Was this the Indians?"—he meets Sudbury Haynes at the Fairhaven Cliffs "come a-fishing. . . . He represents the Indian still. . . . I feel he is as essential a part of our community as the lawyer in the village. He tells me he caught three pickerel here the other day that weighed seven pounds all together. . . . The weather concerns him. He is an observer of her phenomena" (*PJ* 4:337–38). This is the Indian wisdom Thoreau sketched at the end of "Natural History of Massachusetts," a web of knowledge not abstracted and isolated from the environment but seen from inside its meshes. Yet while Thoreau celebrates this trove of ecological knowledge, he seems untroubled that Native people are largely a memory in Musketaquid and that the "wild" people he meets in his walks are settlers and arrivants who may have become more indigenous to this place but are not Indigenous people themselves.

Thoreau goes back in time in his Journal to see how this wisdom has evolved, looking through some eighteenth-century ledgers for traces of its native roots. From the credits for the skins of wildcats, squirrels, foxes, and deer, he can better know his brute neighbors of yore, and in noting a wampum belt exchanged for fifteen shillings, he finds that this edge world had a long colonial transition (*PJ* 7:264). If wampum is no longer accepted currency on the Mill Dam in Thoreau's day, older ways persist along the river. Thoreau is fascinated watching the spearfishers on Fairhaven Bay, looking for prey in the nighttime waters by the light of fires mounted off the bows of their boats—a technique learned from Native people. "It reminds me of the light which Columbus saw on approaching the shores of the New World" (*PJ* 5:29). This wisdom helps weave these settlers into the land. "The Indians generally," Thoreau notes after a visit to Clamshell Bank on the Concord River, "make a very extensive use of the muskrat for food–& from these heaps [of shells], it would seem that they used the fresh-water clam extensively also—these 2 peculiarly *native* animals" (*PJ* 7:190; italics in the original). By eating these animals—by living close to the land—the Musketaquid people made a ceremony of their indigeneity. Thoreau never quite claims indigeneity for himself, but he crafts his own ceremonies of subsistence. His long fascination with wild apple trees, which would culminate in the late essay "Wild Apples," begins in this era too. While he admires the native crab apple, "our wild apple is wild perchance like myself, who belong not to the aboriginal race here—but strayed into the woods from the cultivated stock—where the birds where winged thoughts or agents have planted me" (*PJ* 3:232). He has been *planted*—the passive object of a sentence whose subjects are multiple and increasingly elusive: "birds" or "winged thoughts" or "agents." The ambiguity of this sentence suggests the price of naturalization. Gone here is the triumphant individualism and self-reliant agency with which *Walden* begins. To become more native to his place, Thoreau must surrender to the wild.

More-Than-Brute Neighbors

From this vantage point, Thoreau is able to gain new perspective on both the village and the woods. In *Walden*, he notes that he traveled to the center of Concord every day or two, but it was not exactly a return home: "As I walked in the woods to see the birds and squirrels, so I walked in the village to see the men and boys; instead of the wind among the pines I heard the carts rattle. In one direction from my house there was a colony of muskrats in the river meadows; under the grove of elms and buttonwoods in the other horizon was a village of busy men, as curious to me as if they had been prairie dogs" (*W* 167). This is a crucial insight. From the Walden Woods, nature is not the opposite of the village, the wilderness that served as the binary counterpoint to civilization in the late nineteenth century, a space cleared of its Native inhabitants and declared "pristine."[10] Nature instead becomes a field that includes both the village and the woods, and its wild edges everywhere show through. The edge decenters the village and the human world it embodies, and in the Journal, Thoreau finds the equivalency works in both directions. This insight builds gradually—in 1839, he asks, "Why should we not cultivate neighborly relations with the foxes?" (*PJ* 1:135), and some years later, hearing a fox "barking raggedly, wildly, demoniacally in the night," Thoreau suggests that "he is but a faint man" (*PJ* 2:188). In 1850, on seeing a muskrat come out of a hole in the ice, Thoreau remarks, "He is a man wilder than Ray or Melvin. While I am looking at him, I am thinking what he is thinking of me. He a different sort of man, that is all" (*PJ* 3:151). When a neighbor shows him a heron he had shot, Thoreau declares, "I am glad to recognize him for a native of America,—why not an American citizen?" (*PJ* 3:111). As the Journal progresses, Thoreau gradually extends personhood from animals to trees. In December 1851, he describes seeing white pines illuminated in the evening sun, "a soft feathery grove with their grey stems indistinctly seen—like human beings come to their cabin door.... The trees indeed have hearts. With a certain affection the sun seems to send its farewell ray far and level over the copses to them, & they silently receive it with gratitude, like a group of settlers with their children. The pines impress me as human" (*PJ* 4:211–12). Thoreau's simile here, of trees as settlers, points to an obvious problem in his project, which I will return to below. For now, I want to stress that here, Thoreau erases the barrier between trees and humans—both are people. In *Walden*, he would make that bond even more intimate. In "Solitude," he describes a passing moment of loneliness when he wonders briefly whether human neighbors are essential to one's health. Instead, he becomes "suddenly sensible of a sweet and beneficent society in Nature.... Every little pine needle expanded with sympathy and befriended me. I was so distinctly made aware of the presence of something kindred to me, even in scenes which we are accustomed to call wild and dreary, and also that the nearest of blood to me and humanest was not a person nor a villager, that I thought no place could ever be strange to me again" (*W* 132). Thoreau was home, weaving himself into natural world by extending to it a domestic network of feeling.[11]

This growing sense of animals and plants as persons, neighbors, and fellow citizens is hardly unique to Thoreau, though it was unusual in a Western world that more typically saw animals as dumb brutes at best and as Cartesian machines at worst, liable to exploitation at any human whim and without any ethical qualms. Trees and plants had their advocates, but they had little standing.[12] There was a small but visible movement against the exploitation of animals in this era framed primarily in terms of averting pain in animals deemed capable of suffering—Thoreau no doubt heard these arguments worked out at length as Bronson Alcott and Charles Lane honed their plans for their short-lived Fruitlands utopian community in 1843, and this ethic infuses the chapter "Higher Laws" in *Walden*. Eating animals "is a miserable way, as anyone who has gone to snaring rabbits and slaughtering lambs will learn" (*W* 216). His focus in this chapter is not so much the sentience or suffering of animals or the sympathetic connection to the more-than-human world that infuses the pine needle passage above. Here, Thoreau focuses on the moral pollution of humans engaged in such gross subsistence, habits that tether the soul to a corrupt world—an attitude more characteristic of the Hindu scriptures he devoured at Walden Pond and other idealist philosophies. "We are conscious of an animal in us, that awakens in proportion as higher nature slumbers" (*W* 219), he writes, framing an irreconcilable dualism between an ideal soul and a gross materiality.

Yet even as he utters this sentence, he has second thoughts about demeaning our animal nature. "It is reptile and sensual, and perhaps cannot be wholly expelled; like the worms which, even in life and health, occupy our bodies" (*W* 219). Thoreau recognizes that humans may be pure but not well—that our animal nature is essential to our full being and that a true purity, a real chastity, must unite both. Thus the hermit, in the opening of "Brute Neighbors," immediately following "Higher Laws," must turn from his ethereal meditations to the matter of digging worms for fishing. This act of subsistence weaves the spiritual impulse into the materiality of the world. Not by chance, a particular plant serves as a marker of this process—he advises the poet to "set in the spade down yonder among the ground-nuts, where you see the johnswort waving" (*W* 224). The act of digging worms among the groundnuts and Saint-John's-wort sets the hermit's meditations on a more proper path: "Why do precisely these objects we behold make a world? Why has man just these species of animals for his neighbors?" (*W* 225). These objects, these *neighbors*, this community, and what it means to belong to it, are what matters. The question Thoreau poses here is not really one of animal rights but of relations. Kristen Case has termed this "knowing as neighboring," drawing on Bruno Latour's actor-network theory and Karen Barad's sense of posthuman performativity to capture the relational, transactional quality of Thoreau's engagement with the more-than-human world.[13] In replacing the word "objects" with "neighbors" in this passage, Thoreau marks a shift from seeing animals and plants as fixed objects of study to relational beings, part of network in which he, too, is fully engaged. Thus Thoreau-the-hermit doesn't classify the groundnuts or fishworms but uses them to engage with the world around him, a movement in his thinking that aligns closely with the newly emerging field of Indigenous animal studies. In "Brute Neighbors," Thoreau becomes enmeshed in what Dorion Sagan calls a multispecies community, a networked set of sociobiological relations. As Kim TallBear has noted, this stance is quite close to Native American views of the connections between the human and the more-than-human world—what Vine Deloria Jr. calls the "American Indian metaphysic" of "all my relations." In this Indigenous worldview, according to TallBear, the same immaterial life force animates everything—animals and plants, water and earth. There is no dualism separating the spiritual and the material, and unlike many Western formulations of animal studies, the starting point is not human consciousness, with its distinct capacities to know and feel, but a shared, interwoven ontology that greatly expands the scope of the community.[14]

In *Walden*, and even more so in the Journal, animals appear not as objects of study or sources of profit but as fellow beings going about their business. In his walks about the Concord landscape, particularly in the early 1850s, Thoreau resembles less a scientist off to study a particular organism than as someone scouting the land, looking for signs that might open a window into natural phenomena.[15] That might entail observing the date when a plant flowers, noticing the composition of trees in a swamp, following the tracks of a fox in the snow, or holding the gaze of a woodchuck for a long half hour. In this, he followed the pattern of premodern hunters and gatherers learning to read the landscape. It was this rooted, interwoven, living knowledge that Thoreau sought, what many Indigenous people learn as part of their birthright and what serves for a settler like Thoreau as the mark of being naturalized on his home ground. In *Walden*, the animals he meets cross his path. Mice and rabbits and wasps set up housekeeping in his home, squirrels and chickadees share his food, and foxes and loons engage in a delicate dance played out on the local geography. They are neither subject and object nor predator and prey. They are *neighbors*, and Thoreau is eager to learn from them, whether to wonder at the motivations of ants engaged in battle or to stare into the eyes of a partridge chick holding still by some deep instinct while its mother tries to lure away a potential predator. "All intelligence seemed reflected in them. They suggest not merely the purity of infancy, but a wisdom clarified by experience. Such an eye was not born when the bird was, but is coeval with the sky which it reflects. The woods do not yield another such a gem" (*W* 227). This is, again, knowledge at once material and spiritual, embedded, and relational, not gained by the dry exercise of logic or ethics or the narrowed gaze of science. And although Thoreau ultimately turns away from hunting and fishing in "Higher Laws," he recognizes that such activities offer a better pathway toward this wisdom than philosophical musings or the dissection table. Only by walking, watching, listening, and attending to everything that crossed his path could Thoreau begin to grasp the rich interplay of his many brute neighbors.

If Thoreau mourns the loss of some neighbors—bears, wolves, deer, and beavers that were exterminated in colonial times—he celebrates the fact that other neighbors thrive. Rabbits and partridges "are among the simple and indigenous animal products . . . of the very hue and substance of Nature, and nearest allied to leaves and to the ground," he writes at the end of "Winter Animals," in a comment that playfully undercuts the market sense of "products" and restores the word to its sense of "offspring." "Our woods teem with them both, and around every swamp may be seen the partridge or rabbit walk, beset with twiggy fences and horsehair snares, which some cow-boy tends" (*W* 281). Such emblems of indigeneity are everywhere, and those human neighbors who see them best are those who seek them as food.

If Thoreau approves of encouraging young people to hunt and fish as the best way of making their "closest acquaintance with Nature," so much more knowledge comes from setting these age-old snares. This is not hunting to supply the market but a kind of ceremony, a kind of food that ties one to the earth itself. Subsistence, then, is the sacrament of indigeneity.

This process of immersion and connection, of recognizing the personhood of nature and building an empathetic bond with one's more-than-human neighbors in the edge community, comes with real costs. It puts Thoreau in conflict with his less-wild neighbors, and it exposes him to a sense of sharp loss to which the village seems immune. There was a cruel irony in Thoreau learning to love trees in the mid-nineteenth century, as Massachusetts cut its remaining woods at a ferocious rate. In December 1851, Thoreau bore witness to the cutting of one of the last mature pines on Fair Haven Hill, "which waved in solitary majesty over the sproutlands." He watches the sawers gnaw like "beavers or insects at the trunk," until, after long minutes, the tree begins to fall. "It rushes to embrace the earth, & mingle its elements with the dust. And now all is still once more & forever." Thoreau measures the corpse as if for its shroud ("4 feet in diameter where it was sawed—about 100 feet long"), even as the chopper prepares it for the mill. "And the space it occupied in the upper air is vacant for the next 2 centuries. It is lumber He has laid waste the air. . . . A plant which it has taken two centuries to perfect rising by slow stages toward the heavens—has this afternoon ceased to exist. . . . Why does not the village bell sound a knell?" (*PJ* 4:227–29). The more Thoreau weaves himself into this community on the edge of his native town, the more he grieves its loss. The more he sees, the more he mourns.

One result, then, of Thoreau's growing empathy with the human and the more-than-human members of this edge community is new environmental ethics. Another is a new ontology. It is no coincidence that the passage on the cutting of the pine in the Journal is followed immediately by an extensive description of the thawing sand on the bank of the Deep Cut that would become the climax of *Walden*. The first draft of the book contains a short paragraph on the phenomenon, one that drew him again and again to the railroad bank; the full version begins to take shape in Version F, written in 1853–54.[16] It draws extensively on the Journal entry written on December 31, 1851, the day after Thoreau witnessed the cutting of the great pine. The thawing sand, he writes, "suggest[s]—that there is motion in the earth as well on the surface; it lives & grows. It is warmed & influenced by the sun—just as my blood by my thoughts. . . . The earth I tread on is not a dead, inert mass. It is a body—has a spirit—is organic—and fluid to the influence of its spirit—and to whatever particle of that spirit is in me. . . . Concord is a worthier place to live in—the globe is a worthier place, for these creations This slumbering life—that may wake. Even the solid globe is permeated by the living law. It is the most living of creatures" (*PJ* 4:230–31). This is one of Thoreau's clearest expressions of the pantheism that runs through his work. That he seized on this idea the day after watching one of the great treasures of Musketaquid summarily turned into lumber was no accident—Thoreau's ethical outrage fueled his ontological insight. Trees have standing, Thoreau suggests, not because of their aesthetic value in a picturesque landscape or through some gradual extension of the doctrine of rights beyond the purview of propertied white males, but because everything on this earth is alive and filled with spirit. It is a stance rooted not in logic but in empathy—a shared experience of what it means to be alive in Concord, on the globe. At the end of the sandbank passage in *Walden*, Thoreau makes this insight clear. The melting sand "is somewhat excrementitious . . . but this suggests at least that Nature has some bowels, and there again is the mother of humanity." Affect, like "the frost coming out of the ground," flows throughout "a living earth" (*W* 308–9).

This perspective is not easily gained along the commercial hive of Concord's Mill Dam, and as Thoreau finishes his meditation on the sand foliage, he notes that on the same walk, he saw "an old Irishwoman at the shanty in the woods—sitting out on the hillside bare headed in the rain & on the icy though thawing ground—knitting. She comes out like the ground squirrel at the least intimation of warmer weather. She will not have to go far to be buried—so close she lives to the earth.—While I walk still in a great coat & under an umbrella—Such Irish as these are naturalizing themselves at a rapid rate—and threaten to displace the Yankees—as the latter have the Indians" (*PJ* 4:231). This is a striking version of racial succession: if Thoreau here accepts as a given the displacement of one race with another, by privileging Irish immigrants, he upends any notion of Anglo-Saxon superiority or Manifest Destiny. He upends, too, the terms of this succession. What matters most in this example is one group's ability not to better exploit the resources of the earth but to live close to it, to naturalize, to grow wild. The measure of success at the edge of Concord is not how efficiently a people can transform the earth but how fully they can be transformed by it.

This process of becoming naturalized carried risks that Thoreau knew all too well. He had, after all, burned at least a hundred acres of woods in 1844, between Fairhaven Bay and Walden Pond, after a carelessly set campfire got out of control. He and Edward Hoar had been trying to travel "Indian-style," living off the fish they caught on the river, but they badly misjudged the safety of their campsite. It took him until 1850 to write about the episode (It was a source of deep shame, and he notes that the hissed phrase "burnt woods" followed him for years around Concord), but he resolves at the end of the passage to "attend to the phenomenon before me—determined to make the most of it" (*PJ* 3:78). And he does. A few days after this entry, he joins a man named Ray in a carefully prescribed burn in the woods. Though Ray is low in social standing, Thoreau is pleased that "however poor miserable, intemperate & worthless he may appear to be a mere burden to society—but you will find at least that there is something which he understands & can do better than any other." He then explains how such burning should be done: against the wind, with a fire line prepared, and enough people set around to snuff any embers (*PJ* 3:79–80). And then, he revels as new life appears—strawberries and huckleberries and shoots of grass. On September 10, 1851, he notes that "in the spring I burned over a hundred acres till the ground earth was sere and black, and by midsummer this space was clad in a fresher and more luxuriant green than the surrounding even. Shall man then despair?" (*PJ* 4:68–69). By then, Thoreau had recorded numerous accounts in the Indian Notebooks of the Native practice of burning the woods in the spring and fall to provide better habitat for berries and for deer, and he had learned to do the same. Burning the woods was a sign, finally, of becoming naturalized. Thoreau was learning, slowly but surely, how to speak the language of trees and meadows, of ponds and rivers, a language best learned on the edges of Concord, where people who lived different kinds of marginal lives shared their insights and built a new, if terribly fragile, community.

Naturalizing Mythology

Transformation is one motif of the sandbank passage in "Spring"—correspondences are everywhere in this vision, and form ceaselessly blends into form. In "Walking," Thoreau complains that English literature "cannot adequately express this yearning for the Wild"; he turns to classical mythology instead, for "mythology is the crop which the Old World bore before its soil became exhausted" (*Exc* 209). In the Journal that is the source for this passage, written in January 1851, Thoreau exclaims, "The West is preparing to add its fables to those of the East" (*PJ* 3:180), and in the finished essay he adds, "the poets of the world will be inspired by American mythology" (*Exc* 209). "Walking" is a keystone in Thoreau's effort to incorporate indigenous materials into this mythology, drawn not from his Indian Notebooks but from the landscape itself. This happens gradually, as his walks in the wooded edges of Concord slowly reveal what has been there all long. Toward the end of the essay, as Thoreau describes walking through a pine grove one evening on the edge of Spaulding Farm, his prose lifts into the register of mysticism—beings appear, emblems of an enchanted world just visible to those who have learned to become native.

The Spaulding Farm passage has its sources in a number of Journal entries. An afternoon walk on October 31, 1850, when Thoreau was "looking through a stately pine-grove I saw the western sun falling in golden streams through its aisles—Its west side opposite to me was all lit up with golden light; but what was I to it?" (*PJ* 3:124). On November 11, "the west side of every wood & rising ground gleamed like the boundary of elysium" (*PJ* 3:138). On November 21, Thoreau finds that the sun in a pinewood "reinspires the dreams of my youth. . . . It was like looking into dream land" (*PJ* 3:148). And on February 27, 1851, Thoreau muses over the pure oddness that a deed gives title to a swamp he recently surveyed "to Spaulding his Heirs & Assigns . . . at all times & forever after . . . [for them to] have, hold, use, occupy and enjoy the said swamp." What is that absurdity, he asks, compared to "the shadow of the wings of thought" that suggest events of greater importance in the world? (*PJ* 3:198–200).

Thoreau weaves these thoughts into a vision of a reenchanted world. In the finished essay, he describes walking through a pinewood at sunset, where he half-glimpses, half-imagines a family of ethereal beings who live on the edge of the material world: "I was impressed as if some ancient and altogether admirable and shining family had seated there in that part of Concord, unknown to me; to whom the sun was servant; who had not gone into society in the village; who had not been called on. . . . The pines furnished them with gables as they grew. Their house was not obvious to vision; the trees grew through it. I do not know whether I heard the sounds of a suppressed hilarity or not. They seemed to recline on sunbeams. They have sons and daughters. They are quite well. . . . Nothing can equal the serenity of their lives" (*Exc* 218). Thus the "shadow of the wings of thought" takes form, transmuted into beings described with a warmth and wonder that make the passage a fundamental basis of Thoreau's growing understanding of nature. It is, first, an intuited understanding—this moment is emblematic of Thoreau's insistence on his transcendentalism even as he mastered the emerging practice and discourse of science. It is, second, better described not as a moment of transcendence, like Emerson's transparent eyeball passage in "Nature," where the subject sees the world dissolve into its ideal essences, but one of immanence. In this moment of enchantment, Thoreau doesn't see through or beyond the material world; he sees it spring to life, its spiritual essence suddenly made visible. And this vision is, finally, one of wholeness, pleasure, serenity, and even suppressed hilarity, rather than terror or dissolution. This pinewood on the edge of Concord is the Holy Land to which his walks all lead, where "the subtle magnetism in Nature which, if we unconsciously yield to it, will direct us aright" (*Exc* 195), not the West of Manifest Destiny but the westering impulse in all of humankind—in a word, the wild. Elysium is not beyond some far distant horizon but on the western side of every pinewood.

This is the great treasure of Spaulding's farm, though Spaulding himself is blind to it, and Thoreau can see it only by glimpses: "But I find it difficult to remember them. They fade irrevocably out of my mind even now while I speak and endeavor to recall them, and recollect myself. It is only after a long and serious effort to recollect my best thoughts that I become again aware of their cohabitancy" (*Exc* 219). This passage resonates throughout Thoreau's work: The wide traveling in Concord. The wild spaces at the town's margins. The animate earth, alive, organic. The familiar world grown transcendent. The ethereal family in the pines, however, strikes a new note. Who are these beings? Not quite the faeries whose lore fascinated the young Louisa May Alcott, nor New World relatives of the Greek god Pan, survivors of the long tradition of British folklore and classical myth that Timothy Morton terms the "arche-lithic."[17] Nor, exactly, are they symbols of a more formal pantheism that Thoreau invoked when bemoaning the unthinking felling of a Chesuncook pine, a spirit of nature that was, by the mid-nineteenth century, a comfortable foil for Protestant orthodoxy, with a heritage reaching back beyond the monism of Baruch Spinoza to Lucretius and the pre-Socratic Greeks.

Edward Mooney notes that the Spaulding Farm passage, and the mode of being Thoreau captures therein, is inflected by his extensive reading of

Hindu sacred writing and by his readings in Native American ethnography, and this last area is worth considering in more detail. The Spaulding Farm section is one moment where Thoreau's elusive spirituality comes into focus. More recently, Alda Balthrop-Lewis has traced the ethical dimension of Thoreau's religion in *Walden*, an embodied practice that had a strong moral force; this moment captures his more mystical side, traced by Alan Hodder—the dissolving subjectivity and enlarged perspective that comes from the kind of regular meditative practice Thoreau describes in "Walking."[18] These dimensions are often seen as separate, but the context suggests a link between them forged by contact with Native people.

In the winter when he wrote the journal entries that fueled "Walking," Thoreau visited a Penobscot family camping in Concord—the source of the comment about the effectiveness of their simple shelter in *Walden* and perhaps the story of the Indian basket-maker as well. He recorded a lengthy conversation on November 26 that is full of lore—on moose, caribou, hunting practices, and the uses of animal hides; on spears and spearfishing, birchbark vessels, snowshoes, and traps (*PJ* 3:152–54). His summary of the conversation reads like an entry from one of the Indian Notebooks; indeed, Thoreau seems to be validating his sources by doing his own fieldwork. Yet he learns more from this encounter than a list of ethnographic terms. The Penobscot family were not, after all, simply a repository of Native artifacts but living members of a Native community that may have been far from its center on Indian Island but that clearly included the banks of the Musketaquid among its distant edges. Their journey to Concord may have been primarily economic in nature—they were eager to sell baskets—but it was clearly diplomatic as well, meant to reknit the relations between this settler community and their Native neighbors.[19] In talking with this family, Thoreau came face to face with the Indigenous world that still existed on the outskirts of Concord village. From Thoreau's record, the conversation must have been rather stiff, marked by generosity and patience on the Penobscot side. If this inquisitive visitor to their tent wasn't interested in buying baskets, they seemed happy to cultivate his goodwill and share details of their life in the Maine Woods. It appears that both parties sought to find common ground. The message is driven home two days later, when Thoreau recollects the conversation. "The Indian talked about 'our folks' & 'your folks' 'my grandfather' & 'my grandfather's cousin,' Samoset" (*PJ* 3:155). This is the heart of their exchange—a reworking of the colonial past that is relived and recalibrated. The Wabanaki sachem Samoset arrived in the fledgling Plymouth colony in

1622, greeting the English in their language and showing the Pilgrims that this colonial world would be more complicated than they had imagined. This conversation with a Penobscot family in Thoreau's hometown, too, proved unsettling, jolting him out of his fixation on an Indian past. Samoset's words find their way into *Walden*, Version E, written in 1852–53, which includes Thoreau's greeting at the end of "Visitors": "All honest pilgrims, who came out to the woods for freedom's sake, and left the village behind, I was ready to greet with—'Welcome, Englishmen! welcome, Englishmen!'—for I had had communication with that race" (*W* 154). Thoreau is playing Indian here, to be sure, but he is also applying a lesson learned from a Penobscot elder who welcomed him to his own home at the village edge.

Once within this tent, Thoreau finds that the world he was trying to glimpse in the Jesuit Relations was alive and well on the banks of the Musketaquid, with a Penobscot teacher patiently explaining to his interlocutor what it means to be Indigenous—to know the land and to live off its wild fruits. If there is a difference between "our folks" and "your folks," it is one that can be bridged; indeed, it seems the Penobscot family worked hard to transform what began as an ethnographic encounter into an ethical one, embedded in a long-standing set of relations. Thoreau, interestingly, records no talk of religion, of spirits, or of politics—a discussion of hunting, trapping, and subsistence skills was safer common ground. But those practices of daily life, of subsistence, are inseparable from both religion and politics in Native cultures. Such intimate relations are part of the web of reciprocity that shape every aspect of Native life. These issues were clearly on Thoreau's mind that winter, as the draft of "Walking" took shape. The Indian Notebooks from this period include a wide variety of sources, including a number that focus on Indigenous spirituality: two books by Ephraim Squire on Indian antiquities and an excerpt from David Cusick's *History of the Six Nations* in Notebook 3; descriptions of memorial cairns and *pneise*, or warrior-shamans, stories collected by Henry Rowe Schoolcraft, and a discussion by Squire of the Great Serpent, Manabosho, and Earth Diver traditions in Notebook 4. Notebook 5, written between September 1851 and February 1852, toward the end of the final revision of the "Walking" manuscript, includes more oral traditions—Lenape stories gathered by John Heckewelder and Adrian Van Doren. In Notebook 6, from 1852, Thoreau would quote Schoolcraft again on Indigenous spirituality: they "live in the ancient belief of the diurgus, or Soul of the Universe, which inhabits and animates everything" (IN 6:54). By the time Thoreau copied this passage, that message had grown long familiar.

The key insight of the Spaulding Farm passage is captured by the final word: "cohabitancy." It is an odd word—the *Oxford English Dictionary* includes only this example from "Walking" for this particular form. Thoreau would have been familiar with the older sense of the word, referring to people living together in a sexual relationship outside of marriage; he would have been interested to learn that biologists now use the term to describe different species who share an ecological space. Both senses are at work in Thoreau's use of the word—of different orders of beings juxtaposed almost invisibly on a certain landscape, woven together with a tinge of eros that defies any normative ordering of reproduction. "Cohabitancy" is, in a word, *queer*, and that queerness holds, I suggest, for the larger order of racial succession at the heart of "Walking." The beings of Spaulding farm defy the orderly clock of Manifest Destiny, the steady march of cultural evolution and Anglo-Saxon supremacy, the yielding of savagery to civilization that was the bedrock assumption of its advocates. These beings of ambiguous heritage, not quite faeries, not quite the little people of the Algonquians, *pukwudgees* or *muhkeahweesug*, are better seen not as a cultural memory but as an autochthonous manifestation of place, a mark of being native that defies the orderly division of time into past and future in the same way the wild force of nature defies efforts to mark a swamp with surveying tools.[20] These beings mark an eternal present; they are the grace notes of the wild. Thoreau here begins to see the Native past in Concord as not really past at all. It is no accident that this sliding scale of time took shape as Thoreau conceived of the Kalendar project in the early 1850s, where phenology and succession serve at once as firmly fixed historical data and part of a long, slow cycle of change and renewal. What is true for flowers and forests is true for people. This was not easy to see—the beings at Spaulding Farm are only glimpsed sidelong and fade from view, and this was true, too, of his views of Native people—at times fixed to the simple past tense, at times extended into the past imperfect, at moments understood in the perfect tense, with the past flowing into the present; at key points of time, projected into the region's future.

This layering of timescapes, this interweaving of historical chronology and timeless present, is one of the defining characteristics of myth, what Mircea Eliade calls "sacred time" and identifies as the primary goal of religious ceremony. Myths in any culture bring the sacred, the eternal present, into the profane world of ordinary life.[21] This is what repeatedly drew Thoreau to the well of classical Greek literature, and what drove him to read widely and deeply in Eastern spiritual traditions. By the early 1850s, he was increasingly familiar as well with Native American mythology. From early accounts of English and French missionaries he got his first glimpses of Algonquin cosmologies, and from Ephraim Squier and Henry Rowe Schoolcraft he gained a growing understanding of the scope and nature of traditional Native stories. Yet this body of sacred Native literature plays hardly any role in *Walden*. Suzanne Rose makes a detailed argument that the loon episode in "Brute Neighbors" is deeply informed by Thoreau's reading of Earth Diver myths, but while it is impossible to rule out the connection, it is not one that Thoreau makes explicit, despite his willingness to cite directly from the Indian Notebooks in other parts of *Walden*.[22] And yet the broader elements of Native American sacred stories infuse the pages of both "Walking" and *Walden*. "Walking" is framed as a quest toward Holy Land—a ceremonial vision quest enacted in Thoreau's daily walks that are closer to shamanic ritual than to regular exercise.[23] The beings he glimpses at Spaulding Farm are as close to the totems and spirit animals found across Native American cultures as they are to any similar beings in the Western tradition. And *Walden* might be read as a winter story, the long accounts of the earth's creation and how the natural order of things came to be that were told night after night in tribal communities as a way of reminding the people gathered in the circle of the Original Instructions. Winter stories not only explained the universe to the people who lived at its center, not only cultivated an ethos of connection, respect, and mutual responsibility to everything in creation, but also helped remake the universe and carry it forward. This flexible, interwoven network of stories, told and retold over generations by the most respected story keepers in ways that met the present needs of the community while conveying age-old truths, were, in Robert Bringhurst's phrase, "the old growth forest of the mind," the culmination of a thousand generations of wisdom.[24] They were also, unlike the stories that European settlers brought with them from the Mediterranean world, deeply rooted in place, woven into the land in which the storyteller and audience traveled about in their daily efforts to make a living. These stories were part of what N. Scott Momaday calls "the remembered earth," with the doubled meaning of "re-membered" as both brought forward in memory and reconstituted in the act of telling. Native American storytelling, as Lisa Brooks and Keith Basso have suggested, was essential in creating a place-world, a specific landscape saturated with story that provided practical, ethical, and ontological guidance to those who traveled the land and knew the stories. The main feature of such stories is their rootedness: for the Western Apache who shared their stories with Basso, and for the Southern Algonquian world that Brooks recovers, stories live not in the minds of their tellers but in the interplay of person and place.[25] The stories exist not in some archive of unwritten human memory but are summoned from the elements of landscape itself.

These elements are at the heart of *Walden* as well—the insights and stories rooted in the features of Walden Woods and the pond itself, which are at once vividly real places and vessels for spiritual insight; the interweaving of practical details of living—getting water, building a house, hoeing a bean field, gathering wood—with a ceremonial sense of ritual. The mingling of ethics and ontology. The compressing of two years of living at the pond and some eight years of later walks into the cycle of one year, weaving a human chronology into an eternal present of spring, summer, autumn, and winter. And the rapturous proclamation in "Spring" of the eternal creation, a spiritual insight founded not on a distant revelation in a faraway land but in the workings of the humblest landscape of home—the thawing of sand on a raw railroad bank, the long look into the depths of Walden Pond and seeing, suddenly, that it is Earth's eye looking back. It is worth remembering, too, that the book *Walden* began with Concord's version of winter stories—with Thoreau walking from his small house on pond's shore to the lecture room in the center of his home village to share what he found with his neighbors, to help them live more deliberately on this part of the remembered earth.

This, I suggest, is what Thoreau had in mind in the groundnut passage in "House-Warming." His foraging in the early fall is more ceremony than subsistence, his version of the Creek Busk or a feast of first fruits that he describes in "Economy," a ritual that weaves the year's harvest into the endless cycle of renewal.[26] The grapes, cranberries, and chestnuts please his senses and his imagination more than they feed his appetite; the groundnut, in particular, is a "sort of fabulous fruit" that summons both his half-remembered childhood and the long era of the "hunter tribe." It was once, Thoreau imagines, "the *totem* of an Indian tribe," and its power enables Thoreau to escape the shackles of contemporary New England history and envision a distant future contiguous with a distant past, when English grains will vanish and "the almost-extinct ground-nut will perhaps revive in spite of frost and flourish, prove itself indigenous, and resume its importance and dignity as the diet of the hunter tribe." This will happen "when the reign of poetry commences here" (*W* 239). By poetry, Thoreau means something closer to myth, an art that has become native, that revives and flourishes in the heart of a wild nature, in which a simple, storied food, tasting a bit like a frostbitten potato, becomes a sacrament of nativity for a tribe willing to live on the gifts of nature.

Who exactly this tribe of the future is remains ambiguous. Its members would not be the direct heirs of Tahattawan and the Musketaquid people, long displaced and dispersed by the brutal currents of colonialism. As Lydia Willsky-Ciollo has argued, Thoreau was less interested in helping Native people revive their culture than serving as "a minister of Indian knowledge to whites."[27] In this, Thoreau served the ongoing settler project, adding to the literature of replacement. Thoreau never realizes what Mark Rifkin suggests is the potential for a "queer solidarity with Native self-determination" in *Walden*, a project that would have required a more systematic effort to confront the Native dispossession that made his sojourn at the shore of a quiet pond possible, and a more sustained engagement with the Native people who continued to make their homes in New England and still visited Concord's edge.[28] But it is important to note, too, that Thoreau pushed against the settler colonial ideology that still shapes our world. The people of the new golden age Thoreau imagines would not be the people of Concord village, busily building a capitalist regime and relentlessly uprooting any trace of the wild from the American landscape. They might be the distant heirs of the people who lived on the edge of Concord in Thoreau's day, the wild scions of English, Irish, and French Canadian immigrants, the descendants of enslaved people seeking new kinds of freedom in the Walden Woods, and even the long-scattered members of the Nipmuck, Massachusetts, Pawtucket, or Wabanaki community retracing ancient trade routes and waterways to find themselves on the banks of the Musketaquid. They might not remember the old, old stories that were told in wigwams during the long winters before the English arrived from beyond the far horizon, and this new tribe might tell stories they had gathered in their long wanderings, of a lost garden to the East, of a prince debating his fate on the eve of battle, or of an artist in a mythical city making a staff that was in every way perfect. Such stories would sink roots into the soil and become myth and, like the story of the egg laid in the heart of the apple tree table, from *Walden*'s conclusion, would one day emerge into a new truth.

CHAPTER 4

Indians in Massachusetts
Cape Cod, *Colonialism, and Wampanoag Revitalization*

> *And surely by reason of those sandy cliffes and cliffes of rocks, both which we saw so planted with Gardens and Corne fields, and so well inhabited with a goodly, strong and well proportioned people . . . who can but approoue this a most excellent place, both for health & fertility?*
>
> —John Smith, *A Description of New England* (1616)

A few years ago, I followed one of those scholarly clues that ran into a dead end. I was just beginning to research Thoreau's relationship to Native Americans, and there seemed to be a promising connection to the efforts of the Mashpee, the largest Wampanoag community, to reclaim their independence in the early nineteenth century. Renée Bergland's excellent book *The National Uncanny* (2000) noted the parallels between William Apess's campaign of civil disobedience during the Mashpee Revolt of 1834 and Thoreau's own night in jail, and she indicated that Thoreau stayed at the Hotel Attaquin in Mashpee during one of his trips to Cape Cod. She cited a history of Mashpee, which referenced a memoir by one of the tribe's most respected leaders, Russell Peters, in the mid-twentieth century, and when I found his book (in the children's section of a local library), I saw that Thoreau was listed among a number of celebrities who had stayed at the hotel. It made sense, of course—Thoreau wrote one of the most enduring accounts of nineteenth-century Cape Cod, traveled there frequently, and was fascinated by Native people. And yet the story didn't add up. Thoreau's four visits to the Cape are well-documented in his book and in his Journal, and although he passed nearby Mashpee on two of them, in 1849 and 1857, he didn't mention a visit to the town or the hotel. His other two trips were confined to the Outer Cape, and while he visited his friend Daniel Ricketson in nearby New Bedford frequently and tracked down several Native people in the area, they never made the short journey to the principal Wampanoag town.[1]

The main question is not whether Thoreau visited Mashpee—we can't rule it out, but it is highly unlikely that he did. Neither is it why such a story found its way into the scholarly record—credible people mistakenly thought he had, for good reasons. The key question is why Thoreau *did not* visit Mashpee, the largest and most vital Native community in nineteenth-century Massachusetts.[2] He certainly knew of it, if not during his first visit, then by his later ones in the 1850s. His interest in Native Americans is well-documented, including the ten volumes of Indian Notebooks he gathered during the years *Cape Cod* took shape. And Mashpee was a place that should have fascinated Thoreau—a thriving community of Wampanoags who had won a remarkable degree of political independence thanks to a carefully crafted plan of civil disobedience and who used that independence to build a collectivist economy amid a rising capitalist sea devoted to preserving the tribe's environmental resources from crass exploitation, pioneering a model of sustainable development based in part on ecotourism. Thoreau passed a few short miles from Mashpee at least twice. Why didn't he go a bit out of his way? And what might he have learned had he turned his full attention to this remarkable people and place? We can learn as much about Thoreau, and his understanding of Native people, from what he didn't see as from what he did.

Thoreau and the Wampanoag Homeland

Thoreau grew up learning about the Wampanoag people. The Pilgrim and Puritan settlement of Massachusetts and the many Indian wars that followed, especially Metacom's Rebellion, were ingrained in New England life. And if anyone missed hearing the stories thereof, plenty of people were, in the early nineteenth century, beginning to write them down in local histories that, as Jean O'Brien notes, celebrated every town's first settlers and last Natives. Between Lidian Jackson, Ellen Sewell, and George Marsden, Thoreau was close to several people with strong ties to Plymouth, the site of the Wampanoag village of Patuxet, and he visited frequently, at one point, in 1852, reading letters by Metacom in Pilgrim Hall.[3] Daniel

Ricketson, in New Bedford, was also on traditional Wampanoag land, and he took Thoreau to visit several Wampanoag people. Indeed, Thoreau visited the Wampanoag homeland more than almost any other place aside from Concord, Boston, and Cambridge.[4] Still, the Wampanoag presence for Thoreau was largely historical. Walls notes that while at Harvard, Thoreau briefly studied the language—the short inscription he wrote to place on Fairhaven Hill shows his reading of the *Up-Biblum God*, or Eliot Bible—but there's no evidence that he followed his classmate Horatio Hale in learning some of the closely related Penobscot language from a group camped nearby along the Charles River.[5]

In January 1834, Thoreau had just arrived at Harvard when a delegation from Mashpee visited Boston to argue for independence from their overseer and their minister, appointed by Harvard, giving several public addresses and garnering a good deal of press. The Mashpee Revolt, which had taken place the summer before, in 1833, might have offered an interesting context for the young Thoreau as he navigated the Dunkin Rebellion at Harvard in May of that same year—one of the periodic student uprisings against college discipline—but if Thoreau or any of his classmates drew connections between these acts of resistance, they are unrecorded. Thoreau might have learned that one of the Mashpee leaders, the Pequot minister and writer William Apess, had spent a month in jail for defending the tribe's right to protect its woodlands. His book about the Mashpee Revolt, *Indian Nullification*, was published in Boston in 1835, as Thoreau was immersing himself in the classics. A year later, when Thoreau took a term off to teach school in Canton under Orestes Brownson, Apess delivered his "Eulogy on King Philip" twice in Boston before large crowds, puncturing the saintly aura of the early colonists and valorizing Metacom, or Philip, as a heroic, independent leader and model American. There is no record that Thoreau was aware of any of these keystone events in Wampanoag history.[6]

Thoreau's contact with Native peoples until the late 1840s was confined to the stone tools of their ancestors and a few people passing through Concord. His systematic reading about Native peoples, gathered in the Indian Notebooks, began around 1849. He was still on his first notebook when he traveled to Cape Cod that year; his later trips, in 1850, 1855, and 1857, coincided with his increasingly extensive note-taking. His first Indian Notebook was filled with early European accounts of Native New England, including a note about memory cairns in Mashpee (IN 1:76) and a story about Maushop, the Wampanoag Trickster-Creator, from Yarmouth (IN 1:78); later notebooks circle back to sources about Native peoples in the contact era, alongside just about every other text available on Native peoples in the United States, Canada, and other parts of the world, written by everyone from early explorers and missionaries to contemporary anthropologists and government agents. Thoreau did his homework.

That homework, however, did not include much material on the Native communities that survived in nineteenth-century Massachusetts, of which there were a good number. While Nashobah, home of the Musketaquid tribe after they left Concord, disbanded by the early eighteenth century and the closely related Natick community lost its land base in the late eighteenth century, at least two Nipmuc communities hung on to slender reservations in Thoreau's time, in Dudley and Hassamanisco in south-central Massachusetts. Most Native communities were located in the southeast of the state: Ponkapoag in Canton, Watuppa in Fall River, Herring Pond in Plymouth, three communities on Martha's Vineyard—Chappaquidick, Christiantown, and Aquinnah—and the largest, Mashpee. Many other Native peoples lived in loose communities without a land base or among their Black and white neighbors without a strong tribal connection; many more traveled widely in search of work, as was typical for lower-class people in New England. For Wampanoag men, this often meant long stretches at sea on whaling voyages and long stints in domestic service for women. Most lived quietly on the margins of New England life, for too much attention had rarely been a good thing. Those tribes with a land base had the most government attention—typically guardians (often a minister or lawyer) sometimes appointed and funded by the state of Massachusetts, sometimes appointed and paid for by other charitable organizations. Other tribes built informal relationships with influential whites nearby who helped protect their interests from other nearby whites who sought to profit off Indigenous land and labor. Native people were not eligible for citizenship in Massachusetts, but they were certainly liable for debt, and many ended up in long terms of indentured servitude; their land, too, was always at risk of being seized and sold to pay off debts of often dubious origin.[7]

Conflicts were frequent, and some brought the attention of state government, for good or ill. At least two state commissions reported on the status of Native peoples in Massachusetts during Thoreau's writing life: one a somewhat cursory investigation headed by Francis Whiting Bird in

1848 and published in February 1849, and the other by John Milton Earle, whose more comprehensive report was commissioned in 1859 and published in 1861. Both fall within the general pattern of the scientific reports Thoreau reviewed in "Natural History of Massachusetts"—government-sponsored reports meant to inform legislation while reaching a wider audience. There is no record that Thoreau read them, but given his long and comprehensive gathering of Indian sources, he could certainly have found the Bird report, published six months before his first trip to Cape Cod. Earle's report came too late to be of use to Thoreau, but it demonstrates how much information about Native communities was available to those who cared to know. Bird counted 425 Native peoples on or near the Cape, living in Herring Pond in Plymouth, Mashpee, and Yarmouth; if we include the three communities on Martha's Vineyard and nearby Watuppa in Fall River, the number is 722. Earle's more extensive inquiries in 1859 raised the number by several hundred more. The Native peoples in Southeastern Massachusetts were but a small percentage of a growing settler population, and many earned a living at sea. Yet this number far exceeds that of Penobscot people living in and around Old Town in Maine in the same era, and the two main communities, Mashpee and Aquinnah, were large, distinct, and quite stable during Thoreau's lifetime.

While Thoreau avoided Mashpee, he did meet several Wampanoag people from other communities in his travels. On October 2, 1855, Ricketson took Thoreau to Assawampsett Pond in Middleborough, where they inspected a Native cemetery, gathered a few quartz arrowheads, and met a Wampanoag couple out fishing: Thomas and Sepit Smith.[8] The exchange was an awkward one, as if Thoreau were more comfortable with the grave markings, stone tools, and historical accounts of the three praying villages that once demarcated the Middleborough landscape. Ricketson didn't make things easier. He summarily summoned the couple, and as they approached, said, patronizingly, "Come nearer. Don't be afraid—I ain't a-going to hurt ye." He then proceeded to quiz them on their percentage of Indian blood, "telling the squaw," Thoreau writes, "that we were interested in the old stock, now that they are so few." We can only assume that Thoreau was more discreet, but he was no less interested in blood quantum, noting that Thomas Smith was Black and claimed one-quarter Native ancestry, whereas Sepit Smith was one-half Native. Thoreau description of her is jarringly racist: she was "a regular countrywoman with half an acre of face (squaw-like)." Thomas is patient with his interlocutors, sharing details about the natural history of the pond; Sepit is less so. "I never saw yet the man I was afraid of," she snaps at Ricketson after his greeting; after his comment about how few of the old stock remain, she counters, "Yes . . . & you d be glad if they were all gone" (JM 19:104–5). Thoreau clearly understands her irritation, though while he tries to put some distance between Ricketson's callous, racist questioning and himself, it is clear that the Smiths do not make much of a distinction.

Thoreau appears to waver between the two views of Native peoples that characterize much of his reading. On the one hand is the savagist lens: he sees the couple as the last exemplars of a vanishing race, with too much mixed blood to count as real Indians but still interesting as curious embodiments of lost history. On the other, we glimpse a view of these people he never fully articulates but that took shape during the writing of *Walden* and "Walking." Here, the Smiths are fellow citizens of the edge community, surviving close to the land and fiercely guarding their dignity and independence, all the while possessing, if not legal title to land itself, then a rich knowledge of how to make a living in the still-wild margins of Massachusetts. It is worth noting that the journal entry describing this encounter moves not to a peroration on the last of the Indians but instead to a detailed account of the couple's boat and grapple, an observation of the moss fringing the rocks on the pond's shore, and a general overview of the Middleborough landscape. For Thoreau, at least, this Native couple are firmly anchored in the land.

Thoreau's visit with Martha Simons, whom he describes as the last of the "New Bedford Indians," on June 26, 1856, was similarly ambivalent. Simons may have occupied the last Native-owned parcel of land on Sconticut Neck, outside New Bedford, but she was hardly the last Native person in the area: when Earle held several meetings with local Natives in 1860, he estimated that at least 150 people (most from nearby Wampanoag communities) lived in the city; most worked in whaling or associated maritime trades, and many were eager to press property claims in nearby Dartmouth and Westport.[9] Thoreau's description of their journey hints that Ricketson was aware of this community, as he specifies that Simons was "the only pure-blooded Indian left about New Bedford." Ricketson likely knew of other Indigenous people in the region, like Thomas and Sepit Smith, but did not consider them to be "real" Indians. This distinction mattered more to European Americans eager to mark the end of a race than to Wampanoag people themselves, who measured tribal membership

FIGURE 3: Portrait of Martha Simons, *Last of the Narragansetts*, by Albert Bierstadt, 1857. Millicent Library, Fairhaven, Massachusetts.

by descent and adoption rather than blood quantum. Thoreau notes that Simons's house "is a little hut but not so big as mine"; they knock when she returns from the seaside, and she invites them in. Thoreau describes her using the same racial terms he used to describe Sepit Smith: "A half acre of the real tawny Ind. face, broad with high cheek-bones, black eyes and straight hair. . . . To judge from her physiognomy, she might have been King Philip's own daughter." Yet the conversation is a disappointment. Simons answers her visitors' questions "listlessly, without being interested or implicated, mostly in monosyllables, as if hardly present," an understandable response, given their rather presumptuous appearance at her door. "She could not speak a word of Indian, and knew nothing of her race," Thoreau notes. As the conversation progresses, he begins to understand why: like many impoverished Native people, she was indentured as a servant at age seven, a system that at once enabled settlers to profit from Native people's labor and to erase their cultural heritage. But not all of it. Simons may not have been able to speak her grandfather's language, but she knew the plants that grew in her homeland. When Thoreau asks her about a flower he had stuck in the brim of his hat, she opens up about the uses of husk-root. "I ought to have had my hat full of plants," he writes, after this brief glimpse of the depths of traditional knowledge that still survived on the edge of a prosperous, modern city (JM 21:137–40). Yet though Thoreau visited New Bedford several more times, he never again sought out Simons.

On his last visit to Cape Cod, in June 1857, Thoreau took the train to Plymouth and walked from there along the Cape to Provincetown. On the second day of his walk (June 16), he passed through Herring Pond, a small Wampanoag community, and paused just long enough to ask directions to Sandwich. He had been told by his hosts the night before that they were "worthy people," and Thoreau is impressed enough to see them at work on a new meetinghouse that he underlines the sentence in his journal. He describes the person he speaks with as "a respectable-looking young man not darker than a sunburnt white man, with dark eyes and the usual straight black hair of his race." Thoreau plays the game of identifying blood quantum only half-heartedly: he guesses the young man is of mixed race, and "when I observed to him that he was of the aboriginal stock—he answered—'I suppose so'" (JM 23:140–41). Thoreau then goes on his way, heading on foot to Sandwich and then by railroad to Yarmouth, where he crossed the Cape to Bass River and West Harwich, again bypassing Mashpee along the way. If he hadn't been fully aware of the largest Wampanoag community when he boarded a stagecoach with Channing in the pouring rain in 1849, he surely knew of it by now, having recorded a half-dozen mentions of it in the Indian Notebooks and spent many days with friends in Plymouth and New Bedford who knew about their Native neighbors. Without Channing as a companion and with no firm schedule, he would have had ample time to turn a bit out of his way as he gathered more material for the book he was finishing after the partial magazine publication of the manuscript. And yet Mashpee was never part of those plans.

Other Cape Cods

Cape Cod began as journal entries in 1849 and finished as Thoreau's second posthumously published book, after *The Maine Woods*, in 1865. Like the latter, it was edited by Sophia Thoreau and Ellery Channing from a manuscript that was complete but not finalized; while it is unclear what Thoreau's plans for revision might have been, it is clear his goals changed over time. The three separate journeys gathered into *The Maine Woods* allow us to trace his evolving interests and understanding, but his weaving several different journeys into one makes it more difficult to see how his purposes changed in *Cape Cod*. Part satirical travelogue, part unflinching meditation on death, part systematic takedown of Pilgrim hagiography, part devastating critique of the ravages of settlement and capitalism, part detailed observations on natural history, part transcendental musings on cosmology, *Cape Cod* has attracted a range of responses as varied as its themes. Emerson plugged the material as riotously funny lectures after Thoreau had his Concord audience laughing to tears at his descriptions of prim Cape Cod matrons and parsimonious settlers, and the editor of *Putnam's Magazine*, where Thoreau began publishing the book in 1855, pulled the series after complaints by some of the objects of his satire. Later readers saw it as either Thoreau's lightest or darkest book. More recent accounts have leaned into its darkness, with some, like those of Lawrence Buell and Laura Dassow Walls, focusing on the vast, impersonal nature captured in Thoreau's encounter with the destructive, generative ocean, an early version of naturalism that countered the redemptive spirit of *Walden* and presaged a more Darwinian view of nature to come.[10] Others have focused on Thoreau's critique of Manifest Destiny and the emerging global capitalist system that it cheered on. For John Lowney, the beachcomber (or "wrecker") Thoreau meets eking a living from material salvaged from the regular shipwrecks along the Outer Cape stands as the ambivalent antihero of *Cape Cod*. He lives, like the citizens of Walden Woods, on the edges of a brutal capitalist world but dependent on the commodified wreckage of that system that washes to shore. Alex Moskowitz sees the novel as a broad critique of that system, and Katie Simon argues that the Irish bodies Thoreau coldly inspects from the wreck of the *St. John* summon the ghosts of enslaved African people whose value was amortized and insured on the Middle Passage from the coffeehouses of London.[11]

While the slave trade may be a faint echo in *Cape Cod*, colonization and the displacement of Native peoples was a more central theme. Lowney and, more recently, Michael C. Weisenburg note that Thoreau dives into the literature of exploration—particularly his wide reading in French and Icelandic accounts of early journeys to the New World—to help undercut the literature of English settlement, particularly in the later material that makes up much of the "Provincetown" chapter.[12] There, Thoreau writes what he calls his "Ante-Pilgrim history"—the long record of contact that preceded the arrival of the Pilgrims (*CC* 179). Bartholomew Gosnold, Thoreau notes, was credited by American historians with discovering Cape Cod in 1602, but he was surprised to find Native people dressed in European clothes, using European tools, and far more practiced in cultural exchange than this English crew. It was, observes Thoreau, "a remarkable discovery for the discoverers" (*CC* 179). Linck Johnson has noted that Thoreau's first Indian Notebook began as research to contextualize his first journey to the Cape in 1849—material that provided rich accounts of Native culture and the New England landscape on the eve of settlement—and Thoreau added to them his extensive later research in the French and European literature of discovery. Yet what becomes clear in looking at both the sources Thoreau consulted in making sense of this region, and in the material he wrote, was that his focus in the book was not on the Native people who thrived in this liminal landscape long before the Pilgrims arrived and who fought to survive through Thoreau's time and into the present but on the people who displaced them. What also becomes clear is that Thoreau's focus on the darker forces of nature that he sees embodied in the ceaseless waves crashing into the beaches of the Outer Cape have everything to do with settler colonialism.

Thoreau brought along a good amount of reading material during his 1849 trip. The *Collections of the Massachusetts Historical Society*, volume 8, published in 1802, is not a small book, and it goes some way toward explaining Thoreau's omission of Mashpee. The main article in the volume is a town-by-town survey of Cape Cod that does not include a section on Mashpee—it mentions the Indian territory south of Sandwich, but since it wasn't technically a town when the report was written, Mashpee doesn't register and thus the writer skips over it in his descriptions of neighboring white towns, churches, and nascent industries. Later, as the article moves to Orleans, the author pauses to celebrate the labors of William Treat in the seventeenth century in ministering to the Nauset community, noting that there were some five hundred Native people living in Barnstable County, despite the ravages of disease. Thoreau quotes extensively from this section, using Treat as an exemplum of fire-breathing Calvinism, but the article did not draw his attention to the thriving Christian Indian communities just off his path. In Thoreau's account of his reading in "The Plains of Nauset," he highlights the hellfire and brimstone sermons of Treat but skips the long account of Christian missionary work among the Native communities in Barnstable County in the seventeenth and eighteenth centuries. The author of the article highlights the number of Christian Indian communities on the Cape at the end of the eighteenth century. Most of these had diminished by the mid-nineteenth century, their members having sought work elsewhere or joined relatives at Mashpee, the only Native community that appeared on the principal map of Cape Cod in Thoreau's era. Thoreau traced part of it as a reference for his journeys, beginning halfway along the lower Cape and capturing the outer beach from Chatham to Race Point in detail. Mashpee, quite literally, was not on his map.[13]

If, to speak very broadly, *The Maine Woods* was Thoreau's Indian book, his most sustained published account of his engagement with Native people, informed by years of reading but drawn from careful (if uneven) observations and interactions with his Penobscot guides, then *Cape Cod* might be termed Thoreau's Pilgrim book, his effort to interrogate settler colonial ideology as it was evolving in New England and across the nation. Thoreau used a variety of strategies to undercut the hagiography that was settling around the Pilgrims in this era. The fact that he had lyceum audiences laughing to the point of tears at his depiction of the heirs to William Bradford and Myles Standish and that George Palmer Putnam

FIGURE 4: Thoreau's map of Cape Cod, traced from a map most likely by Simon Borden (1844). Courtesy of the Munroe Special Collections, Concord Free Public Library.

pulled the serial publication after protests greeted the second chapter are good indications that Thoreau wasn't completely toeing the settler colonial line. Thoreau also deftly satirized America's claims to Native land, retelling with pointed humor the story of how the Pilgrim Fathers claimed large chunks of the Outer Cape:

> When the committee from Plymouth purchased the territory of Eastham from the Indians, "it was demanded who claimed Billingsgate?" which was understood to be all that part of the Cape north of what they purchased. "The answer was, there was not any that owned it. 'Then,' the committee said, 'that land is ours.' The Indians answered, that it was." This was a remarkable assertion and admission. The Pilgrims appeared to have regarded themselves as Not Any's representative. . . . Not Any seems to have been the sole proprietor of America before the Yankees. But history says that when the Pilgrims held the lands of Billingsgate many years, "at length appeared an Indian, who styled himself Lieutenant Anthony," who laid claim to them, and of him they bought them. Who knows but a Lieutenant Anthony may be knocking at the door of the White House some day? At any rate, I know that if you hold a thing unjustly, there will be the devil to pay some day. (*CC* 33)

This is hardly the searing critique of Thoreau's antislavery writing, and it is striking in part because this commentary on stolen land is so singular in Thoreau's writing. His goal here is less to redress this foundational injustice by making appropriate amends to the Native peoples who remain in Massachusetts than it is to unsettle the smug descendants of the Pilgrims.

Thoreau also is careful to trace how much these descendants owe to Native culture and territory. He is clearly fascinated by how people on the Cape make their living on this marginal land and unforgiving sea, and he is careful to note how many of the characteristic lifeways on the Cape—from hunting blackfish to trapping herring to gathering oysters to planting corn to catching seagulls—are directly derived from Native practices described in the earliest literature of settlement. While Thoreau gently derides the Pilgrims for their lack of curiosity about the land they've claimed and their reluctance to explore—"The Pilgrims are not the ancestors of the

American backwoodsman," he notes—by the time they have learned to make a living in this strange country, they are no longer fully English (*CC* 201). They have been transformed by the land and sea itself, having learned to adapt from those who knew it best. This adaptation did not go smoothly. *Cape Cod* is full of grim descriptions of a desolate landscape, barren plains of denuded sandy soil that can barely grow a tree above the height of a man, and Thoreau repeatedly points out that this wasteland is of the Yankees' own making—Cape Cod was, at the dawn of English settlement, a thickly forested landscape with rich soil. The clear-cutting of trees in New England was at its height in this era, but nowhere were the results so bleak as here. Yet Thoreau is also careful to document efforts to bring the land back to health, citing efforts to replant pitch pine forests and sow beachgrass to halt the spread of sand dunes (*CC* 17–18, 163–64). Learning to live in harmony with this severe environment, Thoreau finds, is the work of generations.

The effort to fully understand this unique environment drives the last chapters of *Cape Cod*. Traditional ecological knowledge is a valuable tool in doing so, but for Thoreau, it is the knowledge that matters, not the people who hold it. This is part of what Christa Vogelius has called Thoreau's increasing ahistoricity.[14] Thoreau gradually undercuts the narrow teleology of Manifest Destiny by bringing deep time to the Cape, sketching in greater and greater detail a *longue durée* that places the Pilgrims as one narrow strata of history that includes French and Scandinavian explorers, the long presence of Native peoples, and the geological epochs that shaped this narrow sandbar jutting into the ocean. In the ceaseless rolling of the ocean waves, a few hundred years of settlement are a drop of time, and Thoreau makes it clear that the Yankee hold on this barren coast is no more certain than that of a ship caught in a nor'easter. Thoreau comes to the Great Beach, on the outer edge of Cape Cod, to look long at the ocean, and he learns that human endeavors count for little when seen from this vantage. He sees here "naked Nature, inhumanely sincere," unmoved by any "sniveling sympathies" a person may bring to the shore (*CC* 147, 84). The ocean, Thoreau says, exists beyond historical time; "it was equally wild and unfathomable always. The Indians have left no traces on its surface, and it is the same to the civilized man and the savage" (*CC* 148). In this constant churn of matter, Thoreau suggests, no species, no race has secure standing. A shipwreck may strew human bodies across a beach, immigrants destined for some farther shore, and, perhaps, scatter foreign seeds that stand a better chance of putting down roots in new soil. "Vessels, with seeds in the cargoes, destined for particular ports, where perhaps they were not needed, have been cast away on desolate islands, and though their crews have perished, some of their seeds have been preserved. Out of many kinds a few would find soil and climate adapted to them, become naturalized, and perhaps drive out the native plants at last, and so fit the place for the habitation of man" (*CC* 131). This is a troubling meditation of colonization. Seeds and shipwrecks are not part of some divine plan but instead part of nature's ceaseless, remorseless churn. As with seeds, so with people: Nature disperses them as she will, Thoreau suggests, folding humans deeply into the web of a Darwinian nature that seems to leave little room for care or thought for narrower questions of national identity or political justice. It is this view of nature's wildness and power that unsettles the colonial ideology central to U.S. politics and culture and allows Thoreau to "put all America behind him" when gazing over the ocean. It is not a view that has much to offer the people of Mashpee.

Thoreau in Mashpee: An Imagined Indian Notebook

What would Thoreau have found in 1849 if he and Channing had left the stagecoach between Sandwich and Barnstable and braved the rain to head south some ten miles to Mashpee? Something rather remarkable that would have had some striking correspondence with the primary themes of his writing. What Mashpee would have offered is much deeper than dry satire and more hopeful, perhaps, than a dark naturalist vision scored with the ceaseless roar of the surf. Mashpee provides a counter story of settlement that preserves a Native view of colonization and deftly rebuts the narrative of Indian vanishing. Mashpee, in the 1840s and 1850s, was a small but thriving community that was charting an Indigenous course through the nineteenth century and offering a compelling alternative to market capitalism. I would like to touch on several aspects of the Mashpee project in tracing what never was but is useful to imagine—an Indian Notebook centered on Mashpee.

Imagine, for one, that Thoreau had found a copy of William Apess's *Indian Nullification* (1835). He might have been surprised to learn this was Apess's third book. His first, *A Son of the Forest* (1829), was the first full-length autobiography by a Native American; it recounts his birth in Colrain in western Massachusetts, his impoverished childhood in Connecticut, chafing against indentured servitude, and his travels in Upstate New York and Upper Canada during and after the War of 1812, before he returned to New England and began his career as an itinerant Methodist minister. His second book was a group biography of Native peoples around his home in the Pequod territory of southeastern Connecticut, *The Experiences of Five Christian Indians* (1833), which included an indictment of settler colonialism: "An Indian's Looking-Glass for Whites," as searing as anything that came from Thoreau's pen. Apess's work as a minister took him to Mashpee, where he found the tribe deeply frustrated by their appointed minister and joined the movement that became known as the Mashpee Revolt.[15]

If Thoreau had read Apess's account of the revolt, he would likely have transcribed Apess's description of arriving at the church in Mashpee, where he had been invited to preach. Apess admires the setting: "The sacred edifice stood in the midst of a noble forest, and seemed to be about a hundred years old; circumstances which did not render its appearance less interesting. Hard by was an Indian burial ground, overgrown with pines, in which the graves were all ranged North and South. A delightful brook, fed by some of the sweetest springs in Massachusetts, murmured beside it." Thoreau would have been pleased to find a church placed in such harmony with nature—a sharp contrast to the meetinghouse he describes in Dennis, set on a barren plain surrounded by a hollow square of dead poplar trees. Thoreau might also have copied Apess's disorienting description of the congregants—not the rich, tawny hues of the Indians he knew but the pale, wan faces of the settlers who had crowded out the Mashpee from their own church. "I turned to meet my Indian brethren and give them the hand of friendship; but I was greatly disappointed in the appearance of those who advanced. All the Indians I had ever seen were of a reddish color, sometimes approaching a yellow; but now, look to what quarter I would, most of those who were coming were pale faces, and, in my disappointment, it seemed to me that the hue of death sat upon their countenances."[16] Thoreau might have admired the way Apess makes the appearance of white people in a New England church seem unnatural, a skillful shock to conventional expectations. Apess's upending of the "naturalness" of white supremacy would have been new to Thoreau,

FIGURE 5: Portrait of William Apess, from the frontispiece of his autobiography, *A Son of the Forest* (1831).

who gathers plenty of examples in his reading of Native disdain for the behavior of European settlers and plenty, too, where colonists engage in duplicity or carry out atrocities that belie any innate racial superiority. But these generally involve Native peoples in traditional societies resisting the onslaught of colonization. Apess's normalization of a contemporary Christian Native community and his defamiliarization of whiteness were different, and they might have suggested to Thoreau that there was as much to be learned from contemporary Native communities living within settler society as there was from their precontact culture.

One of those lessons appeared shortly after the church set piece. Apess goes on to describe the origin of the Mashpee Revolt, a highly organized and politically savvy campaign to win independence for the Mashpee. Apess joined a group of Wampanoag leaders—Israel Amos, Isaac Coombs, and Ezra Attaquin—in building a movement that was part spiritual (the Mashpee wanted to discharge their appointed Calvinist minister, Phinneas Fish, and follow their own Methodist minister, Blind Joe Amos); part political (the campaign focused on replacing their state overseers with their own leadership, and the Mashpee ultimately won independent status as a special district); and part cultural (forced to make a living among the broader white society, tribal members were eager to control the terms of their adaptation). These elements were, at their core, environmental as well. The conflict focused on regaining tribal control of their land base: the woodlands that were an increasingly rare and valuable commodity, a source of both fuel and timber and a home to animals like white-tailed deer that had been hunted out of eastern Massachusetts, and the lakes and stream that were increasingly famous for their herring runs and sea-run brook trout. This environment was, from the perspective of the market capitalism that increasingly defined New England, an unexploited source of wealth; for the Mashpee, it was the foundation of a spiritual connection to the landscape that survived colonization in the form of complex subsistence patterns held together by a dense network of story, medicine, and ceremony.

Mashpee—the place and the people—were shaped by an intricate pattern of use that wove community members together in a way unrecognizable to an ownership system of private property. Daniel Mandell describes how the tribe managed their land communally, carefully allowing families to farm, hunt, fish, and harvest timber in a manner that preserved the overall health of the landscape. Lisa Brooks suggests the Mashpee continued to burn the undergrowth in this pitch pine forest into the nineteenth century to allow for more grass and understory plants and, hence, more large game. By all accounts, both the Mashpee woods and waters were a unique resource in eastern Massachusetts, full of deer at a time when they had long been exterminated in places like Concord and full of fish that were a marvel to visitors.[17] This was the nexus of Mashpee politics: an organic resistance movement rooted in deep communal traditions and founded on a people's intimate connection to a specific landscape. Part of the genius of the Mashpee Revolt's leaders was to frame this movement in terms that were recognizable to European American society while remaining faithful to the tribe's distinct provenance.

Thoreau might also have been drawn to the Mashpee declaration of sovereignty, with terms that echoed the founding documents of the United States as well as the tradition of Native American covenants that inspired them; he might have noted that they took effect on July 1, 1833, eleven years almost to the day before Thoreau took up residence at Walden Pond. Their movement in opposition to an exploitative, soul-killing capitalist system, like his, centered on a woodland environment that offered a very different ontological and economic orientation. Their resolutions were simple and powerful:

> *Resolved*, That we, as a tribe, will rule ourselves, and have the Constitution so; for all men are born free and equal, says the Constitution of the country.
> *Resolved*, That we will not permit any white man to come upon our plantation, to cut or carry off wood or hay, or any other article, without our permission, after the 1st of July next.
> *Resolved*, That we will put said resolutions in force after that date, (July next,) with the penalty of binding and throwing them from the plantation, if they will not stay away without.[18]

These resolutions are carefully pitched to white readers, couched in the language of U.S. governance. Thoreau might have admired the careful dance of allegiance and sovereignty here—appealing to the Declaration of Independence and Constitution as guarantors of basic rights but also asserting the Mashpee's right to rule themselves. This is an early example of what Audra Simpson, in *Mohawk Interruptus* (2014), has described as nested sovereignty, the overlapping allegiances that shape Native sovereignty, and although it seemed unruly to Massachusetts politicians, it might have resonated with a writer who sought to carve out a space apart from the state and national legal systems through measured acts of civil disobedience.[19]

Thoreau's experiment sparked the modest curiosity of his neighbors, but the Mashpee Revolt brought a quick and venomous backlash, particularly after Apess and some others forcibly unloaded wood from a cart that had been gathered without the tribe's permission. This act of nonviolent resistance caused a hue and cry among the neighboring whites, some of whom quickly raised the specter of an armed outbreak; others, however, recognized it as something different: an act of civil disobedience rooted in a higher principle of justice that was meant not only to address a specific action (taking wood from tribal land) but also to call other members of the community to confront the broader injustice of the Mashpee tribe's colonial status. To underscore this principle, Apess himself was charged with riot and spent a month in the Barnstable jail for refusing to accept civil government authority—the one place, he claimed, where a just man could be in Massachusetts: "Since this affair took place, I have been kindly informed by a gentleman of Barnstable, that my punishment was not half severe enough. I replied that, in my mind, it was no punishment at all; and I am yet to learn what punishment can dismay a man conscious of his own innocence. Lightning, tempest and battle, wreck, pain, buffeting and torture have small terror to a pure conscience. The body they may afflict, but the mind is beyond their power."[20] The protest, gradually, worked. A prominent local attorney joined the tribe's cause, helping it navigate the legal framework that anchored this colonial structure; several newspaper editors, including William Lloyd Garrison, picked up the story and argued on the tribe's behalf, tapping into the broad outrage among reform-minded New Englanders at the Cherokee removal. After the tribe petitioned the state legislature, a delegation visited Mashpee, and Mashpee leaders went to Boston to make their case before the legislature and the public. Ultimately, Mashpee was granted district status in Massachusetts, with rights to self-government. The tribe was not granted status as a town with full citizenship of tribal members, which would come later in the nineteenth century and with it the loss of the tribe's separate political status. In 1834, the tribe was instead recognized as a distinct political entity, with its land base set apart for the tribe to manage as it saw fit and its affairs largely under its own control, including the ability to elect its own government, choose its own minister, and manage the modest allotment of state funds for schools and roads. With the change in status, many tribal members who had been working in the different corners of the American economy available to people of color—as sailors or laborers—returned to Mashpee; most received a portion of the tribal reserve as allotments to manage as farm or timberland. Some quickly cut their woodlots, but most felt the obligation to use the land as a tribal resource rather than as an individual possession.

Mandell argues that Mashpee served as an anti-capitalist haven, a community that organized itself along more communal and inclusive values that reflected, in part, the older values of New England towns and, in part, the communitarian principles of traditional tribal life. Mashpee, like other Native communities, stood out as well for its multiracial aspect, welcoming African and European Americans into communal life, something rather new (or long ignored) in America. In the late 1840s and 1850s, Mashpee may not have been exactly what Thoreau had in mind when he imagined, at the end of "Resistance to Civil Government," a more ideal democratic community, "a State which can afford to be just to all men, and treat the individual with respect as a neighbor," but Mashpee certainly offered a better model than the quiet desperation and callous indifference to injustice that he criticized in Massachusetts (*RP* 89). It was closer in many ways to the edge community he described in the "Former Inhabitants" chapter in *Walden*—a world constructed in Walden Woods by the formerly enslaved and the refugees of empire and capitalism, who built their lives among sandy pine barrens on the outskirts of Concord alongside the Native ghosts of Musketaquid. The main difference is that Mashpee thrived, unlike the imagined community of Walden Woods and unlike several of the other fragile Native communities that struggled to keep their land and people together in the nineteenth century. This Wampanoag community quickly took advantage of its hard-won independence, growing in numbers and prosperity in the decades that followed.

Mashpee might also have provided several examples to add to Thoreau's list of representative men: the detailed biographical sketches that occur throughout Thoreau's writing, typically common people who serve as a more democratic counterpoint to Emerson's collection of essays about world historical figures. This list includes people like Nathaniel Rodgers, the abolitionist editor; Alek Therien, the Canadian woodchopper; Joe Polis, Thoreau's last Penobscot guide; and John Brown. It's not hard to imagine Thoreau adding William Apess to this list. Had he read Apess's *A Son of the Forest*, Thoreau perhaps would have highlighted his birth in the Catamount Hill section of Colrain, an edge community very much like Walden Woods; the trying circumstances of his childhood; his misadventures in the War of 1812; and his recovery of a Native identity among a Mohawk community near Montreal. He would surely have noted his principled protest during the Mashpee Revolt.

Thoreau might also have turned from Apess's writings about his own life and the story of the Mashpee Revolt to his last publication, "A Eulogy for King Philip" (1836).[21] Romantic era reappraisals of Metacom, or King Philip, as an American icon were relatively common—a version of playing Indian that helped affirm a settler colonial identity in the early National era, even as local histories of New England highlighted the trials and triumphs of settlers during Metacom's Rebellion. Thoreau, interestingly, pays little attention to Metacom or the war he led in the Indian Notebooks, though he did transcribe two letters by Metacom held at Pilgrim Hall in Plymouth. We don't know whether Metacom's absence in Thoreau's Indian material was due to his impatience with both Puritan demonization and Romantic mythologizing or whether his focus on precontact culture meant that Metacom was outside the purview of his research. Had he read Apess's account, he may have paid more attention. Apess uses Philip, and the long string of injustices he sought to redress, to systematically dismantle the Pilgrim hagiography taking shape in the nineteenth century, a project that Thoreau engages with equal vigor in *Cape Cod*. For Apess, too, Philip is a model idealist, a principled leader who devotes his considerable political and military skill toward serving the cause of justice—a figure, in other words, who would fit comfortably alongside Thoreau's depiction of John Brown.

Had Thoreau and Ellery Channing headed to Mashpee in 1849, they might have met a third candidate for a representative man. Solomon Attaquin was twenty-three when he signed a petition during the Mashpee Revolt; like many others of his generation, he stayed in Mashpee to make a living within this renewed tribal community. He spent several years in coastal trading, typically shipping wood from Mashpee to Nantucket and other nearby towns; with the proceeds, he built the Hotel Attaquin in Mashpee in 1840, which became the nucleus of several other businesses; the most profitable soon became environmental tourism. By the mid-1850s, after Attaquin and others appealed to state authorities to stop whites from poaching on tribal land, the Mashpee sold fishing licenses for up to $5 per day for the opportunity to catch prized trout in the Mashpee River; others paid local Mashpee guides for the opportunity to hunt deer in the woodlands. The fact that Daniel Webster and Grover Cleveland visited Mashpee, stayed at the Hotel Attaquin, and employed Solomon Attaquin as a guide might not have held much sway with Thoreau, but such celebrated clients indicate the growing prominence of Mashpee, and they show, too, that Native guides who could teach visitors about traditional Algonquin culture while skillfully navigating the demands of nineteenth-century American life were not confined to Maine. Attaquin might never have replaced Joe Polis in Emerson's list of the people most influential in Thoreau's life, but had he met him in 1849 or 1857, he might have come earlier to the key lesson he began to learn from Polis: that Native people could fully master life in the contemporary United States and still be fully Native. Attaquin may have been, to borrow Philip Deloria's term, an example of "Indians in unexpected places," and had Thoreau met him, the Indian Notebooks might have taken a very different shape.[22] The Notebooks are primarily an effort to reconstruct the Native world as it existed before contact, with the implicit assumption that the Native world as it survived settler colonialism was less authentic and invariably degraded, a reminder of a great injustice, perhaps, but not one worthy of attention on its own terms. The example of Attaquin, as well as the larger Mashpee community, might have shown Thoreau that this contemporary Native world was not without interest or merit. Time has shown that Mashpee in the 1850s laid the groundwork for a Wampanoag revitalization movement that continues to flourish to this day.[23]

The main insight Thoreau might have gained by visiting Mashpee, however, would not have come from reading texts but from walking the land and talking with its people, most likely over the course of many different visits. That insight is the perspective of a people whose lives and culture are fully embedded within a certain environment, where humans see themselves as only one among many nonhuman people, where the trees and rocks and rivers are as alive as the humans themselves and all stand in a relation of reciprocity that is at once material and spiritual. As Leanne Betasamosake Simpson describes among the Anishinaabe, the land itself is the teacher; as Lisa Brooks argues, the Native world of the Northeast is a dizzying network of relations, a "common pot" traced out by the everyday practice of material life and woven together by story and ceremony rooted in the landscape.[24] It's not clear whether Thoreau would have seen this. As his visits to other Wampanoag people in the region show, such encounters were too often marred by prejudice. His talk with Sepit and Thomas Smith in Middleborough was cut short by Ricketson's

FIGURE 6: Solomon Attaquin, Native Northeast Portal, https://nativenortheastportal.com/bio/bibliography/attaquin-solomon-1810-1895.

hostile question about blood quantum, while his talk with Martha Simons in New Bedford, which quickened to real exchange when the conversation turned to plants, soon withered. Solomon Attaquin might have happily entertained Thoreau and Channing and taken their money without letting them into the heart of Mashpee culture, in the same way that Attean and Polis, as I will discuss in the next chapter, carefully took the measure of man they guided through the heart of the Penobscot world, sharing some aspects of their culture while keeping others very much to themselves.

But had Thoreau been a good student and a respectful guest, he might have seen that his own project in Concord—an effort to see the myriad connections among the many features of the natural environment, to build a new model for living rooted in a rich and respectful relationship among all the members of the community, human and more-than-human, where all could flourish without regard to race, gender or species—was a shared one, and that Indigenous wisdom had not entirely vanished from Massachusetts. Perhaps Thoreau would have seen in Cape Cod something other than a degraded landscape and a diminished people, grasping for dollars in a global capitalist system that left even the wealthy deeply impoverished. He might have found that he had friends in Mashpee—if only he had looked.

CHAPTER 5

Lost in the Maine Woods
Henry Thoreau, Joseph Nicolar, and the Penobscot World

Not until we are lost, in other worlds, not until we have lost the world, do we begin to find ourselves, and realize where we are and the infinite extent of our relations.
—Henry Thoreau, *Walden*

K'-d-achowi mojibna kpiwi / *We have to go into the woods.*
—Joseph Laurent, *New Familiar Abenaki and English Dialogues*

For all his lifelong fascination with the Native people of Musketaquid, Thoreau's first documented conversation with a Native person took place in Maine, where he looked, unsuccessfully, for a teaching position in 1838. On the shore of the Penobscot River, across from Indian Island, Thoreau talked with "an old Indian, who sat dreaming on a scow at the water side.... Talked of hunting and fishing and old times and new times. Pointing up the Penobscot, he observed, 'Two or three miles up the river one beautiful country!' And then as if to come as far to meet me as I had gone to meet him—he exclaimed—'Ugh one very hard time!' But he had mistaken his man" (*PJ* 1:46). This unnamed Penobscot was the first of several transformative guides who would take Thoreau beyond the edge of the settler colonial world to see a different country. It would indeed be a hard time—Thoreau would never shed his prejudices easily or fully, and whether he would learn to come as far to meet Native people as they came to meet him was, in 1838, no sure thing. But Thoreau was eager to prove that this fortuitous teacher, at once tutelary spirit and living person, was not pointing the way upriver in vain.

As I have discussed earlier, Thoreau's experience with Native people was limited. Thus any account of his relationship with Native Americans must turn to his most sustained record of such encounters in the three essays collected after his death in *The Maine Woods*. In these essays, Thoreau charts his efforts to confront what he terms, in "Ktaadn," "the red face of man," and they reveal an attitude that is shifting, ambivalent and elusive, marked in turn by primitivist celebration, savagist scorn, and transformative contact (*MW* 79). Thoreau's encounters with the Penobscot world were, like most meetings across this cultural frontier, marked by moments of sudden insight and profound misunderstanding; they were, in a word, disorienting, and if they didn't spark the kind of political advocacy that marked his antislavery writing, they did help to unsettle his notions of "the Indian," and of America itself.[1]

More important, a careful reading of *The Maine Woods* suggests that this encounter went both ways. Thoreau's Native guides were neither passive servants nor simple objects of study but custodians of Penobscot culture who worked carefully to fit Thoreau into their changing world. The reprint of *Life and Traditions of the Red Man* (2007), edited by Annette Kolodny, first published by the Penobscot elder Joseph Nicolar in 1893, provides a rich opportunity to place a comprehensive statement of the Penobscot world alongside Thoreau's work. Nicolar's account of tribal tradition is derived from decades of listening to an earlier generation of storytellers and *meteoulin* (shamans)—a group that included Thoreau's guides, Joe Attean and Joe Polis.[2] Nicolar's book offers unique insight into the world of these guides, allowing us to overlay a crucial map onto the cross-cultural journeys Thoreau took through the Maine Woods. It captures the long history of the Penobscot people in their homeland, an ongoing effort to adapt to a variety of ecological and political challenges of which the arrival of whites is only one in a long series. The book is a landmark in the tribe's continuing effort to preserve its cultural and political sovereignty in the face of U.S. expansionism. Attean and Polis were important players in this effort, and their journeys with Thoreau need to be read with this struggle in mind. What is most striking from this Penobscot perspective is how often Thoreau gets lost in the woods—at times literally disoriented in the physical landscape but more frequently swamped in the labyrinth of an unfamiliar cross-cultural environment that took shape along this frontier between the United States and the Penobscot world. Thoreau and his Penobscot guides learn to navigate a landscape that is at once recognizable and strange, serene and unexpectedly lethal, and together they learn an old truth—that one must first become lost to see the world anew.

The Clock and the Map

The Maine Woods contains a certain chronology. Its three essays span the last fifteen years of Thoreau's life, from "Ktaadn," based on his 1846 journey, to "Chesuncook," based on the trip in 1853, to "The Allegash and East Branch," an account of his trip in 1857; he drafted "Ktaadn" at the end of his stay at Walden Pond and was revising "The Allegash and East Branch" on his deathbed in 1862. As Robert Sayre and Linda Frost have noted, the three essays lend themselves to an evolutionary narrative. "Ktaadn" is the most infused with the ideology of American progress, a discourse that maps geographic movement toward an unfurling western frontier onto the steady development of civilization, with the primitive forest gradually yielding to the gun, the axe, the plow, and the mill (or, as Thoreau puts it at the end of "Ktaadn," the canoe, the batteau, and the steamer [*MW* 82–83]). "Chesuncook" and "The Allegash" gradually undermine this narrative, at moments attacking the assumption that civilization represents progress at all, at times countering the notion of chronology itself, until, by the end of "The Allegash," Thoreau presents an understanding of time and space utterly at odds with a teleology that ends in American civilization.[3] This narrative is useful, but it is important to note from the start that it imposes an overly rigid progression on this series of essays. Rather than see *The Maine Woods* as a steady evolution toward a radical rethinking of savagist ideology, a better model might be to see the book as operating according to different clocks, alternative senses of time that are layered on top of each other and feed into different chronological frameworks.

One of those clocks runs on national time. At the end of "Ktaadn," Thoreau remarks, "I am reminded by my journey how exceedingly new this country is. You have only to travel a few days into the interior and back parts even of the old States, to come to that very America which the Northmen, and Cabot, and Gosnold, and Smith, and Raleigh visited" (*MW* 81). Geography here recapitulates chronology, with the city of Bangor representing the fulcrum of civilization. "The bear and deer are still found within its limits," Thoreau writes. "Twelve miles in the rear, twelve miles of railroad, are Orono and Indian Island, the home of the Penobscot tribe,

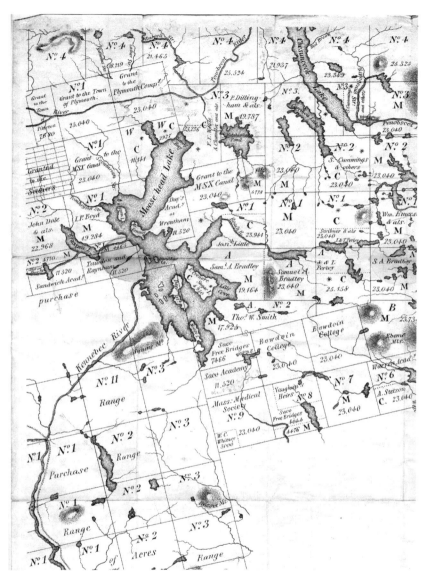

FIGURE 7: Portion of Thoreau's map of Maine, *from A Plan of the Public Lands in the State of Maine*, by George W. Coffin, Boston, 1835. Courtesy Munroe Special Collections, Concord Free Public Library.

and then commence the batteau and the canoe; and sixty miles above, the country is virtually unmapped and unexplored, and there still waves the virgin forest of the New World" (*MW* 83). The journey west is a journey back in time, with the summit of Katahdin a point of origin, for "the tops of mountains are among the unfinished parts of the globe" (*MW* 65). Thoreau's journey helps fill in that map. He eagerly records the first signs of settlement within this virgin forest, imagining the landscape as it will look years hence, cleared and settled. The very mountain cranberries he gathers on the slopes of Mount Katahdin, he speculates, will one day be articles of commerce (*MW* 66). The view from Katahdin is, he says, "the State of Maine, which we had seen on the map," a huge expanse of wilderness "that was a large farm for somebody, when cleared" (*MW* 66).[4] In preparing for (and writing up) his journey, Thoreau carefully read Charles Jackson's 1838 *Report on the Geology of Maine*, a text that eagerly adopts its official charge to advance the settlement and economic development of this new state, and while Thoreau doesn't quite mimic the eager strains of Jackson's boosterism, he often falls into his teleology. Jackson's gestures toward a distant geological past frame a distinctly American future. Describing the Aroostock Plateau, he asserts with calm confidence, "That region will become, as it is destined by Nature to be, the granary of the North."[5]

Jackson was guided by the Penobscot leader Louis Neptune, who also agreed to guide Thoreau's party to the top of Katahdin. Neptune failed to show up at the appointed time, and when Thoreau meets Neptune on his return, his ire no doubt fuels his description of the tribal elder as a "degraded savage" (*MW* 78). Yet the description is also part of the logic of evolutionary time used by Jackson himself and affirmed, as Joshua Bellin notes, by such early ethnologists as Henry Rowe Schoolcraft and Samuel Morton.[6] The proper place for the Indian is the distant past. This is the only charity Thoreau can muster when describing Neptune's departure: "For there turns up now a still more primitive and ancient man. . . . He is but dim and misty to me, obscured by the aeons that lie between the bark canoe and the batteau" (*MW* 79). Neptune and his companions have no place in the present; Thoreau can only deal generously with Neptune when he sees him (dimly) as a relic of a vanishing era. In this chronology, Thoreau was very much in keeping with mainstream American writing—*Sartain's Union Magazine*, where "Ktaadn" was published, enthusiastically endorsed Manifest Destiny; edited by Caroline Kirkland, western settlement was a recurrent theme and literary tourism a staple.

Yet in "Ktaadn" and the other essays in *The Maine Woods*, Thoreau also frequently disrupted this nationalist clock, sprinkling throughout his narratives sharp critiques of the notion of progress. At the beginning of "Ktaadn," when passing by the sawmills in Old Town, he bewails the fate of white pine from the shores of Chesuncook sold to the New England Friction Match Company; in "The Allegash and East Branch," he mulls wryly over lumbermen whose highest praise for a tree is that a team of oxen can stand on its stump. "Is their elevated position intended . . . as a symbol of the fact that the pastoral comes next to the sylvan or hunter life?" (*MW* 229). Such rhetoric, of course, is a romantic truism, a form of nostalgia that may only have served to grease the wheels of industrial progress. Yet such moments also show that other clocks were running in the Maine Woods, ones not set to the chronology of American nationalism. On his second and third trips to Maine, he gradually comes to realize that Native time and space don't fit within European parameters. Joe Polis remarks at one point that he can walk from where they are to Old Town in three days in the winter, across a wilderness unfathomable to Thoreau, who realizes that within this nation are "places where he might live and die and never hear of the United States, which makes such a noise in the world" (*MW* 236). The present tense is crucial here—although Neptune is consigned to a dim, irretrievable past, Polis lives very much in the present, and by the end of the passage, the pronoun "he" has expanded to include not just Polis but any traveler who can set his coordinates, and his clock, by this ageless expanse of nature.

This happens again in "Chesuncook" when Thoreau, listening to Joe Attean talking with a group of Native hunters late into the night, finds himself transported far beyond the present: "These Abenakis gossiped, laughed and jested in the language in which Eliot's Bible is written, the language which has been spoken in New England who shall say how long?" (*MW* 136). This passage captures Wai Che Dimock's notion of "deep time," a frame of reference that looks beyond a narrow synchronic context to place literature in a global exchange that reaches across many centuries. This particular moment of cross-cultural encounter links Thoreau into the networks of the Wabanaki world, weaving his location in U.S. history into the vastly different time frames and reference points that shape this particular region. "Deep time," as Dimock conceives of it, is an antinationalist concept, but it is important to note that it can cut different ways. For while the *longue durée*, the span of centuries, better allows for study of deep structural changes that move across any one nation, such a perspective was also central to the work of most nineteenth-century historians and anthropologists who were the architects of savagism. Deep time was, all too often, the handmaiden of Indian removal and other projects of U.S. imperialism. By the time Thoreau journeyed to Maine, the *longue durée* was firmly ensconced in American literature, with writers like Longfellow eagerly turning Native American history and story into what Paul Giles has called "medieval American literature."[7] America's native past became the primitive ground against which the new nation defined itself. Thoreau's work shares this medievalist sense of deep time. At the end of "The Allegash and East Branch," when, camping at a well-established spot, he suddenly realizes that "not long since, similar beds were laid upon the Connecticut, the Hudson and the Delaware; and longer still ago, by the Thames and the Seine, and they now help make the soil where private and public gardens, mansions and palaces are" (*MW* 287). The passage constructs a past that undergirds a European American present, safely burying a primitive history under the successive strata of civilization. This is also the logic behind his call, at the end of "Chesuncook," for national preserves where the wild forests might survive, where the landscape of the deep past, neatly contained, might nourish the present. Such preserves, of course, are trophies of modernity, remnants of an earlier time that survive to be admired (or gawked at) by civilized tourists who come ultimately to affirm their distance from a deep past. Surely, *The Maine Woods* is partly this effort to use the woods to anchor American history.[8]

Yet *The Maine Woods* also rejects this chronology, crafting an alternate view in which past and present are not separate points on which to tether national identity but instead parts of an intertwined whole. Mythic time is a category that became increasingly important to Thoreau as his career developed—while not uncommon in transcendentalist thought (particularly Emerson's), it remained at odds with a more common progressive strain that meshed more closely with mainstream notions of American teleology.[9] The essays in *The Maine Woods* are increasingly filled with moments that undercut this diachronic model of time as depth and instead place events from the distant past onto the synchronic axis of an eternal present. There are many. The climactic scene in "Ktaadn" puts Thoreau in the "cloud factory" of the mist-shrouded peak. On top of the mountain, a scene of ongoing creation that ultimately overcomes any attempt to subdue these elemental mythic forces with the discourses of geography and history. It is only on the way down from the mist-shrouded peak that the force of the experience strikes Thoreau. Walking through an area of burnt land, he writes, "I looked with awe at the ground I trod, to see what Powers had made there, the form and fashion and material of their work. This was the Earth of which we had heard, made out of Chaos and Old Night. Here was no man's garden, but the unhandseled globe. . . . It was the fresh and natural surface of the planet Earth, as it was made forever and ever" (*MW* 70). The passage is saturated with awe, with a sense not just of the stately, ongoing creation unfolding over geologic time but also of the manifestation of the world's originary powers. At the beginning of the journey to Katahdin, when Thoreau asked Louis Neptune to guide his party, he had made a patronizing crack about leaving an offering to Pomola, the thunder spirit Penobscot traditions associated with the mountain; by the time Thoreau has reached the mountaintop, his tone shifts. There, he recognizes that for Native people, such places "are sacred and mysterious tracts never visited by them. Pomola is always angry with those who climb to the summit of Ktaadn" (*MW* 65). On his descent, he trembles with the full force of this sacred awe. "What is this Titan that has possession of me?" he asks (*MW* 71). The answer is myth, for in dissolving the span of ages that separates him from creation, Thoreau feels the ecstatic force of nature in its eternal present tense.

This moment is hardly singular—the very essence of such experiences of mythic, ceremonial, or sacred time, after all, is their circularity—and such instants tend to follow passages where Thoreau replicates the settler colonial ideology of the vanishing Indian. In "The Allegash and East Branch," after mocking Joe Polis for the "dumb wonder" with which he tells a traditional legend about the origins of Mount Kineo, Thoreau finds himself struck with wonder at seeing phosphorescent wood at their campsite. "The woods," Thoreau realizes once again, "were not tenantless, but chokefull of honest spirits" (*MW* 181). This personified landscape, I suggest, is part and parcel of Thoreau's shift in tense from a distant past to a living presence. By having past and present feed into each other through the nexus of myth, he replaces time that is deep with time that is *thick*—layered with meaning and rich with associative connection. Such a perspective transforms his experience of the landscape through which he travels, which becomes not the leading edge of history and nation but instead a topos saturated with meanings and associations that head off into a myriad of directions where past and future offer no useful points of reference.

While the deep time of the *longue durée* is useful in expanding the narrow chronology fixated on modern nationhood, it is important to recognize that the process of stretching the diachronic axis of historical development can replicate an ideology of cultural evolution, misrepresenting particularly cultures that are not organized around teleology. "Thickness," I suggest, better focuses attention on the complex interplay of cultures and crisscrossing chronologies that shape America at key junctures like the nineteenth-century Maine frontier. Such a focus is far more open to the competing cultural frameworks that shaped this landscape, and reading *The Maine Woods* with this concept in mind suggests that Thoreau learned more from his Penobscot guides than even he himself could acknowledge. Mark Rifkin explores how different chronologies can deepen the "legitimacy crises" of settler history: "Indigenous forms of time push against the imperatives of settler sovereignty," he argues, noting that "temporal multiplicity" could help unravel the ideological threads of Manifest Destiny.[10] Thoreau certainly couldn't sustain this perspective—every moment where thick time shapes his narrative is followed by another where the discourse of maps, surveys, and other elements of national ideology secured by a particular notion of deep time reasserts itself. Yet these moments that reset the national clock are themselves followed by episodes that fold time back onto itself, tangling any rigid chronology, if only for a moment. Deep time and thick time never align. They stand, instead, as separate clocks keeping time in the Maine Woods.

Nature and Personhood

European American notions of time were not the only things Thoreau lost in the woods. The killing of a cow moose stands as the deeply ambivalent center of "Chesuncook," and following Thoreau's rapidly shifting ideological frameworks in writing about the episode is disorienting indeed. Thoreau traveled with his cousin George Thatcher, a Bangor lumber merchant, and Joe Attean partly to visit an environment relatively untouched by white settlement and partly to learn about Native culture firsthand. Hunting moose was part of his cousin's plan, not his, and Thoreau describes the initial sighting of the moose and her calf, and Thatcher's frantic shots, with a veteran travel writer's ironic detachment. Thatcher, "our Nimrod," is no mighty hunter. This is quickly supplanted by his ethnographer's interest as

Attean tracks the wounded animal, and then later by his naturalist's compulsion to minutely measure the carcass, for "I did not wish to be obliged to say merely that the moose was very large" (*MW* 113). He describes in gothic detail the butchering of the animal: "the rent udder, and the ghastly naked red carcass appearing from within its seemly robe" (*MW* 115). An aesthetic revulsion slowly grows—"The afternoon's tragedy, and my share in it, affected my innocence and destroyed the pleasure of my adventure" (*MW* 119)—until he finally settles on a reformist plea. He could imagine living in the woods and hunting just enough to survive. "But this hunting of the moose merely for the satisfaction of killing him . . . is too much like going out by night to some wood-side pasture and shooting your neighbor's horses. These are God's own horses, poor timid creatures" (*MW* 119). It is from this stance that he condemns his Native guide: "What a coarse and imperfect use Indians and hunters make of nature!" (*MW* 120). Yet these shifting and entirely recognizable frames never quite contain the oddity of the first sighting of the moose. Thoreau describes them as "half-frightened rabbits, with their long ears and half-inquisitive, half-frightened looks; the true denizens of the forest (I saw at once), filling a vacuum which now I first discovered had not been filled for me,—*moose-men, wood-eaters,* the word is said to mean, clad in a sort of Vermont gray, or homespun" (*MW* 110).[11] Later, after measuring the carcass, Thoreau writes, "This was the kind of man that was at home there; for, near as I can learn, that has never been the residence, but the hunting-ground of the Indian" (*MW* 115). In a few short pages, Thoreau's view of the moose has moved from tourist trophy to full personhood.

Other moments in "Chesuncook" similarly place Thoreau outside the bounds of contemporary discourse about the environment. Most famous is his description of the pine tree, the heart of the Maine lumber industry, best known, he argues, not to the sawyer or lumberman but to the poet: "It is not their bones or hide or tallow that I love most. It is the living spirit of the tree, not its spirit of turpentine, with which I sympathize, and which heals my cuts. It is as immortal as I am, and perchance will go to as high a heaven, there to tower over me still" (110). The passage was jarring enough that James Russell Lowell, who had solicited "Chesuncook" for the *Atlantic Monthly*, deleted it as far too pantheistic for his readers, to Thoreau's deep chagrin. Speaking of plants as "people" was something of a Romantic commonplace, appearing in the work of James Thompson a generation before Thoreau's birth and in that of John Muir a generation after his death;

Thoreau's formulation, however, went far beyond playful anthropomorphism to a more fundamental assault on Judeo-Christian cosmology.

In "The Allegash and East Branch," descriptions of a living landscape grow more uncanny still. Paddling along Moosehead Lake and looking into the surrounding wilderness, Thoreau describes an ominously animate landscape: "Only solemn bear-haunted mountains, with their great slopes, were visible; where, as man is not, we suppose other powers to be. My imagination personified the slopes themselves, as if by their very length they would waylay you, and compel you to camp again on them before night. Some invisible glutton would seem to drop from the trees and gnaw at the heart of the solitary hunter who threaded those woods; and yet I was tempted to walk there" (*MW* 184). Such moments are as far in spirit from the beneficent spirit of nature that Thoreau learns to see in his Concord environs as Walden Pond is from Moosehead Lake.

This note of difference that creeps into *The Maine Woods*, I suggest, reflects more than the natural evolution of Thoreau's thinking, fueled by both his deep immersion in natural history writing and his careful observation of his environment. These moments, even more than his revisions of the European American clock and map, reflect his contact with the Penobscot world. Thoreau's Maine essays don't reproduce Penobscot traditions, but they do mark his growing awareness of an alternative cosmology that structures this particular environment. After seeing phosphorescent wood for the first time when camped on the shore of Moosehead Lake, Thoreau has a sudden realization of this expansive world: "Nature must have made a thousand revelations to them which are still secrets to us" (*MW* 181). Thoreau never learns most of these secrets; he does, however, gain a sharpened sense of what he does not know. He indicates this most directly in the letter he wrote to H. G. O. Blake after his trip with Polis: "The Indian, who can find his way so wonderfully in the woods, possesses so much intelligence which the white man does not,—and it increases my own capacity, as well as faith, to observe it. I rejoice to find that intelligence flows in other channels than I knew. It redeems for me portions of what seemed brutish before" (*Corr* 491). This awareness opens up his experience of the Maine Woods, enabling him to encounter this environment in a manner quite different from that of white travelers who came knowing what to expect and therefore were unable to see the unexpected. It also, I suggest, allowed for the Penobscots themselves to teach this outsider something about their world without trading away their cultural sovereignty.

Penobscot Encounters

Thoreau went to Maine in large part to study Native people; his journal and his essays record just about every scrap of information he learned in talking with his Penobscot guides. What is clear from the large body of Penobscot traditions now available is how little they told him. Their reticence is not surprising—by the 1840s, when Thoreau first traveled to the Maine Woods, the region's Wabanaki tribes had been vastly reduced by warfare and disease. The Passamaquoddy and Maliseet lived in several villages on the Canadian border, while the Penobscot gathered in one village of several hundred people in Old Town, a few miles from the burgeoning lumber town of Bangor. The State of Maine treated the tribe with indifference when it wasn't systematically shrinking their hunting grounds on the upper Penobscot, supposedly guaranteed by treaty. Almost every white person who dealt with the Penobscot assumed they would soon vanish and acted accordingly; the tribe itself wrestled with how best to cope with the changes ripping through their society and their environment. Most had accepted some measure of Christianity, Catholic or Protestant, but most still held firm to their own traditions. John Neptune, the last of the traditional *meteoulin*, remained a powerful figure, and most still hunted and carried on traditional crafts even as they experimented with farming, lumbering, marketing goods to whites, and guiding the increasing stream of white hunters and tourists. Tribal members argued about whether to embrace Protestantism, whether to send their children to white schools, and how best to work with the state government; many sought to forge tactical alliances with sympathetic whites.[12]

They did not, however, share much of their culture—few whites cared to ask, and the few who did often treated Penobscot traditions with ridicule. It wasn't until 1884 that Charles Leland published the first collection of Penobscot literature. Fannie Eckstorm, an ethnographer whose family members were close to John Neptune, notes that her father refused to believe that Leland's collection was authentic, because he had never heard of any of these tales in all his years of visiting and hunting with his Penobscot friends. According to Eckstorm, "It was their secret, which enabled them to be a race despised and yet to walk with dignity among their condemners because they knew something white people did not know. They had fought with spirits; they had vanquished demons; they held the power of life and death over enemies; nothing was impossible to those among them who had acquired 'spiritual power.'"[13] During the period of Thoreau's travels, two things are clear: the traditional knowledge of the Penobscot was very much intact, and the Penobscots were careful to keep it from whites. They had lost much of their political sovereignty over their tribal territory; indeed, surveying parties guided by the Penobscots themselves redrew traditional boundaries and apportioned land for lumbermen and settlers who cut trees, cleared farms, and built dams and mills that altered the riverine ecosystem. Yet they held onto their cultural sovereignty, a cosmology that structured a uniquely Penobscot relationship to the environment, shaped both by story and by the rhythms of a life that reached far beyond white contact. It is this Penobscot world that shadows Thoreau's encounter with the Maine Woods.

Nicolar and Cultural Sovereignty

The republication of Joseph Nicolar's remarkable compilation of Penobscot traditions offers a useful opportunity to read the dynamics of the cultural exchange that took place in the Maine Woods. Dimock's formulation of "deep time" and Rifkin's term "temporal multiplicity" are useful here because Nicolar was particularly interested in contesting European American notions of history. He opens his books by declaring, "In offering this work which will give the public the full account of all the pure traditions which have been handed down from the beginning of the red man's world to the present time, I deem it proper to state that there have been no historical works of the white man, nor any other written history from any source quoted" (*LTRM* 96). The Native world, for Nicolar, is not only distinct but also, for whites, impenetrable: "Because when his ways and habits are learned it will be found that they are so peculiar it has spread a veil over the eyes and minds of the learned of these modern dates, and have caused many to enquire, 'Where did the red man come from?' This is the question we intend to answer!" (96). Nicolar's account of the Native world begins by asserting the inability of European norms to account for its time and structure. Like other Native histories by, for example, David Cusick (Tuscarora) and Sarah Winnemucca (Paiute), Nicolar represents the precontact Indian world not so much as different from European culture but as wholly other, operating outside European constructions of time and history.[14]

FIGURE 8: Photograph of Joseph Nicolar from *Life and Traditions of the Red Man* (1893). Public domain.

Such claims were not merely of anthropological interest. The ambitious tone of Nicolar's preface makes it clear that his project is meant not to preserve a record of a vanishing culture but to guarantee that Penobscot history and geography continue to shape Penobscot territory. Nicolar anticipates by a century the call of the contemporary Penobscot anthropologist Darren Ranco for a Native anthropology that "theorizes from within," framing his account according to Penobscot needs.[15] "I have been crowned with success," he boasts, in having done his part to ensure that the Penobscot culture hero, Gluskabe (which Nicolar spells "Klose-kur-beh"), remains the defining presence in a changing Maine landscape. "The works of Klose-kur-beh were wonderful," Nicolar writes, and by preserving his story, he continues his efforts to make this earth "a happy land for the people" (*LTRM* 96). The Penobscots had long relied on warfare and diplomacy to protect their homeland; by the nineteenth century, their efforts focused on other means. Politics was one arena, and Nicolar, as a long-standing Penobscot representative to the Maine legislature, was instrumental in securing his people's standing in civil society. Culture was another, and Nicolar's retelling of Penobscot traditions needs to be understood as part of the long struggle for Penobscot sovereignty—an example of the decolonizing work that Sylvia Winters has called "ontological sovereignty."[16]

Nicolar's account of Penobscot traditions is aimed squarely at keeping this tribal past very much alive in a world increasingly defined by modernity. Penobscot politics in the nineteenth century were complex, with members divided over religion (Protestant, Catholic, or traditional); education (public schooling, Christian schooling, or traditional upbringing); and tribal governance (hereditary or elected chiefs). Nicolar was part of the "Old Party," which was largely Protestant, in favor of public schooling and supporting hereditary leadership. Like most Penobscots, he sought a balance between traditional and modern culture.[17] (Attean and Polis were also associated with the Old Party.) *Life and Traditions of the Red Man* was part of this effort—while addressed to sympathetic white readers to a degree, it was primarily addressed to his own community. Some of that message was intensely traditional. In gathering and preserving such an extensive body of Penobscot tradition, Nicolar made sure that, despite the passing of tribal elders and a decline in Native speakers of their language, the Penobscot world would survive. The mythic presence at the root of these stories is a crucial element of that culture—Evan T. Pritchard's (Micmac) title of his Algonquian ethnology, *No Word for Time* (1997), neatly captures its centrality. In his essay "Crossing Moosehead Lake," Chris Sockalexis, an archaeologist and the Penobscot tribal preservation officer, describes the sense of belonging and connection fostered by story and anchored in the landscape that continues to weave the Penobscot community, past and present, together.[18] Nicolar's account also describes a world in which Europeans barely register. Most of his book centers on events before the arrival of whites, and even after contact, the narrative centers on conflicts among Native groups. Nicolar's world is apart in both time and place from contemporary American society, with a long cycle of change, struggle, and survival that offers a potent context for the tribe's status at the end of the nineteenth century, a *longue durée* that is a powerful rebuke to any indication of imminent vanishing.

Yet in countering Eurocentric notions of history that consign Indians to a "medieval" past, Nicolar also refashions Penobscot chronology. Frank Speck, who lived among the Penobscot in the 1910s, notes that a number of elders were critical of Nicolar's reworking of traditional stories, partly because of his introduction of Christian elements.[19] More radical, perhaps, was his shift in medium. Penobscot stories were traditionally transmitted orally, often in ritualized settings to specific audiences at certain times of the year; they were invariably adapted to the unique circumstances of the setting, with various episodes woven together to meet the needs of the situation.[20] Penobscot traditions were less history than language, with elements assembled according to a coherent grammar but taking shape only in the act of utterance and always in the present, governed not by an immutable chronology but the complex demands of the contemporary world. Their time frame was, thus, thick rather than deep. By weaving these stories into a fixed narrative, Nicolar organized them along a diachronic axis that emphasized depth. Such a chronology, reaching back to a separate creation and carrying at every point the cultural knowledge that shaped the Penobscot world, served to rework the foundations of the Penobscot nation. Kolodny notes that most white scholars have largely ignored Nicolar, "frustrated by the difficulty of aligning his narrative with any corresponding Euroamerican chronology."[21] This is because Nicolar fashions his chronology, I would argue, as a counterpoint to the construction of deep time that helped buttress the American nation. In Nicolar's telling, the Penobscots, too, had a history that authorized their nation, culture, and claim to exist as a separate people with sovereign ties to their own territory. His formulation of deep time establishes a discrete past that serves, in the Penobscot national imaginary, as a place apart, a span of time that exists without reference to the politics of contact, colonization, and cultural hegemony. Deep time, for Nicolar, becomes a focal point for Penobscot national identity. This reframing the Penobscot past was also a key strategy for securing tribal status among whites, making it recognizable while asserting its difference. Nicolar sought to make their traditions available to, in his words, a wide "public," sharing Penobscot culture with whites on his own terms.

Penobscots who guided white explorers, surveyors, hunters, and tourists had long been the conduits of such cultural transmission, and their varying approaches suggest the ambivalence in their community about the terms and contexts through which their knowledge of the Penobscot world was conveyed. Joseph Treat, traveling with the Penobscot chief John Neptune during his 1820 survey of Penobscot territory for the new state of Maine, notes that an earlier surveying expedition found its maps defaced and its efforts to demarcate the land as U.S. territory consistently thwarted.[22] On the other hand, Treat's journal shows Neptune detailing Penobscot names and traditions for every lake, mountain, and waterfall, ensuring that this state survey was saturated with Penobscot culture. James Francis, the Penobscot tribal historian, describes how deeply rooted the Penobscot cosmology is within the Maine landscape; their ethic of mutual obligation to a land full of spirits, animal-people, and daunting power is fundamentally geographic, every place-name helping to orient a traveler in relation to both physical space and spiritual power, mapping the resources needed for subsistence and reaffirming ties of kinship to the more-than-human world.[23] Thoreau himself glimpsed this—"So much geography is there in their names," he notes in "The Allegash and East Branch," in finding that Penobscot place-names invariably indicated key descriptive features that help members of the tribe find their way through the landscape (*MW* 270).[24] He is less attuned to the way the Penobscot key their tribal traditions to features in the landscape, recalling stories associated with a specific place and recasting them to meet the needs of the moment—a nexus of geography and culture Keith Basso has termed a "place-world." Penobscot guides throughout the nineteenth century clearly saw themselves as diplomats; it is, perhaps, no accident that the three Penobscots Thoreau stumbled across as guides were among the most important tribal leaders of the era. Louis Neptune, who guided the state geologist Charles Jackson in the 1830s, provided a thick Penobscot discourse to Jackson's official report. His refusal to guide Thoreau during his first trip to Maine might well be attributed to his ambivalence about leading outsiders to the most sacred parts of the Penobscot landscape. Thoreau fares better with his second trip—the long interview with tribal chief (and Treat's guide) John Neptune at the end of the trip is a mark of the confidence Thoreau earned from Joe Attean. When Thoreau appeared on Indian Island looking for a guide in 1857, Joe Polis was one of the most important traditional leaders of the Penobscots. Nicolar himself, having long sought out those elders most deeply versed in traditional learning, was certainly familiar with the principles of Penobscot cultural diplomacy. Teaching whites to understand and respect the Penobscot world—its geography, its spirituality, its sense of time—was a key feature of the long struggle to preserve Penobscot sovereignty.

Penobscot Story-Maps

Nicolar begins with the sense of mythic time that only gradually appears in Thoreau's essays. Klose-kur-beh's creation at the hands of the "Great Being" establishes him as the intermediary between the creator and the people who will soon appear; his first journey, to the top of a cloud-shrouded mountain shaken by wind and lightning strikingly evocative of Mount Katahdin, establishes a mythic frame of reference for the Penobscot world. The Great Being's first teaching affirms that the world is a living presence: "There was a living spirit in all things, and the spirit of all things has power over all. . . . The Great Spirit was in the sun—moon—stars—clouds of heaven—mountains, and even in the trees of the earth" (*LTRM* 102). This conception of an animate, personified Nature is one of the key features of Penobscot culture. It is woven into song and ceremony as well as embedded in traditional storytelling and the very structure of the language. Kolodny notes that "the precontact Eastern Algonquian-speaking tribes of the Canadian Maritimes and Maine experienced their world as everywhere alive with spiritual powers and kin-beings. The very grammar of their dialects rendered certain kinds of stones or even a snowball as animate and potentially endowed with personhood."[25] Thus the very act of guiding whites through this territory and marking its features with Penobscot names preserves this sensibility of an animate presence in the land.

Outsiders were not always quick to pick up on such ideas. The story retold by Polis about the great hunter, brusquely dismissed by Thoreau as marked "by a long drawling tone, long-windedness, and dumb wonder, which he hopes will be contagious" (*MW* 169), is a central passage in Nicolar. At first, it clearly isn't contagious—when Thoreau later meets Polis climbing Mount Kineo, he attributes his fatigue in part to "superstition. Perhaps he believed he was climbing over the back of a tremendous moose" (*MW* 177). Nicolar's book suggests that Polis believed exactly that. Stories of Klose-kur-beh were not assigned to a distant past but were very much at the heart of the Penobscot world, informing every leg of their journeys through the woods. Thoreau remarks on his guides' habit of falling silent when traveling rather than engage in idle chatter, and it may be that some of their thoughts were of the stories that shaped the land and whether or how to convey them to their clients. Thoreau's response to Polis's first story was clearly unpromising, and what might have been the first in a stream of stories quickly ended. In their highly circumspect way of telling Penobscot stories, Attean and Polis cast a respectful veil over their tribe's most sacred traditions while still conveying key aspects of its culture. Polis, for example, doesn't tell Thoreau one of the central stories in *Life and Traditions of the Red Man,* the arrival of winter. Pa-poon, the frost spirit, arrives in a Penobscot village in the form of a small boy; ignored, he eventually kills seven children, eating their tongues and surviving every attempt to kill him. "I have been obliged to awaken you by striking a blow where it will be most felt" (*LTRM* 146), he tells the people, and then gives instructions on how to survive the coming winter. It is a troubling and difficult story, one bearing directly on a central event in Polis's life—when hunting as a boy of eleven, he was caught many miles from home by the sudden onset of winter; he and his companions barely survived their return. The Pa-poon story conveys the merciless quality of Maine winters and the cultural resourcefulness needed to survive it; Polis's own story shows that it was an integral part of the Penobscot world, not assigned to a primitive past but very much alive in the present. Polis chose not to tell it, seeing, perhaps, that Thoreau was not prepared to hear it, allowing the story of his formative encounter with winter's fury to stand alone. Reading Nicolar gives us a sense of the weight of untold stories, the rich traditions Polis and Attean decided not to share with their client, and how little of the rich Penobscot world Thoreau was allowed to glimpse.

Yet Thoreau clearly was a potentially receptive student of Penobscot culture. His experience on Mount Katahdin bears striking parallels with Nicolar's description of the mythic mountain at the opening of *Life and Traditions of the Red Man.* Many Penobscot stories, indeed, are eerily close to episodes in Thoreau's essays. In crossing Moosehead Lake, Thoreau echoes Klose-kur-beh's epic battle with the sea serpent who has fouled the ocean. He describes the waves that "will gently creep up the side of the canoe and fill your lap, like a monster deliberately covering you with its slime before it swallows you" (*MW* 171). This description echoes as well one of the central stories about John Neptune. Francis Speck reports that his animal helper was a giant eel, which he called to him one day on the shore of a lake in front of a number of witnesses. Abby Langdon Alger and Fannie Eckstorm record different versions of the story, in which Neptune fought a rival shaman who took the form of a *wiwil'mecq'*, a snakelike water monster that Alger writes "smeared him with slime from head to foot" before he vanquished it.[26] They report that Neptune's helper was a salamander. Thoreau knew none of this when he met with Neptune, though he eagerly recorded the brief traditions Neptune did tell. Their interview

FIGURE 9: Photograph of Joseph Attean from the Fannie Hardy Eckstorm Papers. Courtesy of the University of Maine Fogler Library and the Penobscot Nation.

FIGURE 10: Portrait of Joseph Polis by Charles Bird King, 1842. Courtesy of the Gilcrease Museum, Tulsa, OK.

is a highly charged episode, with Neptune welcoming his visitor, who has clearly earned the trust of Attean, but warily, sounding Thoreau out as a possible ally, trying him with some brief stories, and watching him closely. Few people had come to the Penobscots with a genuine interest in their culture, and one gets a sense of Neptune and other tribal leaders testing the boundaries of a new diplomatic frontier that Nicolar would fully explore a generation later.

This trust was not necessarily misplaced. Thoreau at times genuinely learns from Native culture, never more self-consciously than in "Chesuncook," where he talks of "moose-men" in terms that adopt a Native understanding of animal personhood not as a primitive mark of difference but as a powerful means of countering European American notions of nature as commodity. This understanding of animals as kin is a key feature of Penobscot cosmology. Nicolar's history contains a long list of Klose-kurbeh's animal helpers, and Alger retells a powerful story about a Penobscot who, on a long winter hunt, marries a moose-woman and eventually turns into a moose himself. More recently, James Francis, the Penobscot tribal historian, has published a Penobscot tradition about Joe Polis's father, Awasus, being raised by a bear.[27] Penobscot literature is full of transformation stories, and Frank Speck notes many families trace their lineage to an ancestor who had transformed from animal to human, a belief that underscores the close relationship between humans and animals, with equal powers and equivalent social organization. Animals, like humans, have villages and shamans, and they are discussed in equivalent terms—wolf-folk, bear-folk, moose-folk, and human-folk are all part of one extensive community. Hunting is not harvesting a resource but "ordained killing," an acknowledgment on the animal's part that their spirit has been overcome by the hunter's superior power or that it has offered itself up to feed the people. Thoreau did not hear these stories from his Penobscot guides, but his extensive reading included many such transformation stories. However mediated, they resonated with his own evolving understanding of animals. He returned from his trip with Polis firmly convinced that science had a great deal to learn from Indian knowledge of animals.[28]

Trees, rocks, and geographic features, too, are possessed of spirit and have standing in the Penobscot world. Joseph Nicolar writes of a crucial encounter between Klose-kur-beh and a group of trees early in his wanderings:

When night came this same lonely feeling was upon him, he prepared a place for his night's rest. After the darkness had come and before laying down to sleep, to cheer himself, Klose-kur-beh did sing. When this was done, the seven trees that stood nearest bent their tops and listened to the singing of Klose-kur-beh, and when the singing was over, the largest of the seven straightened its body up and said, "How grateful the heart of man ought to be when he can bring cheer to himself by singing when lonely. When my kind and I sing, we sing in distress; when the fury of the winds shakes our limbs we sing in wailing,—our roots are many and strong and cannot move to avoid the fury of the heavens. Because you can move at your pleasure do not linger here, but on the morrow when the sun rises take your canoe, and with your companion go forth toward the sun and keep the same course seven days and seven nights. . . . When you find land it will be like this land and the trees the same as we. Your work will then be complete because you will have found that there is spirit in all things, and where there is spirit there is power, and as there is knowledge in us, we, the seven trees, will show you the power that is in us and will smooth the way for the whole time of your journey." (*LTRM* 123–24)

The key insight of this story—that there is spirit in all things, and that power comes from understanding and respecting it—occurs again and again in Nicolar's book; it is the linchpin of the Penobscot connection to their environment, the key to their cultural sovereignty. This sensibility is entirely at odds with the extractive economy most evident in the sawmills around Old Town—an economy that employed a large number of the Penobscot tribe. Nicolar's story, then, is an important cultural counterweight to an emergent capitalism, one that had far deeper roots in Penobscot traditions than Thoreau's plea for the "living spirit" of the pine, and one directed at the wide "public" cited in his introduction. Klose-kur-beh's message was crucial both for the whites who came in increasing numbers to the Maine Woods and for the Penobscots themselves.

Crossing Paths

Thus we have the paradox of Thoreau's relationship to the Penobscot. Although he went to Maine for the express purpose of studying Indigenous people, he was, at worst, openly dismissive of their culture, their society, and their beliefs; more frequently, his sympathy was bound up in an ideology of savagism that took as a certainty the inevitable vanishing of "the red face of man" and valued only those aspects of their culture that were firmly tied to a supposedly irrecoverable past. Such a view might enable Thoreau to use his image of Indians to critique an emerging American capitalism, but it hardly provided him meaningful insight into the lives of Native people. He certainly learned from Polis and Attean, but he was allowed only the barest glimpse of the traditions and practices that made up the Penobscot world, and even then, he was often unable to see what was before him. And yet the essays in *The Maine Woods* are nevertheless full of a sensibility, imagery, and language entirely consonant with the Penobscot relationship to the environment—a sense of ongoing creation that counters Western conceptions of teleology; a conception of a natural world that is alive, full of spiritual power and endowed with personhood; and a firm sense of the reciprocal relationship between humans and the environment that later European American writers would term a "land ethic." How did Thoreau appear to learn so much from a people he only saw through a thick layer of prejudice? The answers, I suggest, are best understood from a more nuanced reading of the cross-cultural dynamics that shaped these encounters in the woods.

One response is suggested by Wai Che Dimock's call for a far wider context for American studies, one that reaches not only across the globe but deep into the past. Such a frame of reference complicates the cultural exchange at work in Thoreau's writing, weaving into the problematic dyad of Thoreau and Indian the rich web of cultural borrowing that made up Thoreau's reading, from ancient Greece, India, and China to medieval Islam to the vast corpus of travel writing Thoreau eagerly devoured. Many of the perspectives and beliefs central to the Penobscot world are far closer in spirit to, say, Greek myth or Hindu philosophy than they are to nineteenth-century European culture, and when Thoreau pens his own pantheist ode to the spirit of the pine tree, he may be drawing more on Hesiod than on Joe Attean. In his rapture on top of Mount Katahdin, certainly, Thoreau finds himself reaching beyond Milton to the mythic landscape of Hesiod's *Theogony*, where Chaos, Night, and the Titans give expression to his experience of raw nature. Yet the Penobscot spirit Pomola shoulders his way into this Greek pantheon, suggesting that for Thoreau, at least, the path to understanding his Penobscot neighbors lay through ancient Greece, a cross-cultural triangulation that opens up an entirely new perspective on the environment.

A second response is to focus more carefully on the people who guided Thoreau through this environment. Native peoples have long played passive roles in studies of American writers, and this is true especially for Thoreau. Native critics themselves have argued that we need to fully acknowledge how carefully Native people shaped their world, including their relationship with whites.[29] This holds particularly true for the Penobscots in the nineteenth century, who were engaged in a long struggle to preserve their cultural identity and their unique relationship to their environment in an era when overt resistance to white colonization was no longer tenable. In Nicolar's *Life and Traditions*, Klose-kur-beh's central teaching is clear: "The land the Great Spirit gave them they must never leave" (*LTRM* 102), and it's important to understand Thoreau's guides in light of this imperative. Attean and Polis, after all, were not simply guides but tribal leaders, and their trips with Thoreau are better understood not as wilderness tourism but cultural diplomacy, in which they carefully sized up this naturalist and writer and determined how best he might advance the goals of preserving Penobscot cultural sovereignty. Part of this strategy involved simply keeping key aspects of their culture private, but part involved a careful initiation into the Penobscot relationship with the land, from the web of language that reached into every corner of the environment to the myriad patterns of subsistence that had evolved over the centuries to the subtle ways the Penobscot oriented themselves in time and place.

The Maine Woods is, among many other things, a powerful record of Penobscot pedagogy. Attean and Polis revealed some of their traditions and rituals, waiting, as Native teachers typically did, for the right circumstances to summon an appropriate story and then carefully gauging its effect. Even when Thoreau clearly wasn't ready, as when Polis told of Klose-kur-beh's killing of the moose that became Mount Kineo, the story may still have taken effect—what follows that evening is Thoreau's revelation about phosphorescent wood and his newfound respect for the depths of Indian knowledge. Later, after reaching one of Polis's hunting camps and observing his blazon of a bear in a canoe, Thoreau realizes that "this was one of his homes" (*MW*

200). It is also clear from reading Nicolar that Attean and Polis carefully instruct Thoreau in how to read the Penobscot world. They tell of the same battles between the Mohawks and the Wabanaki that occupy the last chapter of Nicolar's book, they sing traditional songs lying beside the campfire, they explain their language and offer some of the traditional ecological knowledge that shapes their world. When Thoreau demonstrates that he would not be receptive to stories of Klose-kur-beh and Pomola, Polis and Attean prove determined to indirectly pass on the knowledge they learned through the medium of the Penobscot culture hero. If Thoreau won't listen to the story of Klose-kur-beh's hunting, he will watch and listen as Attean and Polis hunt themselves; while these guides grew up learning everything from the uses of plants to the techniques of making a birchbark canoe by listening to the same Klose-kur-beh stories retold by Nicolar, Thoreau is content to learn some of this lore from the guides themselves. Significantly, both Polis and Attean initiate Thoreau into contemporary Penobscot politics only at the end of their journeys, after establishing a relationship and, more important, after carefully guiding him through the extensive territory that the Penobscot still consider their own. The long interview with John Neptune at the end of "Chesuncook" and the detailed account of the struggle between the Old and New Parties at the end of "The Allegash and East Branch" are not merely anecdotes appended to a wilderness sojourn; instead, they show Thoreau how deeply interwoven the Maine Woods are to the Penobscot village at Old Town, with story, language, history, and politics fully embedded within a specific environment to make up the Penobscot world. In both journeys, Thoreau leaves on a primitivist excursion to the deep woods and returns to an Indian Island that is at once fully rooted in Penobscot tradition and very much a part of modern America.

One final way of reading the cross-cultural dynamics of *The Maine Woods* is to place the environment itself at the center of these competing ideologies. By carefully attending to the landscape, by focusing on the flora, fauna, and geology that met his gaze, Thoreau managed (if only temporarily and partially) to escape the narrow ideological perspective of nineteenth-century American expansionism and open himself to alternative ways of understanding this environment. Thoreau was most open to the Penobscot world when he was most open to the Maine environment. Thus the passages in *The Maine Woods* that most closely echo a Penobscot sensibility—invoking Pomola on top of Katahdin, summoning the spirit of a pine tree, or marveling at phosphorescent wood—all occur at moments when the environment surprises him, refusing to be bound by the narrow categories of European American ideology, when Thoreau, in short, gets lost. This is most evident when reading Thoreau's essays alongside accounts by his contemporaries. Charles Jackson's 1837 geological survey of Maine, John Springer's 1851 *Forest Life and Forest Trees*, and James Russell Lowell's 1853 *Moosehead Journal* are far more tame books, framing the landscape in terms of natural resources ripe for development, the rugged progress of industry, or genteel tourism.[30] Thoreau, in being open to seeing an environment that regularly exceeds ready-made categories of knowledge, is open, as these other observers are not, to Penobscot ways of seeing this world.

This openness was carefully cultivated by Thoreau's Penobscot guides. In "The Allegash and East Branch," Thoreau relates a story told by Polis about one of his visits to Boston. He had listened to Daniel Webster's Bunker Hill oration, one of the classic efforts to mythologize American history, and went to pay his respects; after being repulsed, Polis concluded he "was not worth talk about a musquash" (*MW* 253). Polis might have guessed that his client was no fan of Webster—the former statesman had confirmed Thoreau's distaste for politicians by helping pass the Fugitive Slave Law of 1850, and Thoreau clearly agreed with this assessment. Polis and Webster never had the opportunity to compare notes on time and history. A generation later, however, Joseph Nicolar did. His book might be read as a Penobscot reply to an oration that begins with Christopher Columbus and portrays a battle in Charlestown as a decisive point in history. "But we are Americans," Webster wrote. "We live in what may be called the early age of this great continent; and we know that our posterity, through all time, are here to enjoy and suffer the allotments of humanity."[31] Elsewhere, however, Polis remarked that Americans were "very strong, but too fast" (*MW* 246)—too fast to either properly read the landscape or to appreciate the depths of time that preceded European settlement. Nicolar helps us tease out what Polis means: the Penobscot world, deeply rooted in time and place, is strong, too, and offers a crucial alternative to an American project that, even at this "early age," was threatening to careen out of control.

Thoreau, however bound up in the chronology of American nationalism, at least began to see this Native world through a different lens of time. By the end of "Chesuncook," he is able to see the Penobscot community of Indian Island as at once rooted in the past and very much living in the present; he listens respectfully to John Neptune's stories of current politics and traditional lore and sees no dissonance at discovering, in the yard of a modern frame house, a Penobscot making a birch bark canoe. In "The Allegash and East Branch," he is even able to offer something from his knowledge of the past. Long-possessed of a talent for finding arrowheads in Concord, which he delighted in as a record of the region's vanished past, he is delighted to find the same hornstone used to make those arrows on the slopes of Mount Kineo. At a campsite some days later, he points out to Polis that a similar stone was likely carried there a century or more ago to make arrows. Thoreau is thus able to weave his knowledge of an environment marked by a Native past into living present. We don't know Polis's reaction to this insight. He likely had heard the Penobscot story that Gluskabe was even then in his distant abode to the north, manufacturing arrowheads for the day when he would help his people drive the whites back across the sea. We do know, however, that Polis honored Thoreau with a Penobscot name meaning "great paddler" (*MW* 295).[32] The essay ends with Polis and Thoreau shooting the rapids above Old Town, weaving their way deftly down a river that defined the Penobscot world, before Thoreau traded in a birch bark canoe for a railroad and steamer.

This sustained encounter with the Maine Woods and the Penobscot world, I argue, had a lasting effect on Thoreau's work beyond these Maine essays. His travels through this transformative landscape, and the careful teachings of Attean and Polis, contributed to a mythic sense of the environment that developed in the writing of *Walden* and continued as Thoreau began to frame a more systematic study of the environment around Concord. As Thoreau delved ever more deeply into science, he continued to resist calling himself a "scientist"—he insisted that his studies of animals, plants, and the natural features of the landscape were not merely scientific but spiritual and philosophical as well. Such a stance certainly affirmed his allegiance to transcendentalism, but it also evidences his consonance with a Penobscot view of nature, what he termed early in his career "a more perfect Indian wisdom" (*Exc* 28). For Thoreau, ecology is not merely a material science. *The Maine Woods* also underscores the highly charged politics that frame any encounter with the environment. As the Natives who guided the long series of explorers, missionaries, surveyors, lumbermen, hunters, tourists, and writers through their traditional territory well understood, building a relationship with an environment is part of asserting control over it. In Maine, forced to confront in a way he wasn't in Concord that his journeys through a landscape were journeys through a highly politicized environment as well, Thoreau began to learn that Native people were more than mere figures useful to critique the materialist excesses of an emergent capitalism: they were people with their own history, interests, and voices. Any truly thorough account of American history and literature needs to listen carefully to these voices.

CHAPTER 6

Succession
Wild Fruits, The Dispersion of Seeds, *and* *Thoreau's Indian Afterlife*

> *When the whites shall have ceased killing the red man, and got all their lands from them, the great tortoise which bears the island upon his back, shall dive down into the deep and drown them all, as he once did before, a great many years ago; and that when he rises again, the Indians shall once more be put in possession of the whole country.*
> —John Heckewelder, *History, Manners, and Customs of the Indian Nations* (1819)

It is no small irony that Henry David Thoreau's last encounter with Native people was at once his most "authentic" and his most colonial. His visit to the gathering of the Mdewakanton and Wahpekute bands of the Dakota on the Minnesota frontier in June 1861 gave Thoreau his first opportunity to interact with a Native community whose precontact culture was largely intact. Although the Dakota had long navigated the encroachments of French and British traders and had recently ceded large parts of their territory to American settlers, most still sought to live according to their traditional ways, and few spoke English.[1] These were the kinds of societies Thoreau had been reading about for over a decade as he compiled his Indian Notebooks, and he saw them as distinct from the contemporary Wampanoag people, who had learned to survive on the edge of nineteenth-century Massachusetts, and from his Penobscot guides, who moved easily between a world shaped by the timber industry and tourism and their carefully guarded traditions. The Dakotas were on the raw frontier of American settlement; their Lakota relatives to the west would remain, for another decade and a half, fiercely independent. They gathered with U.S. government representatives not as conquered subjects but as a sovereign people demanding their rights guaranteed by treaty. And yet Thoreau traveled to the Redwood Sioux Agency on a tourist junket tacked onto an official government delegation. On the steamboat heading up the Minnesota River with Thoreau and his travel companion, Horace Mann Jr., was the territorial governor, the U.S. Indian agent, close to a hundred tourists, and a dance band. It was a journey up a river into the dark heart of colonialism.

Thoreau's time among the Dakota people was highly circumscribed. Between the speeches by both sides and various ceremonies (including a "monkey dance" by the Dakota men), there was time for trading, as tourists bought souvenirs from the impoverished Dakotas, including ceremonial soapstone pipes and intricately beaded clothing, but little sustained interaction. Thoreau managed to get the gist of the main speeches—"They were quite dissatisfied with the white man's treatment of them, and probably have reason to be so," he wrote to his Concord friend Franklin Sanborn—but nothing in Thoreau's letters or notes indicate that he learned much from his visit with the Dakotas (*Corr* 621). If the Penobscot River serves as a useful metaphor for Thoreau's relationship with Joe Attean and Joe Polis, from whom he learned to navigate its broad lakes and dangerous rapids, the return trip down the Minnesota River aptly figures this particular encounter. Thoreau was confined to a gilded steamboat with a group of drunken tourists imitating Indian dances to the sounds of a hired band as the boat constantly ran aground on the endless meanders of the current. Thoreau certainly realized that this effort to learn from Native people on the American frontier was a failure. He may have had an inkling that Dakota frustration would erupt a year later into a brutal, disastrous war. He likely understood, too, that his trip to the West would not restore his health and that the journey home would end at his deathbed. Thoreau would return to Concord, pick up the thread of his Journal and try to move along his last two major writing projects, *Wild Fruits* and *The Dispersion of Seeds*. Aside from several items of Dakota clothing, the chief treasures he brought back from Minnesota were his notes on botany. If he had plans to write about his trip west, they never materialized. Most of his remaining time and energy would go to preparing his lectures for publication. He was thinking about what would come after him. He was thinking about succession.

It was not the first time that Thoreau wove together thoughts on Native Americans, the more-than-human world, and mortality. On February 3, 1859, his father, John Thoreau, died in the house on Main Street in Concord, and Thoreau's Journal for the day is filled with a loving account of this quiet man's life. His father had never been a driving force in Thoreau's life in a household filled with strong women, and Thoreau is clearly musing over his connection to this man firmly anchored in the village center while his son prowled the town's wild edges. He had succeeded to his father's place as head of the family, but the passage speaks to the profound difference between father and son. This tension between similarity and difference, between what comes before and what succeeds it, drives the abrupt transition that follows this private eulogy. Succession between generations shifts to succession between races and spurs some of the sharpest critiques of settler colonialism in his writing: "Some have spoken slightingly of the Indians," he begins, in a searing critique of both those who murder Native people in cold blood ("the trapper—the mt-man, or gold-digger, who shoots one as a wild beast") and those who practice a more ideological form of murder (historians "wielding a pen instead of a rifle"). Thoreau dismisses claims of Native inferiority—the Indian, he posits, knows at least as much of religion as Henry Ward Beecher, and indeed, "The thought of the so-called savage tribe is generally far more just than that of a single civilized man" (JM 18:173–74). More to the point, Thoreau says, is that their lives feed into his. Walls observes that "by some obscure link his father's death called up the deaths of American Indians."[2] Thoreau doesn't fill in the gap between his reminiscences of his father and his defense of Native people, but he makes it clear that both matter: "Even the indigenous animals are inexhaustibly interesting to us. How much more, then, the indigenous man of America? If wild men, so much more like ourselves than they are unlike, have inhabited these shores before us, we wish to know particularly what manner of men they were, how they lived here, their relation to nature, their arts and their customs, their fancies and superstitions. They paddled over these waters, they wandered in these woods, and they had their fancies and beliefs connected with the sea and forest, which concern us quite as much as the fables of Oriental nations do. . . . It is the spirit of humanity, that which animates both so-called savages and civilized nations, working through a man, and not the man expressing himself, that interests us the most" (JM 28:173–74). Thoreau and his fellow settlers in this land, then, are *interested* in Indigenous people—pressing, as he often does, on the word's multiple meanings. "We" have a sympathetic concern for Native people, a shared human connection deepened by the landscape both settlers and Natives have shared over time. As Thoreau's father is a link to an earlier time, a connection that interests him in the history that shaped his father and thence himself, the Indigenous people of Musketaquid are a link to a deeper history and a more broadly shared humanity. And as John Thoreau's death makes Henry realize that "we die partially in sympathy at the death of each of our friends and near relatives," the long meditation on Native people shows that he feels their loss too. He is *interested* in this loss in pecuniary terms as well—after all, like any settler, he makes his living on what was Native land. This moment of succession—when Henry succeeds his father as head of the Thoreau household, marking the passing of a generation—sharpens Thoreau's Indian problem, his recognition that his inheritance depends on the dispossession of another people, and the ghosts of Musketaquid haunt his claims to this new role. He shares their deep connection to this landscape he calls home, this native ground, but he is troubled by this broken succession.

What exactly this means is not entirely clear to Thoreau himself, and as was his wont, he thinks through issues of race, conflict, and loss by meditating on the natural world. Natural succession helps him quiet the ghosts of familial and racial succession. Over the next days, he turns in his Journal to the natural phenomena that capture his interest and clear his mind: on February 7, four days after his father's death, he pens a long meditation on rock tripe, a lichen that figures the elemental appetite of nature, writing that "to study lichens is to get a taste of earth—& health—to go gnawing the rails and rocks" (JM 28:176); on February 11, on the churning appetite of the ice gnawing at shrubs and trees along the riverbank; the next day, on the irregular groping after light by trees shaded by different objects. These topics don't cohere but, as Thoreau notes, "pulsate with fresh life. . . . Most that is first written on any subject is more groping after it, mere rubble-stone and foundation. It is only when many observations of different periods have been brought together that [the writer] begins to grasp his subject and can make one pertinent and just observation" (JM 28:175). These journal entries might, then, be termed the "rubble-stone" and foundation of Thoreau's late work, his effort to weave together his research and writing on phenology, wild fruits, and the dispersion of seeds; his expansive Indian Notebooks; his travel writing about Maine, Cape Cod, and Minnesota; and his social protest speeches and writing. As his Journal indicates, these projects took shape in a personal landscape as well, where

Thoreau tended his friendships and built a life on Concord's main street marked by both joy and loss.

Thoreau may never have managed to tie these threads together into "one pertinent and just observation," but several terms helped anchor his thinking in these years. "Indigenous" and "native" are two that recur throughout these works, referring to plants, animals, and humans, as Thoreau wrestled with what it meant to be rooted in the land, to be part of a web of relations woven into a specific place. These terms were important to the virtue ethics that informed his work after the *Walden* years, and they continued to guide his thinking in these later writings. "If a man is to be rich & strong anywhere," he wrote in the Journal on November 20, 1857, "it must be on his native soil. Here I have been these 40 years learning the language of these fields that I may the better express myself" (JM 24:303–4). Thoreau reserves the term "indigenous" for those with a longer claim to the land than his, but Concord is nevertheless his native soil. He claims it, though, not as a birthright but as a process of becoming, of learning to speak its language and understand its riches. The term that signifies this process of rooting himself is the land is another significant word of this period (and half the title of his major unfinished work): "wild." Thoreau makes clear in both "Wild Apples" and the burgeoning manuscript from which it was drawn, later the book *Wild Fruits*, that the process of becoming native entails enmeshing oneself into the more-than-human world, decentering human identity and values, and embracing nature's unruly fecundity. As Thoreau immersed himself in this process, a final key word came into focus: "succession." The word captures both the power of this "constant new creation," as he phrased it in a Journal passage written after his revelatory reading of *On the Origin of Species*, and the darker insight of Darwin's development theory: that the generative power of nature was interwoven with destruction (JM 32:197). As Annie Dillard observes, "Evolution loves death more than it loves you and me."[3] While this insight was not entirely new for Thoreau—he had been teasing it out at least since the writing of *A Week*—it is one that comes into sharper focus in these later works, and it grew sharper as the triple shadows of civil war, Indian genocide, and his own mortality lengthened. This insight is at once scientific and ontological, carrying profound ethical implications as well. One was immediately obvious the evening Thoreau and a group of friends read through Darwin's book on New Year's Day, 1860: that evolution made a mockery of proslavery arguments. What this insight meant for his relationship to Native Americans is a bit more complicated, and I suggest that the great unfinished works of natural history that filled Thoreau's last years—*Wild Fruits* and *The Dispersion of Seeds*, along with the essays and lectures that were part of this project, "Wild Apples," "The Succession of Forest Trees," and "Huckleberries"—are at once an effort to trace the intricate mechanisms that govern the woods and waters of Musketaquid and an attempt to wrestle with what it means for a white settler to live on Native land. For Thoreau, these botanical studies never led to the clear ethical imperatives regarding Native peoples that fueled his antislavery work, but I posit that they did plant seeds that may yet bear fruit in the long effort to decolonize this land.

Fruits

Thoreau began drafting *Wild Fruits* in 1859, though as Bradley Dean notes, the manuscript had a long gestation, with its first inklings in Thoreau's shift in the Journal to his more systematic phenological observations in the early 1850s. Thoreau's daily walks and Journal entries suggested a form that was not based on the single excursion that shaped most of his essays and books but instead captured the recurring cycle of the seasons. As this project unfolded, Thoreau combined his impressionistic, associative reflections with observational data—species of plants and animals, dates when plants flowered and fruited, the arrival and departure of birds and insects. Eventually, by 1860, Thoreau had begun combing through his earlier journals to gather tables of this data. Thoreau was learning to speak the language of his native fields and experimenting with how best to write it.[4] If the excursion form captured the drama of self-culture, of the individual leaving home to learn some powerful truth, the annual cycle, as Thoreau had discovered in *Walden*, better captured the endlessly renewing power of nature. He never quite finished his task, tying up the unfinished manuscript when he took to his deathbed after returning from Minnesota. What is left is rather uneven—a comprehensive list of fruit-bearing plants from Concord, some described with a few fragmentary notes culled from the Journal, some extensive and polished essays, some in between.[5] What they share is Thoreau's effort to speak the language of his native soil.

It is an effort, Thoreau argues, that we all need to make. In the published edition of *Wild Fruits*, Bradley Dean includes several possible openings to the book. One begins: "Most of us are still related to our native fields as the navigator to undiscovered islands in the sea. We can any afternoon discover a new fruit there which will surprise us by its beauty and sweetness." Such a process of discovery, Thoreau then argues, is essential to living fully in place. "It is not the orange of Cuba but rather the checkerberry of the neighboring field that most delights the eye and the palate of the New England child.... The bitter-sweet of a white acorn which you nibble in a bleak November walk over the tawny earth is more to me than a slice of imported pine-apple" (*WF* 3). The passage is wonderfully inviting, a call to embrace one's native ground by nibbling its fruits. What Thoreau develops is not an excursion or an introduction to phenology but a kind of paideia for new citizens of Concord, a system of education designed to root them in the earth, juxtaposed explicitly against the global capitalist food system that was taking shape in the mid-nineteenth century. Indeed, Lance Newman describes *Wild Fruits* as a utopian project, a "guidebook... to an organic community living in daily communion with the physical body of the land."[6] Rather than an expedition to buy and sell pineapples from the West Indies, Thoreau is interested in "some child's first excursions a-huckleberrying, in which it is introduced into a new world, experiences a new development, though it brings home only a gill of berries in its basket" (*WF* 4). This excursion may not bring much monetary profit, but it offers something far more valuable: "Do not think, then, that the fruits of New England are mean and insignificant, while those of some foreign land are noble and memorable. Our own, whatever they may be, are far more important than any others can be. They educate us and fit us to live here. Better for us the wild strawberry than the pineapple, the wild apple than the orange, the chestnut and pignut rather than the cocoa-nut and almond, and not on account of their flavor merely, but the part they play in our education" (*WF* 5). Thoreau frames this project as "our education"—a possessive pronoun that begins with the "New England child" heading off to pick its first huckleberries but expands to include all of those who enjoy these fruits; by extension, it includes any of Thoreau's readers who want to rebuild their ties to their native fields. Gathering wild fruits, he argues, may not feed the pocketbook, but it sustains the imagination and shifts what it means to be part of a community. Thoreau's goal, then, is ideological rather than scientific or economic. *Wild Fruits* is an effort to teach his readers how to become "native."[7]

The language of the passage has little to say directly about Native people—Thoreau's simile about navigators and undiscovered islands presumes these lands were uninhabited, and though the "tawny landscape" carries a hint of an Indian past, Thoreau takes the emptied landscape as a given, the "New England child," like Thoreau himself, clearly in the line of colonial succession. The role of Indigenous people becomes more explicit, and more complicated, in the first extended entry. After brief comments on the elm, dandelion, willow, and sweet flag, then the mouse-ear and maple, Thoreau turns to the strawberry, "our first edible fruit to ripen" (*WF* 10). They take, he notes, some practice to find. One needs a careful eye for sandy hillsides and a good nose for "an indescribably sweet fragrance . . . the sweet scent of the earth of which the ancients speak," for "strawberries are the manna found, ere long, where that fragrance has been" (12). This kind of knowledge is rare: "Only one in a hundred know where to look for early strawberries," he calculates. "It is, as it were, a sort of Indian knowledge acquired by secret tradition" (13). This is Thoreau's last iteration of the "Indian wisdom" he posited at the end of "Natural History of Massachusetts," and here it is again positioned against a merely scientific knowledge. It is also situated against the traditional ecological knowledge of Native people—it is "as it were" a version of Indian knowledge, not actually passed down by communal tradition but continually rediscovered, a kind of settler self-reliance that occludes its debt to the land's Indigenous inhabitants. The process of "learning to speak the language of his native fields" is cast as a settler project, informed by Thoreau's study of Native people but separate from any social or political connection with them. The goal is to build a relationship with the land, not to the people dispossessed from it. Thoreau doesn't learn to find strawberries by following his elders on their rounds of gathering. He learns instead by walking the land and trying to speak its language. This sort of "Indian knowledge" is not a tradition, a part of a distinct culture, but a practice available to anyone willing to walk the earth with an attentive eye—and nose. Finding strawberries requires a sensory education, not a historical one, and its politics are those of racial succession.

 This is not to say that traditional ecological knowledge doesn't inform Thoreau's understanding of strawberries. He draws widely on the Indian Notebooks. He quotes from Samuel Hearne, John Franklin, and John Tanner for various Native names and spiritual traditions about the strawberry. From William Wood, Roger Williams, and George Loskiel, Thoreau gathers accounts of the fruit's former abundance when the land was tended by Native hands, as well as Native recipes for bread or pudding made from strawberries and cornmeal.[8] The more he learns to speak the language of strawberries, the more he summons the people who had spoken it long before Europeans arrived on these shores. Yet this information, like the quotations from English poets and botanists on the English strawberry, serves as a supplement to knowledge Thoreau has gained from his own wanderings. They deepen his education in strawberries, but they are not the core of it—that belongs instead to the reddened fingers and lingering taste that mark his initiation into these native fields. It is because he knows the strawberry by his experience that he proposes swapping its name: "But let us not call it by the name of 'strawberry' any longer because in Ireland and England they spread straw under their garden kinds. It is not that to the Laplanders or Chippewayan; better to call it by the Indian name of heart-berry, for it is indeed a crimson heart which we eat at the beginning of summer to make us brave for all the rest of the year, as Nature is" (*WF* 17). Strawberries have their own name, and although the Cree and Ojibwe understand it better than the English and Irish (it's worth noting that Thoreau uses the present tense to describe this Indigenous knowledge), Thoreau does not choose the term in a Native language but the essence of that name translated into his own tongue. This is the gleaning from the long years of study gathered in the Indian Notebooks. He acknowledges the Native wisdom that helps him know strawberries, but in *Wild Fruits* they become a settler ceremony. This, says Thoreau, is how you claim a landscape: by eating its crimson heart.

A similar pattern structures "Huckleberries," an entry that serves as the source of the essay of the same name. The fruit is another keystone in the native paideia Thoreau develops: "I served my apprenticeship and have since done considerable journeywork in the huckleberry field," he notes wryly; "it was some of the best schooling that I got, and paid for itself" (*WF* 55). Gathering huckleberries is both education and nature religion: "We pluck and eat in remembrance of her," he writes. "It is a sort of sacrament, a communion—the not forbidden fruits, which no serpent tempts us to eat." Instead of dividing humans from nature, this fruit "entitle[s] us to her regard and protection." In eating huckleberries, we realize that "man stands at length in such a relation to Nature as the animals which pluck and eat as they go" (*WF* 52). Thoreau, again, draws widely on his Indian Notebooks in his effort to know huckleberries. Their range, he notes, is "coterminous with what has been called the Algonquian Family of Indians," and it was an important fruit for them. To show that European settlers learned their use from Native people, not the other way around, he cites widely from early explorers. Samuel de Champlain, Gabriel Sagard, Paul Le

Jeune, Roger Williams, and John Josselyn testify to the Native use of fresh and dried huckleberries in their cooking; Le Jeune notes that "some figure for themselves a paradise full of bluets" (*WF* 47).[9] It wasn't just Thoreau who followed in the path of the Indian—any white cook who used the bounty of the huckleberry patch to make a simple cake did so as well. "We have no national cake so universal and well-known as this in all parts of the country where corn and huckleberries grew. They enjoyed it all alone ages before our ancestors heard of their Indian corn and their huckleberries, and probably if you had travelled here a thousand years ago it would have been offered you alike on the Connecticut, the Potomac, the Niagara, the Ottawa, and the Mississippi" (*WF* 50). This is an inviting vision, an alternative encounter shaped by hospitality and reciprocity, where Europeans were the grateful guests of Indigenous hosts eager to share the bounty of their land. It's a vision that quickly fades—unstated, though implied, is that the same would not be true for Native people traveling along those same rivers in Thoreau's day. While the reader may imagine some reciprocal hospitality, it is clear that Thoreau's thoughts are of a Native past, and his goal is to acknowledge racial succession. Instead of the huckleberry as a vehicle for reconciliation, Thoreau offers it as a memorial: "I think it would be well if the Indian names were as far as possible restored and applied to the numerous species of huckleberries by our botanists, instead of the very inadequate Greek and Latin or English ones at present used. It would serve both a scientific and popular use" (*WF* 50). This would be a science that recognizes traditional ecological knowledge and reminds settlers learning their homeland botany that others had long tended these lands. Thoreau may not be able to fully imagine Native and white people sharing a huckleberry cake on land that had room for both, but he recognizes that names have power and that memory is a first step toward justice.

Yet the focus of *Wild Fruits* is not Indigenous people but indigenous *plants*. Thoreau recalls learning from his Penobscot guides which woodland berries are edible, and he cites widely from white travelers on Native territory in his era, but his references to Native people are generally in the past tense. If he cannot quite imagine their revival, he is eager to promise the revival of native plants. "If you look closely you will find blueberry and huckleberry bushes under your feet, though they may be feeble and barren, throughout all our woods, the most persevering Native Americans, ready to shoot up into place and power at the next election among the plants" (*WF* 44).[10] Do these indigenous plants symbolize Native people, pointing to their resilience and eventual resurgence? Or, as the reference to the Native American, or Know-Nothing, Party suggests, are they emblems of a settler nativism? The irony in the reference makes it hard to tell, but it is clear that Thoreau's interest in what happens in the understory of the local woods is not simply botanical. Plants are political.

Thoreau is careful to note that other plants, too, can naturalize themselves, sink roots into the earth, and become native. It is this latter process that captures the imagination of Thoreau—the mysterious alchemy of becoming "native." In his entry on the European cranberry, Thoreau revels in these small fruits, which he distinguishes (perhaps not accurately) from the closely related American cranberry.[11] He finds them in the swamps scattered about the Concord landscape, "little oases of wildness in the desert of our civilization." The passage then takes an odd turn toward the pagan: "I believe almost in the personality of such planetary matter, feel something akin to reverence for it, can even worship it as terrine, titanic matter extant in my day. We are so different we admire each other, we healthily attract one another. I love it as a maiden" (*WF* 168). Thoreau revels in these wild places and wild plants in the midst of settled towns, describing them with an erotic charge that channels the fecundity of nature. They break down the boundary between civilized and wild, human and more-than-human, and offer a sudden revelation of universal attraction, of nativity. Feeling, here, is inextricable from knowledge; what emerges is not so much science as a new (or old) way of being.[12] Thoreau unearths the ontology of his effort to become native to this place. "These spots are meteoric, aerolitic, and such matter has in all ages been worshipped. . . . It would be the regeneration of mankind if they were to become elevated enough to worship sticks and stones" (*WF* 168). This may be, for the moment, a stretch for most of mankind, though Thoreau noted many examples of sacred places in his Indian Notebooks. Yet rather than have this moment of rapture bring to mind the Musketaquid people whose spirituality was deeply woven into the same landscape, Thoreau universalizes this experience, gesturing beyond settler and Native to encompass all mankind. The result is not an historical accounting of settler society but a universal indigeneity that, for Thoreau, transcends the forces of history. "So many plants, the indigenous and bewildering variety of exotics, you see in conservatories and nurserymen's catalogues, or read of in English books, and the Royal Society did not make one of them, and knows no more about it than you! All truly indigenous and wild on this earth" (*WF*

169). Every plant, Thoreau realizes, is indigenous and wild, and each offers a lesson to its human kin.

This insight is also central in "Wild Apples." Thoreau returns to a sentence that first appeared in his Journal in 1851: "Our wild apple is wild only like myself, perchance, who belong not to the aboriginal race here, but have strayed into the woods from the cultivated stock" (*WF* 79; *PJ* 3:232). Thoreau is careful to distinguish himself from the Native inhabitants of the land—he is not aboriginal—but, like the apple tree, he can become native. He is thrilled to find the indigenous crab apple tree on his journey to Minnesota and proud to claim a "corymb of flowers" for his herbarium in the same spirit of ownership, perhaps, as he collects several items of Dakota clothing, yet this is not the object of the entry. "But though they are indigenous, like the Indians, I doubt whether they are any hardier than those backwoodsmen among the apple trees, which, though descended from cultivated stock, plant themselves in distant fields and forests where the soil is favorable to them" (*WF* 80). These naturalized trees are Thoreau's main subject, the anchor to his identity. "I pluck them as a wild fruit, native to this quarter of the earth," dying trees that nevertheless replant themselves, bearing a puckering fruit that sweetens in the frost, unnamed by science but given two dozen names by him, who has learned their language (*WF* 84). It is this fruit that makes him native to this quarter of the earth, helping him adapt to this new world and, in a process Darwin will help him see, transforming his very being.

Wild Fruits thus lays out a process for becoming native, an educational program that includes extensive reading and study, drawing from the traditional knowledge of Native peoples as well the classical literature of the Mediterranean and the contemporary science of Europe and America, but based first and last on observing, gathering, and tasting the wild fruits of one's own native ground. Thoreau knows that this process is at once laborious and fragile. "The era of wild apples will soon be past," he warns, as old orchards are replanted in nursery trees and wild scrubland turned to pasture and field (*WF* 91). Global capitalism has more interest in the orange, the pineapple, and the almond than the huckleberry and its kin, and Thoreau is horrified to hear of a machine that will turn the huckleberry bushes that sprout from cutover woodlands into cheap fuel. Instead, he proposes an alternative to the mad rush of capital. "Among the Indians the earth and its productions generally were common and free to all the tribe, like the air and water, but among us who have supplanted the Indians, the public retain only a small yard or common in the middle of the village, with perhaps a graveyard beside it" (*WF* 235). In "Chesuncook," he argues for national preserves where the forest and the hunter race might survive and help renew all America; here, he argues for a more radical rethinking of private property—a sense of land not as the anchor of individual gain but as a communal good—for its aesthetic value ("such things are beautiful"), its sacred value ("a mountaintop . . . even to the Indians a sacred place"), and its educational value. Walden Woods and Easterbrooks Country could be "a common possession forever, for instruction and recreation. After all, "we are all schoolmasters, and our schoolhouse is the universe" (*WF* 238). In such a school, Thoreau suggests, we might all learn to become native.

Much depends, of course, on who Thoreau means by "we." As Glen Sean Coulthard has noted, any commons in a settler world was once another nation's sovereign territory, and if Thoreau constantly acknowledges the long tenure of the Musketaquid people in Concord and the continued presence of the Penobscot people in his proposed national preserves in Maine, he can't quite imagine this commons as anything other than American territory. And by making the commons the focus of a settler paideia of place, he removes an essential element of Indigenous decolonization—its focus on territorial sovereignty and the land-based practices that inform every aspect of Indigenous culture. Even Thoreau's proposal to preserve "the hunter race" in his national preserve, although it avoids the often genocidal dispossession that accompanied the creations of the U.S. national parks, still locks Indigenous peoples into a Romantic reservation for the benefit of settlers.[13] But the "all" in Thoreau's promise offers a possibility of inclusion and Native sovereignty that he himself couldn't fully imagine.

Seeds

Becoming native for Thoreau does not mean becoming Indigenous. He is quite clear about this distinction in "Wild Apples"—he is eager to learn from a Native American past, yet he has little interest in trying to replicate it. This was always the case, even when he was playing Indian with John or following Attean and Polis through the Maine Woods. The stance was reinforced by his reading of Darwin, which shifted his focus away from memorializing a static, vanishing race and toward a more fluid, malleable understanding of species, humans among them. This stance infuses his last work, *The Dispersion of Seeds*, and the essay drawn from it, "The Succession of Forest Trees."[14] In the latter, he opens his address to the Middlesex Cattle Show of 1860 by saying, "I wish to see once more the old familiar faces, whose names I do not know, which for me represent the Middlesex country, and come as near to being indigenous to the soil as a white man can" (*Exc* 165). He invites his listeners (and readers) not to play Indian but to learn to become become more native to the soil; not to claim Indigeneity, but to become something new. And they do so by learning about succession.

"The Succession of Forest Trees" has lots to say about acorns and pine cones, squirrels and blue jays; it has little to say directly about Native Americans. Thoreau's goal may have been to explain why an oak forest springs up when a pine forest is cut down, but the insights apply to both the human and the more-than-human world. His meticulous and inspired observations of the spread of seeds and the behavior of animals provide ample evidence that the answer is found in the regular processes of nature and not spontaneous generation, as was popularly held. In the unfinished *Dispersion of Seeds*, left alongside *Wild Fruits* among his papers after his death, he states more firmly that "our forest trees are planted by Nature," and he adds more information from his extensive reading in the Indian Notebooks (*FS* 24).[15] As he considers the pitch pine plains in the Concord area, he suggests an Indigenous origin: "Who knows but the fires or clearings of Indians may have originated many of these bare plains, and so account for the presence of these trees there? We know that they not only annually burned the forest to expedite their hunting, but regularly cleared extensive tracts for cultivation, and these were always level tracts and, where the soil was light, such as they could turn over with their rude implements. When the thin soil was exhausted in one place, they resorted to another" (*FS* 157). If the forests are planted by Nature, then the Indians were doing Nature's work. It was, of course, not a huge leap for European Americans who were used to seeing Native people as wild savages to portray them as part of the natural world, but this passage is a bit different. For one, Native people are engaged in sophisticated (even if "rude") agriculture, rather than being described solely as hunters, as most settler histories did; for another, they are consciously shaping the environment, nurturing a landscape and helping it flourish. This is not quite the "tangled bank" that Darwin uses to anchor the conclusion of *On the Origin of Species*, a riotous cacophony of life that nevertheless unfurls according to the rules of natural selection; nor is it quite a cultivated garden. The Musketaquid had learned how to strike a fruitful balance between the wild woods and cultivated fields of their native ground.

And so might white settlers. Thoreau summarizes his research into European forestry practices and notes that the best methods are those that most closely mimic what Nature itself does when given room and time. "The results to which planters have arrived remind us of the experiences of Kane and his companions at the North, who, when learning to live in that climate, were surprised to find themselves steadily adopting the customs of the natives, simply becoming Esquimaux. So, when we experiment in planting forests, we find ourselves at last doing as Nature does" (*FS* 134). These Arctic explorers were not playing Indian; they were learning to adapt to a new environment from those who had long experience in living in a particularly harsh land. The phrase "becoming Esquimaux" is telling. Kane and his companions were not being initiated into Inuit culture and society, forging the kinds of personal and political alliances that weave newcomers into a tribal fabric. But they also were not simply Europeans who purchased the most effective clothing and tools for the job at hand (at, one hopes, a fair price). By adapting their habits to a new environment, they were themselves changing, becoming native to a new place.

This process of adaptation was the linchpin of Darwin's *On the Origin of Species*, which Thoreau read a few months before drafting *Dispersion*, quickly grasping its import. Reading *Origin* marked, as he phrases it in *Walden*, a new era in his life. The book had just been published when Charles Loring Brace brought the Harvard botanist Asa Gray's copy to Concord on New Year's Day in 1860; Brace, Franklin Sanborn, Bronson Alcott, and Thoreau read it together. Their reactions varied. Brace and Sanborn focused on the book's implications for antislavery work—since most proslavery arguments relied on the theory of separate creation advocated by Louis Agassiz, among others, Darwin's suggestion of a common descent for all humans struck at the heart of their racist argument for slavery. Alcott was rattled by the materialism of Darwin's theory—it left little room for his expansive idealism. Thoreau quickly recognized that natural selection offered the key to his studies of the Concord environment, and he quickly borrowed the book when it arrived at the Concord library. As Randall Fuller notes in his 2017 study of the reception of *On the Origin of Species* in New England, the book quickly reshaped the region's intellectual landscape. Thoreau was immersed in rereading Darwin when Thomas Wentworth Higginson lectured in Concord on slavery later that winter. Inspired by Darwin's more fluid sense of race, Higginson argued that barbarism and civilization were not fixed categories of a racial hierarchy but malleable, with the most profound examples of barbarism coming from the "civilized" region of the American South. Fuller suggests that Thoreau was nettled as well, citing a comment by Alcott that Darwin undercut "Thoreau's prejudice for Adamhood" and, more broadly, his admiration for precontact Native culture. But Fuller notes that Thoreau's main interest lay in applying Darwin's ideas to his own observations about phenology and forest succession. "*Origin*," Fuller writes, "seemed to finish a sentence he had long been struggling to write."[16]

Thoreau mulled over the details and implications of Darwin's theory as he continued his observations of the shifting and evolving landscape on the edge of Concord. In his Journal, and again in *The Dispersion of Seeds*, he captures this central insight: "The development theory implies a greater force in Nature—because more flexible & accommodating—& equivalent to a sort of constant *new* creation" (JM 32:197; *FS* 101–2). This is true for forests and it is true for people—humans are part of this force, changing and accommodating themselves to new environments and new contexts, never fixed into immutable races but always in the process of becoming something new themselves. But as Walls notes, this force of nature came, in her phrase, "with not one key but two: the fecundity of nature and the pressure of mortality."[17] Thoreau watched this force in action as he observed a bumper crop of acorns wither in an early frost, a type of random destruction showing that nature didn't play by human rules. Succession is a process of creation that depends wholly on the vagaries of death. Thoreau does not make the connection between the succession of trees and the succession of races explicit in *The Dispersion of Seeds*, nor does he work out an early version of a social Darwinism. As Branka Arsić's collection *Dispersion* (2021) suggests, Thoreau's project was focused more on science and had some profound implications for ontology. In Arsić's words, these inquiries into vegetal life suggest that "human life—all animal life—is such a continuity of thoughts and bodies, a flow of the heterogenous." Antoine Trainsel, in his contribution to the volume, suggests that this project "unsettles" contemporary notions of individualism and agency, hinting at a new ethics and politics.[18] Juliana Chow, in her study of natural history discourse in the literature of the nineteenth century, highlights Thoreau's long fascination with this churn, with the wreckage he sees everywhere on the shores of Cape Cod—human and natural—paired with the brutal generative processes he sees in the woods of Concord haunting his emerging biogeographic imagination. Dispersion (a geographic process) and succession (a chronological one) weave a web of creation that reaches across time and space, driven by decay and rebirth.[19]

It is clear that forest succession and racial succession are linked in his work. William Howarth notes that Thoreau's late Journal counters a narrative of American triumphalism: "The country was not immortal, moving always onward and upward, but caught in cycles of birth and death, the law of natural succession." Cristin Ellis argues that "Thoreau explicitly understood the migration of seeds and the migration of races to be conceptually of a piece."[20] He had used the term "succession" in the context of European settlement in the past—a journal entry from January 29, 1856, for example, notes that "the saw-miller is the neighbor and successor to the Indian," and on October 22, 1857, he says of the Musketaquid, "these were our predecessors" (JM 20:79, 24:550). As late as January 23, 1858, two years before he read *Origin*, he used the language of fixed racial difference and inevitable vanishing: "Everybody notices that the Indian retains his habits wonderfully,—is still the same man that the discoverers found. The fact is, the history of the white man is a history of improvement, that of the red man a history of fixed habits of stagnation" (JM 25:55). This is not Thoreau's only word on racial succession—he deplores the savagery of white traders who debase Indians and turn them into "vermin-catchers and rum drinkers," and in the white heat of his outrage during the aftermath of John Brown's raid at Harper's Ferry, he stops to decry how "Christian" newspapers tally up the Native people killed by California settlers as if they were deer (JM 30:90). Overall, however, Thoreau's comments suggest that he saw the vanishing of Native Americans as inevitable, even if deplorable. Reading Darwin and understanding the connection between fecundity and mortality, the churn of death and life at the heart of this constant new creation, may have only reaffirmed this view. But his encounter with evolutionary theory may also have changed his thinking about racial categories. His comments about Middlesex farmers and Arctic explorers suggest that he began, after reading Darwin, to see races not as fixed and easily ranked quasi-species but as fluid and flexible categories endlessly responding to the forces of Nature. As Chow notes, Thoreau was primed for this insight from his reading of Charles Pickering's *The Races of Man* (1848), which offered, in contrast to the more strict racial hierarchy described by Arnold Guyot, in *The Earth and Man* (1849), a more variable, fluid, and environmentally responsive view of human races.[21] And Thoreau was not alone in taking this message from *Origin*. Randall Fuller notes that Charles Loring Brace, who brought that first copy of Darwin's book to Concord, was fascinated by this vision of malleable races of humans; his *Races of the Old World* came out in 1863, over a year after Thoreau's death, but his central thesis resonates with Thoreau's emerging view of race: "Scarcely any marks of a human variety are permanent. . . . They continually shade into one another, or are changed or pass away." What this means for American racial politics is not entirely clear—if Brace is eager to undercut the racial ideology of slavery, he is less certain about what will replace it, gesturing toward a vague "organic Kingdom of God" as the goal of humanity that he seems to assume will be Christian, American, and white.[22] Thoreau took a similar premise about the mutability of race in response to environmental conditions and imagined a rather different future.

This is most clearly expressed in a remarkable Journal passage written not long after his insight about Darwin and the constant new creation. On November 23, 1860, after weeks of entries that trace the details of forest succession and count the rings of the chestnut sleepers under the rails (most of which predate European settlement), Thoreau drafted the passage that would open *Wild Fruits*, celebrating the virtues of wild berries over imported tropical fruits. Then there follows an inserted page with the following text, imagining the Concord landscape if its inhabitants simply vanished:

> At first perchance there would be an abundant crop of rank garden weeds & grasses in the cultivated land—rankest of all in the cellar holes sumach & pin-weed hard-hack, blackberry thimbleberry raspberry &c would grow vigorously along old garden limits lines main streets & roads—Garden weeds & grasses would soon disappear—Huckle berry & blueberry bushes—lambskill—hazel—sweet fern—barberry elder, also shadbush, choke berry, andromeda thorns &c would rapidly prevail in the deserted pasture At the same time the wild cherries—birch poplar—willows—checkerberry would re-establish themselves——Finally the pines, hemlock—spruce, larch—shrub oaks—oaks—chestnut—beech—& walnuts— would occupy the site of Concord once more—the apple & perhaps all exotic trees and shrubs & a great part of the indigenous shrubs named above would have disappeared—&

the laurel & yew would to some extent be an underwood here, & perchance the red-man once more thread his way through the mossy swamp-like primitive wood. (JM 33:4)

It's not clear whether this page was inserted here by Thoreau or by a later reader of the Journal, but the placement is fitting. The passage serves as a summation of his work on forest succession, with its richly observed understanding of how an ecosystem moves from gardens and fields to a mature old growth forest, limned in the details of some two-dozen native and exotic plants. It matches well with the day's entry, arguing that the Concord Social Club should celebrate native wild berries rather than imported oranges and pineapples—this vision of a restored native woodland is where such thinking leads. And with this restoration of a thriving "primitive wood" comes the "red man." This vision is striking: for one, it imagines not the relentless progress of the Anglo-Saxon but the opposite. For another, it takes as its focus not the human world, with its cultures and technologies, but the more-than-human world, seeing humans as only one part of the fullest natural expression of the landscape. Third, it makes no effort to imagine how these Indigenous inhabitants appear. There's no inkling of a secure Native refuge from white civilization from which they might reclaim their land or of the long resistance of the land's original inhabitants, patiently surviving in the margins of New England society. It is not even clear that these "red men" are the direct descendants of those displaced by white settlers. They might themselves have arrived from elsewhere. They might even be the descendants of the white settlers themselves, now fully native to the soil. A white Middlesex farmer could never be fully indigenous, but perhaps his great-great-grandchildren could be. And perhaps, at that point, they would no longer be "white." Thoreau may have gleaned this vision of an Indigenous future from his reading in the Indian Notebooks, where he records several different prophecies of Native resurgence after the time of white settlers has passed. Such prophecies were sometimes rooted in tribal traditions, such as the Anishinaabe story of the eight fires; others, like those of the Lenape Neolin and the Shawnee Tenskwatawa, were individual visions that helped fuel Native resistance to colonialism. These visions of Indigenous renewal came to Thoreau from the pens of settler writers, but they may nevertheless have shared a common origin with his own—a vision of a people living deeply rooted in a thriving land.

Such people might be the counterpart of the one wild fruit that does not make it into his manuscript—the arrowheads he gathers everywhere from the Concord soil. He writes a long Journal entry on the subject on March 28, 1859, where he considers it as a future writing project; in the meantime, he ponders the nature of this most unusual item. It is, he notes, remarkably abundant: "Some time or often, you would say, it had rained arrowheads, for they lie all over the surface of America. . . . They are sown like a grain that is slow to germinate broad cast over the earth—like the dragons teeth that bore a crop of soldiers—these bear crops of philosophers & facts; and the same seed is just as good to plant again. It is a stone fruit. Each one yields a thought" (JM 28: 311–13). These are, indeed, a perennial fruit, destined to outlast both their maker and their collector. Curtis Runnels, in assessing Thoreau's archaeology, notes that he seems to have missed the important insights emerging in Europe about stratigraphy, chronology, and cultural evolution—rather than carefully locating artifacts in discrete layers of soil, Thoreau generally plucked lithics from disturbed soil, which made them rather useless in reconstructing precontact history.[23] But as emissaries from the past, the handiwork of Thoreau's predecessors made visible in every freshly plowed field or eroded streambank, they are powerful relics of the long human presence in Musketaquid, embodiments of people living in close harmony with the land. As Ross Martin argues, these arrowheads were not dead artifacts but living thought—a strange paleontology today, but one that fit within the vitalist school of science traced by Arsić. For Martin, arrowheads are signs not of racial succession but of the constant flux of things. Thoreau's collection of lithics is neither archaeological nor ethnological but ontological—an emblem of the interconnectedness of the human and more-than-human world, where mind and matter intersect, where thought takes shape in a fragment of rock. Gathering lithics is a way for Thoreau to "re-member" the Native world that had long flourished in Musketaquid, one that might, with careful nurturing, flourish again.[24]

This is a radical revision of the politics of racial succession that structured settler colonial thought in Thoreau's era—a powerful counter to the strict teleology of cultural development that was taking shape in Europe, where the schema of Stone Age, Bronze Age, and Iron Age was being developed, and in America, where Lewis Morgan's model of cultural evolution would soon become the foundation of the emerging field of anthropology. Martin suggests that Thoreau's vitalism carries with it a progressive ethics, though the Native people in New England whose ancestors crafted the artifacts gathered by Thoreau might disagree. Thoreau might undercut the narrative of Anglo-Saxon superiority and gesture toward a very different future from the global industrial capitalist world taking shape in New England, but his emerging view of racial malleability, where culture is rooted not in genetic typology but emerges organically from a complex of biogeographic forces, offers little help to the political status of struggling Native communities. Indeed, by rooting human identity in the landscape, Thoreau makes it easier to dismiss the claims of any one group to their homeland. The logic of succession, which folds the death of individuals and species into the churn of a constant new creation, naturalizes Indian vanishing. Arrowheads, the mind-prints that convey a powerful biogeographic ontology, are available to anyone who picks them up. They are markers not of political continuity, connecting the living descendants of the Musketaquid tribe to their long inheritance, but of the malleability of living in place. By showing anyone how to be native to a place, they erase the claims of Native peoples to their traditional land.

Yet it is important not to dismiss the progressive potential of this vitalist ethics. Thoreau may not have fully understood that the intense relationality inherent in this vitalist stance includes an obligation to the descendants and relatives of Musketaquid people, but he does offer a powerful alternative to the settler narrative of his era. The Darwinian timescale, for one, dwarfs the triumphalist narratives of settler histories, reframing the story of Anglo-Saxon settlement as one brief example of the great churn of creation, where seeds and races disperse, take root, wither, or flourish in turn, unwittingly acting out the larger forces of natural law. For another, his vitalist world emerges in opposition to the exploitative logic of nineteenth-century capitalism, offering a vision of the human and more-than-human world flourishing together and hinting at an Indigenous future unimaginable to titans of industry and trade celebrating their dams along the Concord and Merrimack Rivers or their railroads cutting through the sandhills around Walden Pond. Thoreau's alternative future is the outcome of the kind of gradualist change Ellis describes as characteristic of Thoreau's late political writings—a shift in ethics that relies not on sudden conversion but on the "cascading ramifications of minimal events," a social counterpart to Thoreau's immersion in Darwinian theory. Such change will emerge from the embodied perspective of a race fully immersed in the environment, and it may take generations.[25] Thoreau imagines these arrowheads, sharp as the day they were made, making their way back to the soil when the houses and museums of those who collected them rot and fall back into the earth. These ancient, ageless artifacts, these stone fruits, operate according to different calendars and clocks than were common in nineteenth-century America. As with the Kalendar project and *Wild Fruits*, Thoreau attempts to think outside the narrative of personal excursions or the teleology of European progress. The constant new creation laughs these more ordinary time frames to scorn. These arrowheads will bear new fruit, help a new forest and a new people, succeed the old ones, in their own time.

These seeds of a new-old forest would not offer much hope to those helping move the process of settler colonialism forward. Nor would this vision of a distant regeneration offer much comfort to those Native peoples caught in the vise of conquest. Thoreau notes quietly in "Huckleberries" that one of the largest battles in Metacom's Rebellion took place when Benjamin Church attacked a group of Wampanoag old men, women, and children gathering berries. Thoreau was sick with what would prove to be his last illness when he drafted this lecture in the winter of 1861; by summer he had traveled up the Minnesota and heard the Dakota leaders rail against an unjust U.S. government, and two years later Little Crow, whose sharp critique of U.S. Indian policy Thoreau noted during his visit, and who became the reluctant leader of the Dakota Uprising, was shot by a settler while picking huckleberries with his son. The episode is a grim echo of the murder of six Nashobah Indians at the end of Metacom's Rebellion, killed while picking huckleberries on the edge of Concord.[26] Thoreau did not live long enough to make this connection. By then, his posthumous life was well underway, beginning with a eulogy by Emerson that celebrated his deep connection to the Indian, followed by a series of essays published in the *Atlantic* that brought a new vision of the New England woods to a war-torn country, then by the first publications of *Cape Cod* and the *Maine Woods*, and then by a new edition of *Walden*. Thoreau's words gradually took root, and they continue to bear fruit that he could hardly imagine.

Nor could he have imagined the fate of Little Crow's seed. His son, Wowinape, was in his teens when his father was killed; he was with him in the fatal huckleberry patch but escaped the scene, though he was later captured and sentenced to be hanged. He converted to Christianity in prison camp and took the name Thomas Wakeman. Pardoned in 1865, he moved to the Dakota Territory and eventually founded the Sioux YMCA, an organization that continues to serve families and youth on the Cheyenne River Reservation. In 1971, Thomas's grandson, Jesse Wakeman, convinced the Minnesota Historical Society to return Little Crow's remains to his family; they were reinterred in Flandreau, South Dakota—one key episode in the gradual but growing revival of Dakota culture.[27]

Leanne Betasamosake Simpson recounts the long-cherished Anishinaabe prophecy of the eight fires that define Indigenous history. Keyed into the very different timescape of Native tradition, the prophecy doesn't align easily with European chronology, and the dark era of colonization, though it plays its part, is far from the whole story. We are, Simpson says, living in the time of the Seventh Fire, when the Oshkimaadiziig generation emerges to help revive Indigenous culture and decolonize Native society. When that work is completed, the people will enter the time of the Eighth Fire, "an eternal fire lit by all humans. . . . In order for the Eighth Fire to be lit, settler society must also choose to change their ways, to decolonize their relationships with the land and Indigenous nations, and to join with us in building a sustainable future based on mutual recognition, justice, and respect." This is at once simple to say and difficult to imagine. Indeed, it was almost impossible for Thoreau to imagine, but not entirely. As Simpson notes, the task of the people of the Seventh Fire is "planting the seeds of resurgence" and letting them gradually bear fruit.[28] Thoreau never fully decolonized his relationship with Native people, never fully advocated for their political equality, never fought to help them retain their land, never fully joined in their effort to preserve their cultural sovereignty in a modernizing United States. But he did remain mindful of the long Native presence in America, learned what he could of Indigenous wisdom, worked ceaselessly to help settler society change its ways, and thought deeply about what it might mean to decolonize America's relationship to the land. He, too, planted seeds of resurgence, and it is our task to help them grow.

Notes

Preface: Reading Thoreau on Native Ground

1 The Thoreau-Wabanaki Anniversary Tour was organized by Mike Wilson of the Northern Forest Center in 2014.
2 For several essays stemming from this journey, see my edited collection *Rediscovering the Maine Woods: Thoreau's Legacy in an Unsettled Land* (Amherst: University of Massachusetts Press, 2019). James Finley's contribution, "Pilgrimages and Working Forests: Envisioning the Commons in *The Maine Woods*," includes a discussion of the Katahdin Woods and Waters National Monument. Two essays in the collection capture Penobscot perspectives on the trip and the region: Chris Sockalexis, "Crossing Moosehead Lake," and James Francis, "Carrying Place: Penobscot Language, Land, and Memory."
3 The literature on decolonization is broad, and I refer here to work focusing primarily on Indigenous people in the Americas, New Zealand, and Australia, rather than the Asian and African decolonization movements that began in the mid-twentieth century. This Indigenous focus has a long history, as Ned Blackhawk, *The Rediscovery of America: Native People and the Unmaking of U.S. History* (New Haven, CT: Yale University Press, 2023), makes clear, but its modern focal point is the United Nations Declaration on the Rights of Indigenous People, adopted in 2007. Advocates of decolonization focus on both changing cultural norms and social institutions, such as Linda Tuhiwai Smith in *Decolonizing Methodologies* (London: Zed Books, 1999), as well as on tribal land restitution and political agency, such as in Eve Tuck and Wang Yang, "Decolonization Is Not a Metaphor," *Decolonization: Indigeneity, Education and Society* 1, no. 1 (2012): 1–40. A good more recent book that weaves these threads together is Patty Krewac's *Becoming Kin: An Indigenous Call to Unforgetting the Past and Reimagining Our Future* (Minneapolis, MN: Broadleaf Books, 2022).
4 Lisa Brooks, *The Common Pot: The Recovery of Native Space in the Northeast* (Minneapolis: University of Minnesota Press, 2008); Siobhan Senier, *Sovereignty and Sustainability: Indigenous Literary Stewardship in New England* (Lincoln: University of Nebraska Press, 2020).

Introduction: Thoreau's Indian Problem

1 Brent Ranalli's "Henry Thoreau's Lifelong Indian Play" appears in *Thoreau in an Age of Crisis: The Uses and Abuses of an American Icon*, ed. Kristen Case, Rochelle L. Johnson, and Henrik Otterberg (Leiden: Brill, 2021). His essay "Thoreau's Indian Stride" was published in the *Concord Saunterer* 27 (2019): 89–110, and "Reading Thoreau's Gait" in the *Thoreau Society Bulletin*, no. 296 (Winter 2017): 1–3. Emerson and Hawthorne

are quoted in Walter Harding, *Thoreau as Seen by His Contemporaries* (Mineola, NY: Dover Publications, 1989), 68, 121.
2 Joshua Bellin, "In the Company of Savagists: Thoreau's Indian Books and Antebellum Ethnology," *Concord Saunterer* 16 (January 2008): 1–32; Richard Schneider, *Civilizing Thoreau: Human Ecology and the Social Sciences in the Major Works* (Rochester, NY: Camden House, 2016).
3 Philip J. Deloria, *Playing Indian* (New Haven, CT: Yale University Press, 1998). For a thorough, more recent account of savagism in the context of Native dispossession, see Roxanne Dunbar-Ortiz, *An Indigenous People's History of the United States* (Boston: Beacon Press, 2015).
4 Patrick Wolfe, "Settler Colonialism and the Elimination of the Native," *Journal of Genocide Research* 8, no. 4 (2006): 387–409; Mark Rifkin, *Settler Common Sense: Queerness and Everyday Colonialism in the American Renaissance* (Minneapolis: University of Minnesota Press, 2014); Jodi Byrd, *The Transit of Empire: Indigenous Critiques of Colonialism* (Minneapolis: University of Minnesota Press, 2011); Renée L. Bergland, *The National Uncanny: Indian Ghosts and American Subjects* (Hanover, NH: Dartmouth University Press, 2000).
5 Robert Sayre, in *Thoreau and the American Indians* (Princeton, NJ: Princeton University Press, 1977), suggests that Thoreau found it easier to assist African Americans in part because he had little investment in slavery, whereas Indians "were essential to his own sense of history" (25). Duncan Caldwell, in "Mind Prints, Arrowheads, the Indians and Thoreau," duncancaldwell.com, 2018, notes that in "Civil Disobedience," Thoreau includes Native American injustice among his reasons for refusing to pay his poll tax: "The Indian come to plead the wrongs of his race would do better to appeal to a just man imprisoned by the State than to the government itself" (*RP* 76). This is the only clause in the essay that addresses Native people, which underscores Thoreau's reticence on this issue.
6 Native writers include David Cusick: Indian Notebook 3; Samson Occom and John Konkapot: Indian Notebook 2; Squier: Indian Notebook 4; Morton: Indian Notebook 5; Schoolcraft: Indian Notebook 5. I follow Richard Sayre's numbering and dating of the Indian Notebooks, which are labeled differently in the Morgan Library collections. In this book, I have relied heavily on the transcripts of the Indian Notebooks completed in the 1930s by a number of graduate students (all women) under the direction of Arthur Christy. I am grateful to Brent Ranalli and the staff of the Morgan Library for making these transcripts available to me. On Copway, see my "Thoreau's Reading of George Copway: An Additional Indian Notebook," *Thoreau Society Bulletin*, no. 302 (Summer 2018): 1–5.
7 See JM 23:140–41.
8 For a detailed account of Mashpee in the nineteenth century, see Daniel Mandell, *Tribe, Race, History: Native Americans in Southern New England, 1780–1880* (Baltimore, MD: Johns Hopkins University Press, 2008), esp. 35–38; see also Lisa Brooks's chapter on Mashpee in *The Common Pot: The Recovery of Native Space in the Northeast* (Minneapolis: University of Minnesota Press, 2006). There are a number of histories of Mashpee and other Wampanoag communities written by Wampanoag people. Russell Peters's *The Wampanoags of Mashpee* (Mashpee, MA: Indian Spiritual and Cultural Training Center, 1987), is the most extensive; Earl Mills Sr. and Alicja Mann's *Son of Mashpee: Reflections of Chief Flying Eagle, a Wampanoag* (Tuscon, AZ: Word Studio, 1996) and Joan Taveres Avant's *People of the First Light* (Barnstable, MA: West Barnstable Press, 2010) offer rich accounts of the Mashpee community. Linda Coombs has written and spoken extensively on Wampanoag history, with a particular focus on correcting misconceptions of early contact between English colonists and Wampanoag people. Her book for young readers, *Colonization and the Wampanoag Story* (New York: Penguin Random House, 2023), offers a rich overview of a difficult topic.

9 Robert Sattelmeyer, *Thoreau's Reading: A Study in Intellectual History with Bibliographical Catalogue* (Princeton, NJ: Princeton University Press, 1988), 108–9.
10 Robin Wall Kimmerer, *Braiding Sweetgrass: Indigenous Wisdom, Scientific Knowledge, and the Teachings of Plants* (Minneapolis, MN: Milkweed Editions, 2013), 9.
11 Jace Weaver, "Indigenousness and Indigeneity," in *Companion to Postcolonialism*, ed. Henry Schwartz and Sangeeta Ray (Hoboken, NJ: Wiley, 2003); Jean O'Brien, *Firsting and Lasting: Writing Indians Out of Existence in New England* (Minneapolis: University of Minnesota Press, 2010), 6; Byrd, *Transit of Empire*, 54; Taiaiake Alfred and Jeff Corntassel, "Being Indigenous: Resurgences against Contemporary Colonialism," *Government and Opposition* 40, no. 4 (October, 2005): 597–614.
12 Kimmerer, *Braiding Sweetgrass*, 213.
13 "Arrivant" is a term usually applied to Africans brought to the Americas as slave labor, following the work of the Barbadian poet Edward Kamau Brathwaite, and is meant to complicate the settler/Indigenous binary. Jodi Byrd discusses the term in *The Transit of Empire*, and Yael Ben-zvi explores its implications in *Native Land Talk: Indigenous and Arrivant Rights Theories* (Hanover, NH: Dartmouth University Press, 2018). Where Irish and other immigrants fit within this framework is more complicated; for a thoughtful account, see Roxanne Dunbar-Ortiz, *Not a Nation of Immigrants: Settler Colonialism, White Supremacy, and a History of Erasure and Exclusion* (Boston: Beacon, 2021).
14 For a detailed account of Maungwudas, see Donald B. Smith, *Mississauga Portraits: Ojibwe Voices from Nineteenth-Century Canada* (Toronto: University of Toronto Press, 2013). On Joe Polis's brothers, see Pauleena M. Seeber, "The Maine Indian Guide," *Papers of the Nineteenth Algonquian Conference* (Ottawa: Carleton University, 1988), 180.
15 Audra Simpson, *Mohawk Interruptus: Political Life across the Borders of Settler States* (Durham, NC: Duke University Press, 2014).
16 Kim TallBear, *Native American DNA: Tribal Belonging and the False Promise of Genetic Science* (Minneapolis: University of Minnesota Press, 2013), 46; Kevin Bruyneel, *Settler Memory: The Disavowal of Indigeneity and the Politics of Race in the United States* (Chapel Hill: University of North Carolina Press, 2021). Daniel Mandell describes how debt, indenture, and the meager wages of farm labor helped impoverish Native communities in *Tribe, Race, History*. William Apess gives a harrowing account of his time as an indentured servant in the early nineteenth century in *A Son of the Forest* (1831). Apess, *On Our Own Ground: The Complete Writings of William Apess, a Pequot*, ed. Barry O'Connell (Amherst: University of Massachusetts Press, 1992), 5–26.
17 Philip Cafaro, *Thoreau's Living Ethics: "Walden" and the Pursuit of Virtue* (Athens: University of Georgia Press, 2004.
18 Bernd Peyer's *The Tutor'd Mind: Indian Missionary-Writers in Antebellum America* (Amherst: University of Massachusetts Press, 1997) is an early anchor of this scholarship; Kristina Bross and Hilary Wyss, both of whom have written excellent studies of Native writers in the colonial era, gathered a range of Native texts in *Early Native Literacies in New England* (Amherst: University of Massachusetts Press, 2008). Robert Allen Warrior, *The People and the Word: Reading Native Nonfiction* (Minneapolis: University of Minnesota Press, 2006), offers a reading of William Apess, among others, that explores how narrative nonfiction reshapes Native experience. Betty Donohue, *Bradford's Indian Book: Being the True Roots and Rise of American Letters as Revealed by the Native Text Embedded in "Of Plimoth Plantation"* (Gainesville: University of Florida Press, 2011), recovers a Native voice within this key Pilgrim text.
19 Dennis Tedlock, *The Spoken Word and the Work of Interpretation* (Philadelphia: University

of Pennsylvania Press 1983), pioneered efforts to capture the literary nuances of oral traditions. Brian Swann has edited a number of anthologies of Native American oral literature; *Algonquian Spirit: Contemporary Translations of the Algonquian Literatures of North America* (Lincoln: University of Nebraska Press, 2005) is the most relevant to Thoreau. Margaret Bruchac has written widely on anthropology and decolonization; her "Broken Chains of Custody: Possessing, Dispossessing, and Repossessing Lost Wampum Belts," *Proceedings of the American Philosophical Society* 162, no. 1 (March 2018): 56–105, is a good introduction to her work with wampum.

20 Barry O'Connell, *On Our Own Ground: The Writings of William Apess* (Amherst: University of Massachusetts Press, 1992); Philip Gura, *The Life of William Apess, Pequot* (Chapel Hill: University of North Carolina Press, 2018); Drew Lopenzina, *Through an Indian's Looking-Glass: A Cultural Biography of William Apess* (Amherst: University of Massachusetts Press, 2017); Joseph Nicolar, *Life and Traditions of the Red Man: A Rediscovered Treasure of Native American Literature*, ed. Annette Kolodny (Durham, NC: Duke University Press, 2007); Siobhan Senier, ed., *Dawnland Voices: An Anthology of Native Voices from New England* (Lincoln: University of Nebraska Press, 2014).

21 Robert Allen Warrior, *The People and the Word: Reading Native Nonfiction* (Minneapolis: University of Minnesota Press, 2005); Jace Weaver, Craig S. Womack, and Robert Warrior, *American Indian Literary Nationalism* (Albuquerque: University of New Mexico Press, 2006); Lisa Brooks, *The Common Pot: The Recovery of Native Space in the Northeast* (Minneapolis: University of Minnesota Press, 2008); O'Brien, *Firsting and Lasting*.

22 The Wôpanâak Language Reclamation Project, founded by Jessie Little Doe Baird, has a rich website: https://www.wlrp.org/. There is also an excellent documentary film about the project, *We Still Live Here—Âs Nutayuneân* (2011).

23 James Francis, the Penobscot tribal historian, has documented the tribe's cultural resurgence in artwork, films, and numerous publications, including "Carrying Place: Penobscot Land, Language, and Memory," in *Rediscovering the Maine Woods: Thoreau's Legacy in an Unsettled Land*, ed. John J. Kucich (Amherst: University of Massachusetts Press, 2019). Darren Ranco's work has focused on the intersections between tribal culture and environmental stewardship, including "Science in Indigenous Homelands: Addressing Power and Justice in Sustainability Science from/with/in the Penobscot River," co-authored with Birdie McGreavy, John Daigle, Suzanne Greenlaw, Nolan Altvater, Tyler Quiring, Natalie Michelle, Jan Paul, Maliyan Binette, Brawley Benson, Anthony Sutton, and David Hart, in *Sustainability Science* 16 (2021), 937–47, and "The Indian Ecologist and the Politics of Representation: Critiquing the Ecological Indian in the Age of Ecocide," in *Perspectives on the Ecological Indian: Native Americans and the Environment*, ed. Michael Harkin and David Rich Lewis (Lincoln: University of Nebraska Press, 2007) 32–51. Siobhan Senier, *Sovereignty and Sustainability: Indigenous Literary Stewardship in New England* (Lincoln: University of Nebraska Press, 2020).

24 O'Brien, *Firsting and Lasting*, 113, 118. On the Penobscot, personal communication from Chris Sockalexis, James Francis, and Jenny Neptune. On the Wampanoag, personal communication from Linda Coombs, Kerri Helme, Donna Mitchell, and Joyce Rain Anderson, all of whom have been generous in sharing their Wampanoag wisdom. The Plymouth 400th anniversary offered many opportunities for the Massachusetts Native community to push back against settler narratives and tell an Indigenous story, including historical videos (https://www.plymouth400inc.org/our-story-exhibit-wampanoag-history/) and the powerful Indigenous History Conference (https://www.bridgew.edu/event/indigenous-history-conference). Kristen Wyman (Nipmuc) has also helped me think through these

NOTES TO PAGES 19–28   197

issues during her presentation in the Decolonizing Thoreau webinar held by the Thoreau Society on October 31, 2020.

25 Patrick Wolfe helped inaugurate the field with *Settler Colonialism and the Transformation of Anthropology: The Politics and Poetics of an Ethnographic Event* (London: Cassell Publishing, 1999). Mark Rifkin's *Manifesting America: The Imperial Construction of U.S. National Space* (New York: Oxford University Press, 2009) is the first of his several key works in the field. Jodi Byrd's *The Transit of Empire* traces settler colonial dynamics in a wide range of settings, while Jean O'Brien's *Firsting and Lasting* delineates its presence in nineteenth-century local histories. Kevin Bruyneel's work has centered on the political and legal structures of settler colonialism, most recently in *Settler Memory*.

26 Elise Lemire, *Black Walden: Slavery and Its Aftermath in Concord, Massachusetts* (Philadelphia: University of Pennsylvania Press, 2009); Sandra Habert Petrolionis, *To Set This World Right: The Anti-Slavery Movement in Thoreau's Concord* (Ithaca, NY: Cornell University Press, 2006); Robert A. Gross, *The Transcendentalists and Their World* (New York: Farrar, Strauss and Giroux, 2021).

27 Rebecca Solnit, "The Thoreau Problem," *Orion*, July 10, 2015, https://orionmagazine.org/article/the-thoreau-problem/; Lance Newman *Our Common Dwelling: Henry Thoreau, Transcendentalism, and the Class Politics of Nature* (New York: Palgrave Macmillan, 2005); Philip Cafaro, *Thoreau's Living Ethics: Walden and the Pursuit of Virtue* (Athens: University of Georgia Press, 2006).

28 See Bruno Latour, *The Politics of Nature* (Cambridge, MA: Harvard University Press, 2004); Jane Bennett, *Thoreau's Nature: Ethics, Politics, and the Wild* (Latham, MD: Rowan and Littlefield, 2002); Timothy Morton, *Dark Ecology: For a Logic of Future Coexistence* (New York: Columbia University Press, 2016); Laura Dassow Walls, *Seeing New Worlds: Thoreau and Nineteenth-Century Natural Science* (Madison: University of Wisconsin Press, 1995); Rochelle Johnson, "'This Enchantment Is No Delusion': Henry David Thoreau, the New Materialisms, and Ineffable Materiality," *Interdisciplinary Studies in Literature and Environment* 21, no. 3 (2014): 606–35; Kristen Case, "Thoreau's Radical Empiricism: The Kalendar, Pragmatism, and Science," in *Thoreauvian Modernities: Transatlantic Conversations on an American Icon*, ed. François Specq, Laura Dassow Walls, and Michel Granger (Athens: University of Georgia Press, 2013); James Finley, "'Who Are We? Where Are We?': Contact and Literary Navigation in *The Maine Woods*," *Interdisciplinary Studies in Literature and Environment* 19, no. 2 (2012): 336–55; and Branka Arsić, *Bird Relics: Grief and Vitalism in Thoreau* (Cambridge, MA: Harvard University Press, 2016).

29 Alda Balthrop-Lewis, *Thoreau's Religion: Walden Woods, Social Justice, and the Politics of Asceticism* (New York: Cambridge University Press, 2021); Lydia Willsky-Ciollo, "Apostles of Wildness: American Indians and Thoreau's Theology of the Wild," *New England Quarterly* 91, no. 4 (December 2018): 551–91.

Chapter 1: Ghosts of Musketaquid

1 For a detailed account of the archaeological record of the Concord area, see Barbara Robinson's catalog for the 1985 Concord Museum exhibit, *From Musketaquid to Concord: The Native and European Experience* (Concord, MA: Concord Antiquarian Society, 1985). Daniel V. Boudillion offers a careful survey of the archival evidence in *History of the Nashobah Praying Indians: Doings, Sufferings, Survival, and Triumph* (Westbrook, ME: Raven House, 2023), as does

Brent Ranalli in "Tahattawan's World," unpublished manuscript, 2023. For a detailed map of traditional Indigenous territory, see Native Land, https://native-land.ca/, which indicates an overlap of these three groups. Jessie Little Doe Baird, in "Boundaries of the Wampanoag Nation: The Geo-Politics of the Wampanoag," unpublished manuscript, 2020, uses linguistic evidence to argue that the Massachusetts were part of the broader Wampanoag Nation, though it seems clear that Massachusett and Pokanoket were distinct power centers, despite sharing the same Wampanoag language and having strong kinship ties.

2   There are a range of sources on Native Americans in Southern New England. For historical accounts of the contact era, see Kathleen Bragdon, *Native People of Southern New England, 1500–1650* (Norman: University of Oklahoma Press, 1999); Christopher Strobel, *Native Americans of New England* (Santa Barbara, CA: Praeger, 2020), and Howard Russell, *Indian New England before the Mayflower* (Chicago: University of Chicago Press, 1980). For accounts with an environmental focus, see William Cronon, *Changes in the Land* (New York: Hill and Wang, 1983); Brian Donahue, *The Great Meadow* (New Haven, CT: Yale University Press, 2004); and Diana Muir, *Reflections in Bullough's Pond* (Hanover, NH: University Press of New England, 2000). On the ceremonial site in Acton, see James W. Mavor Jr. and Bryon E. Dix, *Manitou: The Sacred Landscape of New England's Native Civilization* (Rochester, VT: Inner Traditions, 1989), and Curtiss Hoffman, *Stone Prayers: Native American Constructions of the Eastern Seaboard* (Dover, NH: Arcadia, 2019). The status and significance of these stone formations are not settled archaeology; many are ambiguous, and governmental organizations are reluctant to identify these abundant and widely distributed features as sacred Native sites.

3   In *History of the Nashobah Praying Indians*, Boudillion traces the dispersal of the Nashobah, descendants of whom still live in Massachusetts as part of the Praying Indians of Natick and Ponkapoag. Jenny Hale Pulsipher offers a detailed account of the Nashobah murders in "Massacre at Hurtleberry Hill: Christian Indians and English Authority in Metacom's War," *William and Mary Quarterly* 53, no. 3 (June 1996): 459–86. Thoreau never mentions the episode—it's likely one that the Hoar family preferred to forget—but he certainly read Daniel Gookin's account, "History of the Christian Indians," copying passages from the work in *A Week* and in Indian Notebook 3:53–54. Thoreau read Gookin in *Transactions and Collections of the American Antiquarian Society*, vol. 2 (Cambridge, MA: Harvard University Press), 423–534.

4   The best recent account of Metacom's Rebellion, or King Philip's War, and its impact on Native communities is Lisa Brooks, *Our Beloved Kin: A New History of King Philip's War* (New Haven, CT: Yale University Press, 2018). The Earle Report, commissioned by the Massachusetts legislature and published in 1861, offers the most comprehensive census of Native peoples in Massachusetts in the era. See John Milton Earle, *Report on the Indians of the Commonwealth* (Boston: William White, 1861). For a detailed history of Native Americans in the aftermath of Metacom's Rebellion, see Daniel Mandell, *Behind the Frontier: Indians in Eighteenth-Century Eastern Massachusetts* (Lincoln: University of Nebraska Press, 2000). Jean O'Brien offers a rich history of the Natick people in *Dispossession by Degrees: Indian Land and Identity in Natick, 1650–1790* (New York: Cambridge University Press, 1997). Thoreau records evidence of one Native person living in nineteenth-century Concord. In his Journal on November 26, 1860, he notes, "Mother says one Lidy Bay, an Indian woman (so considered) used to live near Caesar's, and made baskets" (JM 33:19). Robert Gross notes that Issachar Bay of Hopkinton married Lydia Read of Wrentham in 1796; Issachar was identified as a "black man" and died in Concord in 1817 (email communication, August 22, 2022); I have been unable to locate more information about Lydia Read Bay.

5. Jean O'Brien, *Firsting and Lasting: Writing Indians Out of Existence in New England* (Minneapolis: University of Minnesota Press, 2010), xiv, 20.
6. Patrick Wolfe, "Settler Colonialism and the Elimination of the Native," *Journal of Genocide Research* 8, no. 4 (2006): 388; O'Brien, *Firsting and Lasting*, 40. Lucius Barber, *A Record and Documentary History of Simsbury* (1888), is quoted in O'Brien, *Firsting and Lasting*, 44.
7. Ralph Waldo Emerson, "Historical Discourse at Concord, on the Second Centennial Anniversary" (1835), in *The Collected Works of Ralph Waldo Emerson*, vol. 10, *Uncollected Prose Writings*, ed. Ronald A. Bosco and Joel Myerson (Cambridge, MA: Belknap Press of Harvard University Press, 2013), 61–62.
8. Emerson, "Historical Discourse at Concord," 62.
9. Robert Gross, *The Transcendentalists and Their World* (New York: Farrar, Strauss, Giroux, 2021), 353–54.
10. Lemuel Shattuck, *A History of the Town of Concord, Middlesex County, Massachusetts* (Boston: Russell, Odiorne, 1835), 2–12.
11. Shattuck, *History of the Town of Concord*, 3, 64.
12. O'Brien, *Firsting and Lasting*, 51.
13. Jace Weaver, "Indigenousness and Indigeneity," in *A Companion to Postcolonial Studies*, ed. Henry Schwartz and Sangeeta Ray (Hoboken, NJ: Wiley, 2003), 228; Wolfe, "Settler Colonialism," 388; Jodi Byrd, *The Transit of Empire: Indigenous Critiques of Colonialism* (Minneapolis: University of Minnesota Press, 2011), 53.
14. Laura Dassow Walls, *Henry David Thoreau: A Life* (Chicago: University of Chicago Press, 2017), 67; Henry David Thoreau, *Early Essays and Miscellanies*, ed. Joseph J. Moldenhauer and Edwin Moser (Princeton, NJ: Princeton University Press, 1976), 110.
15. Walls, *Henry David Thoreau*, 91–92; the letter is from *Corr* 1:27–30, November 11 and 14, 1837.
16. Philip J. Deloria, *Playing Indian* (New Haven, CT: Yale University Press, 1998); Kevin Bruyneel, *Settler Memory: The Disavowal of Indigeneity and the Politics of Race in the U.S.* (Chapel Hill: University of North Carolina Press, 2021), 22.
17. Quoted in Walls, *Henry David Thoreau*, 92. The epitaph is from Thoreau, *Translations*, ed. K. P. Van Anglen (Princeton, NJ: Princeton University Press, 1986), 148, 281. The inscription reads "Sculptum [Carved] A.D. 1836," but it survives only on paper.
18. My use of the term "contact zone" draws on Mary Louise Pratt's formulation in *Imperial Eyes: Travel Writing and Transculturation* (New York: Routledge, 1992). See also James Clifford, *Routes: Travel and Translation in the Late Twentieth Century* (Cambridge, MA: Harvard University Press, 1997). For a more recent study that applies the contact zone to contemporary conservation efforts on Mayan land, see Juanita Sundberg, "Conservation Encounters: Transculturation in the Contact Zone of Empire," *Cultural Geographies* 13, no. 2 (April 2006): 239–65.
19. See Jane Bennett, *Thoreau's Nature: Ethics, Politics, and the Wild* (Latham, MD: Rowan and Littlefield, 2002); Laura Dassow Walls, *Seeing New Worlds: Thoreau and Nineteenth-Century Natural Science* (Madison: University of Wisconsin Press, 1995); Rochelle Johnson, "'This Enchantment Is No Delusion': Henry David Thoreau, the New Materialisms, and Ineffable Materiality," *Interdisciplinary Studies in Literature and Environment* 21, no. 3 (2014): 606–35; Kristen Case, "Thoreau's Radical Empiricism: The Kalendar, Pragmatism, and Science," in *Thoreauvian Modernities: Transatlantic Conversations about an American Icon*, ed. François Specq, Laura Dassow Walls, and Michel Granger (Athens: University of Georgia Press, 2013); and James Finley, "'Who Are We? Where Are We?': Contact and Literary Navigation in

The Maine Woods," *Interdisciplinary Studies in Literature and Environment* 19, no. 2 (2012): 336–55.

20 Branka Arsić, in *Bird Relics: Grief and Vitalism in Thoreau* (Cambridge, MA: Harvard University Press, 2016), focuses on material Thoreau copied from the Jesuit Relations into Indian Notebooks 7 and 8 (Morgan Library MA 601 and 602) in 1852, three years after publishing *A Week*. Although he did take extensive notes on this ceremony (about twenty manuscript pages), they are better seen as just one part of hundreds of pages on Huron and other Algonquian cultures gathered from the Jesuit Relations.

21 Linck C. Johnson, *Thoreau's Complex Weave: The Writing of "A Week on the Concord and Merrimack Rivers"* (Charlottesville: University of Virginia Press, 1986), 123; Robert F. Sayre, *Thoreau and the American Indians* (Princeton, NJ: Princeton University Press, 1977), 50–55.

22 Richard Schneider, "'An emblem of all progress': Ecological Succession in Thoreau's *A Week on the Concord and Merrimack Rivers*," *Concord Saunterer*, n.s., 19 (2011): 78–104; Joan Burbick, *Thoreau's Alternative History: Changing Perspectives on Nature, Culture, and Language* (University Park: University of Pennsylvania Press, 1987); Brian Gazaille, "Natural Wrecks and Textual Relics in Thoreau's *A Week on the Concord and Merrimack Rivers*," *ESQ* 60, no. 3 (2014): 451–84; Mark Luccarelli, "Thoreau and the Desynchronization of Time," *Thoreau in an Age of Crisis: Uses and Abuses of an American Icon*, ed. Kristen Case, Rochelle L. Johnson, and Henrik Otterberg (Leiden: Brill Fink, 2021); Renée L. Bergland, *The National Uncanny: Indian Ghosts and American Subjects* (Hanover, NH: University Press of New England, 2000).

23 Arsić, *Bird Relics*, 311.

24 Lisa Brooks, *The Common Pot: The Recovery of Native Space in the Northeast* (Minneapolis: University of Minnesota Press, 2008).

25 In this, *A Week* fits in better alongside what Karen Halttunen identifies as the "topographical histories" of New England towns that made up a fraction of the local histories of the nineteenth century—one aspect of settler place-making that preserved a kind of geographic "Indian wisdom" even as it laid claim to a kind of indigeneity. See Halttunen, "Grounded History: Land and Landscape in Early America," *William and Mary Quarterly* 68, no. 4 (October 2011): 513–32.

26 Arsić, in *Bird Relics*, makes this point in regard to the clam midden in Concord that was a source of fascination for Thoreau (204).

27 Lisa Brooks's history of King Philip's War, *Our Beloved Kin*, traces the relationships among Native communities in the era in revelatory detail, using resources that were available in the nineteenth century, though her project was unimaginable to white historians of the era.

28 Linck Johnson includes the text of the first draft of *A Week* in *Thoreau's Complex Weave*. See p. 65.

29 For a detailed discussion of this survey, see Robert Thorson, *The Boatman: Henry David Thoreau's River Years*. (Cambridge, MA: Harvard University Press, 2017).

30 Leslie Marmon Silko, "Landscape and the Pueblo Imagination," in *The Ecocriticism Reader: Landmarks in Literary Ecology*, ed. Cheryll Glotfelty and Harold Fromm (Athens: University of Georgia Press, 1996), 264–75; Peter Nabakov, *A Forest of Time: Native American Ways of History* (New York: Cambridge University Press, 2002); Arsić, *Bird Relics*, 205–6.

31 Arsić, *Bird Relics*, 129.

32 Arsić, 359. The literature on Native graves is extensive. Since the passing of the Native American Graves Protection and Repatriation Act (NAGPRA) legislation in 1990, there has been a focus on returning burial remains to Native communities for a respectful "return to

earth." For a discussion of Abenaki burial grounds and other sacred sites, see John Moody, "Balance: An Overview of Abenaki and Indigenous Peoples Burial/Site Protection," *Vermont Journal of Archaeology* 12 (2011): 46–84. For a discussion of problems in repatriating excavated grave materials with examples from the Connecticut River Valley, see Margaret Bruchac, "Lost and Found: NAGPRA, Scattered Relics, and Restorative Methodologies," *Museum Anthropology* 33, no. 2 (Fall 2010): 137–56.

33 The literature on Native American captivity is extensive, and even in Thoreau's day it was well-known that many white captives, such as Mary Jemison, preferred to remain with their adopted communities. In the Indian Notebooks (3:63), Thoreau records a visit to Westborough from Timothy Rice, who was captured in 1704 and became a leader in his adopted tribe. He also records many instances of captives (usually men) who were tortured and executed. Margaret Bruchac, in an article for a Haverhill newspaper, describes Dustan's capture as a potential opportunity for cultural exchange blighted by her killing of her captors, including children, with an act of savage violence. "Reconsidering Hannah Duston and the Abenaki," *Haverhill (MA) Eagle-Tribune*, August 24, 2006. Dustan's name is spelled variously; I use Thoreau's spelling here, that is, "Dustan."

34 Nathaniel Hawthorne, "The Duston Family," *American Magazine of Useful and Entertaining Knowledge*, May 1836, 395–97; Benjamin Mirick, *A History of Haverhill, Massachusetts* (Haverhill, MA: A. W. Thayer, 1832), 4, 91, 94.

35 L. Johnson, *Thoreau's Complex Weave*, 128.

36 Margaret Bruchac, "Abenaki Connections of 1704: The Sadoques Family and Deerfield, 2004," in *Captive Histories: Captivity Narratives, French Relations and Native Stories of the 1704 Deerfield Raid*, ed. Evan Haefeli and Kevin Sweeney (Amherst: University of Massachusetts Press, 2006), 262–78."

37 Sayre, *Thoreau and the American Indians*, 52; Schneider, "'An emblem of all progress,'" 93.

38 L. Johnson, *Thoreau's Complex Weave*, 150.

Chapter 2: Savagism and Its Discontents

1 Citing (and even naming) the Indian Notebooks is complicated, as I discuss below. My citations follow Robert Sayre's numbering in *Thoreau and the American Indians* (Princeton, NJ: Princeton University Press, 1977), with the volume number first and the page number after the colon. See the appendix to this chapter for the alignment of the various cataloging systems for the Indian Notebooks, their dates, and their page length.

2 Elizabeth Witherell is the editor of The Writings of Henry Thoreau, which includes an online version of Thoreau's journals not yet printed by the Princeton University Press, dating from 1854 to 1861. See https://thoreau.library.ucsb.edu/writings_journals.html.

3 Sayre, *Thoreau and the American Indians*, 118. William Howarth, in *The Literary Manuscripts of Henry Thoreau* (Columbus: Ohio State University Press, 1974), suggests that the Indian Notebooks may have become, like the Journal, a project of "intrinsic merit" (294).

4 Howarth argues that Blake wrote the titles in his uneven effort to order the manuscripts. Suzanne Rose makes a detailed, though not entirely convincing, argument that the labels on the Indian Notebooks were written by Thoreau himself, not by Blake or Henry Russell, who eventually bought them. Rose, "Tracking the Moccasin Print: A Descriptive Index to Thoreau's Indian Notebooks and a Study of the Relationships of the Indian Notebooks to Walden" (PhD diss., University of Oklahoma, 1994), 54–55.

5 Sayre, *Thoreau and the American Indians*, 219.
6 Richard F. Fleck published *Indians of Thoreau: Selections from the Indian Notebooks* (Albuquerque, NM: Hummingbird Press) in 1974, and Suzanne Rose included detailed summaries of the first five of them in her dissertation in 1994, but most are not in print. In the 1930s, Arthur Christy tasked a group of graduate students, all women, with transcribing the notebooks: Geraldyn Ann Delaney, Josephine P. Eppig, Cornelia MacEwan Gorel, Martha Nowlin, Louise R. Pearson, Alberta Torrence Tate, and Marion Wells. These transcriptions (with the exception of IN 11/MA 605, from 1858–59) are available from the Morgan Library as PDFs, and this effort has made subsequent work on the Indian Notebooks, including my own, vastly easier. The manuscripts themselves have been microfilmed but are not easily accessible.
7 For a more detailed account of Thoreau's use of Copway's book, see my "Thoreau's Reading of George Copway: An Additional Indian Notebook," *Thoreau Society Bulletin* 302, no. 2 (Summer 2018): 1–5.
8 The Sanborn comment is from his biography, *Henry D. Thoreau* (Boston: Houghton Mifflin, 1882), 248. Cited in Sayre, *Thoreau and the American Indians*, 102.
9 Robert Sattelmeyer, *Thoreau's Reading: A Study in Intellectual History with Bibliographical Catalogue* (Princeton, NJ: Princeton University Press, 1988).
10 Sayre, *Thoreau and the American Indians*, 120; Joshua Bellin, "In the Company of Savagists: Thoreau's Indian Books and Antebellum Ethnology," *Concord Saunterer* 16 (January 2008): 8–9.
11 Fikret Berkes, *Sacred Ecology*, 4th ed. (New York: Routledge, 2018), 8–12.
12 George Copway, *The Traditional History and Characteristic Sketches of the Ojibway Nation* (Boston: Sanborn, Carter, Bazin, 1850). For a fuller discussion, including a transcription of Thoreau's marginal notations in *Traditional History*, see my "Thoreau's Reading of George Copway," 1–5.
13 Bellin offers a rich summary of these theories in "In the Company of Savagists" and a longer account in *The Demon of the Continent: Indians and the Shaping of American Literature* (Philadelphia: University of Pennsylvania Press, 2000).
14 The scholarship on Thoreau and Darwin is extensive. For a cogent account of Thoreau's reception of Darwin and the theory of evolution, see Laura Dassow Walls's *Henry David Thoreau: A Life* (Chicago: University of Chicago Press, 2017). Her book *Seeing New Worlds: Thoreau and Nineteenth-Century Natural Science* (Madison: University of Wisconsin Press, 1995), is a fuller account of Thoreau's engagement with science. Robert Kuhn McGregor offers a broader study of Thoreau's engagement with nature in *A Wider View of the Universe: Henry Thoreau's Study of Nature* (Jefferson, NC: McFarland, 2017). For a more general account of Darwin's reception in the United States with a focus on Thoreau's circle, see Randall Fuller, *The Book That Changed America: How Darwin's Theory of Evolution Ignited a Nation* (New York: Viking, 2017).
15 Both Bellin, in "In the Company of Savagists," and Sayre, in *Thoreau and the American Indians*, offer cogent summaries of savagism; Sayre notes his own debt to Roy Harvey Pearce, who laid out the elements of this ideology in 1953 (213). More recent accounts of savagism, including Jean O'Brien's *Firsting and Lasting: Writing Indians Out of Existence in New England* (Minneapolis: University of Minnesota Press, 2010), are better situated within the analysis of settler colonial ideology, drawing on the work of Patrick Wolfe.
16 The literature on Pratt and the Indian Boarding School experience is extensive. A good overview is David Wallace Adams, *Education for Extinction: American Indians and the Boarding School Experience, 1875–1928* (Lawrence: University of Kansas Press, 1995). Pratt's

model of education as cultural genocide had deep roots in New England, from Harvard's short-lived Indian College and John Eliot's praying villages in the seventeenth century to Eleazer Wheelock's Indian Charity School in the eighteenth century and the Cornwall Foreign Mission School in the early nineteenth century.

17 As Sayre observes, "Thoreau took from the literature of savagism a composite picture of Indian life in North America which disproves savagism" (*Thoreau and the American Indians*, 127).

18 Bellin, "In the Company of Savagists," 8, 13.

19 Robert Dale Parker Jr. records this incident in his richly researched collection of Jane Johnston Schoolcraft's work, *The Sound the Stars Make Rushing through the Sky: The Writings of Jane Johnston Schoolcraft* (Philadelphia: University of Pennsylvania Press, 2008).

20 Lewis Henry Morgan, *League of the Ho-dé-no-sau-nee, or Iroquois* (New York: Sage & Brother, 1851), 401. Thoreau took detailed notes on *League* in IN 8:378–401, including history, historical and current population, tribal totems, political structure, the Three Sisters, burial rituals and festivals, clothing, dances, games, principal villages, longhouses, marriage customs, hospitality, food, hunting, tanning hides, weapons, canoe-building, maple sugaring, major trails, and the rebounding population. A classic account of nineteenth-century ethnology is Robert E. Bieder, *Science Encounters the Indian, 1820–1880: The Early Years of Ethnology* (Norman: Oklahoma University Press, 1987), who devotes a chapter to Morgan.

21 Although no record of a lecture on Indians survives, Nathaniel Hawthorne mentions one that Thoreau had discussed in a letter inviting him to lecture in Salem in 1849. Robert Hudspeth suggests this was the Ktaadn lecture Thoreau gave in Concord the year before (*Corr* 2:10). Emerson refers to Thoreau's "broken task, which none else can finish" in his eulogy published in the *Atlantic Monthly*, "Thoreau," in Emerson, *The Collected Works of Ralph Waldo Emerson*, vol. 10, *Uncollected Prose Writings*, ed. Ronald A. Bosco and Joel Myerson (Cambridge, MA: Belknap Press of Harvard University Press, 2013), 431.

22 Sayre, *Thoreau and the American Indians*, 128. Howarth makes this point in the *Literary Manuscripts of Henry Thoreau*, adding that "as his knowledge grew, his ambition to publish seemed to wane" (294).

23 Gregory Cajete, "Native Science and Sustaining Indigenous Communities," in *Traditional Ecological Knowledge: Learning from Indigenous Practices for Environmental Sustainability*, ed. Melissa K. Nelson and Dan Shilling (New York: Cambridge University Press, 2018), 16–17. Cajete develops these ideas more fully in *Native Science: Natural Laws of Interdependence* (Sante Fe, NM: Clear Light Books, 2000).

24 These writers are included (along with Cajete) in Nelson and Shilling, *Traditional Ecological Knowledge*: Simon Ortiz, "Indigenous Sustainability: Language, Community, Wholeness, and Solidarity," 85–94, quotation on 85; Jeanette Armstrong, "A Single Strand: The *Nsyilxcen* speaking People's *Tmix*ʷ Knowledge as a Model for Sustaining a Life-Force Place," 95–108, quotation on 97–99; and Robin Wall Kimmerer, "Mishkos Kenomagwen, the Lessons of Grass," 27–58, quotation on 39.

25 Jace Weaver, "Indigenousness and Indigeneity," in *A Companion to Postcolonial Studies*, ed. Henry Schwartz and Sangeeta Ray (Hoboken: Wiley, 2003), 221–35. On the place-based nature of decolonization, see Glen Sean Coulthardt, *Red Skin, White Mask: Rejecting the Colonial Politics of Recognition* (Minneapolis: University of Minnesota Press, 2014), 12–13. See also Sayre, *Thoreau and the American Indians*, 25, and Patrick Wolfe, "Settler Colonialism and the Disappearance of the Native," *Journal of Genocide Research* 8, no. 4 (December 2006): 388.

26 Robert Sayre offers a detailed account of provenance and numbering of the Indian Notebooks in his appendix to *Thoreau and the American Indians* (217–19); he also offers a useful chart on page 110. William Howarth's *The Literary Manuscripts of Henry David Thoreau*

Chapter 3: Becoming Native

1. Jean M. O'Brien, *Firsting and Lasting: Writing Indians Out of Existence in New England* (Minneapolis: University of Minnesota Press, 2010); Kim TallBear, *Native American DNA: Tribal Belonging and the False Promise of Genetic Science* (Minneapolis: University of Minnesota Press, 2013), 46. This process is discussed at length by Kevin Bruyneel in *Settler Memory: The Disavowal of Indigeneity and the Politics of Race in the United States* (Chapel Hill: University of North Carolina Press, 2021), xiii, 2.
2. Robin Wall Kimmerer, *Braiding Sweetgrass: Indigenous Wisdom, Scientific Knowledge, and the Teachings of Plants* (Minneapolis: Milkweed Editions, 2013), 9, 207, 213–15.
3. Keith Basso, *Wisdom Sits in Places: Landscape and Language among the Western Apache* (Albuquerque: University of New Mexico Press, 1996); Lisa Brooks, *The Common Pot: The Recovery of Native Space in the Northeast* (Minneapolis: University of Minnesota Press, 2008).
4. Margaret D. Jacobs, *After One Hundred Winters: Searching for Reconciliation on America's Stolen Land* (Princeton, NJ: Princeton University Press, 2021). There is a broad debate over how to deal with the legacy of settler colonialism in the United States; Jacobs offers several examples of largely local efforts as well as some guiding principles based on reconciliation projects in other parts of the world.
5. Mark Rifkin, *Settler Common Sense: Queerness and Everyday Colonialism in the American Renaissance* (Minneapolis: University of Minnesota Press, 2014). Thomas King, in *The Inconvenient Indian: A Curious Account of Native People in North America* (Minneapolis: University of Minnesota Press, 2013), offers a characteristically insightful and absurdist account of the relationship between Native peoples and white settlers; his central insight, "The issue has always been land," is certainly germane to Thoreau.
6. Walls offers a cogent and powerful reading of the basket as a figure for Thoreau's own writing in *Henry David Thoreau: A Life* (Chicago: University of Chicago Press, 2017), 254. See also Joshua Bellin, *The Demon of the Continent: Indians and the Shaping of American Literature* (Philadelphia: University of Pennsylvania Press, 2000), 66–67, and Rifkin, *Settler Common Sense*, 122–25.
7. Kimmerer, *Braiding Sweetgrass*, 26; Lewis Hyde, *The Gift: Imagination and the Erotic Life of Property* (New York: Random House, 1979).
8. Frederic Clements, *The Structure and Development of Vegetation*, report of the Botanical Survey of Nebraska No. 7, Studies in the Vegetation of the State (Lincoln: University of Nebraska Press, 1904); Aldo Leopold, *Game Management* (New York: Charles Scribner and Sons, 1933); Monica E. Mulrennan and Véronique Bussières, "Social-Ecological Resilience in Indigenous Coastal Contexts," *Ecology and Society* 23, no. 3 (October 2018): 18; William C. Cronon, "Why Edge Effects," *Edge Effects* (blog), October 9, 2014, https://edgeeffects.net/why-edge-effects/.

(Columbus: Ohio State University Press, 1974) remains the standard guide to Thoreau's manuscripts. Howarth's page numbers vary slightly from Sayre, with the exception of an odd undercount of IN 10 / MA 603, which he lists as 209 pages compared to the 437 of Sayre, which is the correct number. The transcriptions often have different pagination from the manuscripts, in part because Thoreau sometimes included drawings and clippings that were not transferred to the transcripts.

9   N. C. Wyeth, *Men of Concord and Some Others as Portrayed in the Journals of Henry David Thoreau* (Boston: Houghton Mifflin, 1939); Robert Gross, *The Transcendentalists and Their World* (New York: Farrar, Strauss and Giroux, 2021); Elise Lemire, *Black Walden: Slavery and Its Aftermath in Concord, Massachusetts* (Philadelphia: University of Pennsylvania Press, 2009); Laura Dassow Walls, "'As You Are Brothers of Mine': Thoreau and the Irish," *New England Quarterly* 88, no. 1 (March 2015): 5–36. In *Our Common Dwelling: Henry Thoreau, Transcendentalism and the Class Politics of Nature* (London: Palgrave Macmillan, 2005), Lance Newman traces Thoreau's response to the labor crises of the 1840s and notes the long tradition of reading Thoreau's experiment at Walden Pond as a response to Brook Farm and other utopian projects. Edge communities like Walden Woods might be seen as both a symptom of the crisis of marginalized labor and a circumscribed response to it. Thoreau's celebration of his former neighbors certainly captures the Associationist desire to address class divisions, and he doubled down on their goals to spiritualize labor and reconnect to nature.

10 This point was first made by William Cronon in "The Trouble with Wilderness; or, Getting Back to the Wrong Nature," in *Uncommon Ground: Rethinking the Human Place in Nature*, ed. William Cronon (W. W. Norton, 1995), 69–90. Mark David Spence details the history of the parks movement in *Dispossessing the Wilderness: Indian Removal and the Making of the National Parks* (New York: Oxford University Press, 1999). Rifkin, in *Settler Common Sense*, sees Thoreau as participating in this logic of a pristine nature at Walden in opposition to the village, an argument that the robust edge community Thoreau finds around Walden undercuts.

11 Lauren Mielke, in *Moving Encounters: Sympathy and the Indian Question in Antebellum Literature* (Amherst: University of Massachusetts Press, 2008), traces the key role this kind of emotional connection plays in the literature of Indian reform in the era. This sympathetic register is common to Thoreau's writing about the more-than-human world but less typical with the Native one.

12 Karen L. Kilcup traces the efforts of women writers (Native and European American) to build this network of sympathy in *Fallen Forests: Emotion, Embodiment, and Ethics in American Women's Environmental Writing, 1781–1924* (Athens: University of Georgia Press, 2013). Lawrence Buell offers a rich summary of the cultural life of trees in *New England Literary Culture: From Revolution through Renaissance* (New York: Cambridge University Press, 1986).

13 Kristen Case, "Knowing as Neighboring: Approaching Thoreau's Kalendar," *J19: The Journal of Nineteenth-Century Americanists* 2, no. 1 (Spring 2014): 107–29. Bruno Latour details his actor-network theory in several works, most thoroughly in *Reassembling the Social: An Introduction to Actor-Network-Theory* (New York: Oxford University Press, 2007). See also Karen Barad, "Posthuman Performativity: Toward an Understanding of How Matter Comes to Matter," *Signs: A Journal of Women in Culture and Society* 28, no. 3 (Spring 2003): 801–31.

14 Dorion Sagan, *Cosmic Apprentice: Dispatches from the Edges of Science* (Minneapolis: University of Minnesota Press, 2013); Kim TallBear, "Why Interspecies Thinking Needs Indigenous Standpoints," *Fieldsights*, November 18, 2011. Vine Deloria Jr.'s *God Is Red: A Native View of Religion* (Denver, CO: Fulcrum Publishing, 1973) is a foundational text in Native religious studies.

15 Brent Ranalli offers a remarkable reading of Thoreau's walking habits in "Thoreau's Indian Stride," *Concord Saunterer* 27 (2019): 89–110.

16 The Digital Thoreau site (https://digitalthoreau.org/) developed and curated by Paul Schacht,

as part of its suite of projects, includes a powerful digitized compilation of the different drafts of *Walden* as assembled by Ronald E. Clapper in "The Development of *Walden*: A Genetic Text" (PhD diss., University of California, Los Angeles, 1967). William Rossi offers a detailed account of the revision of a key part of the sandbank passage in "Making *Walden* and Its Sandbank," *Concord Saunterer* 30 (2022): 10–58.

17 Timothy Morton, *Dark Ecology: For a Logic of Future Coexistence* (New York: Columbia University Press, 2016), 63.

18 Edward Mooney, "'Sympathy with Intelligence': Thoreau's Reveries of Wonder, Presence and Divinities," *Concord Saunterer* 24 (2016): 63–81; Alda Balthrop-Lewis, *Thoreau's Religion: Walden Woods, Social Justice, and the Politics of Asceticism* (New York: Cambridge University Press, 2021; Alan D. Hodder, *Thoreau's Ecstatic Witness* (New Haven, CT: Yale University Press, 2001).

19 This diplomatic dimension of Native groups traveling through New England is particularly evident in a visit Margaret Bruchac describes, in which descendants of Eunice Williams, captured in the Deerfield Raid in 1704, returned to Deerfield from St. Francis/Odanak in Canada in 1837 to reestablish ties to their relatives. See her "Abenaki Connections of 1704: The Sadoques Family and Deerfield, 2004," in *Captive Histories: Captivity Narratives, French Relations, and Native Stories of the 1704 Deerfield Raid*, ed. Evan Haefeli and Kevin Sweeney (Amherst: University of Massachusetts Press, 2006), 262–78.

20 On the survival of English folk beliefs in early America, see David D. Hall, *Worlds of Wonder, Days of Judgment: Popular Religious Belief in Early New England* (Cambridge, MA: Harvard University Press, 1990). In *Spirit of the New England Tribes* (Hanover, NH: University Press of New England, 1986), William S. Simmons gathers a range of accounts of Algonquin little people.

21 Mircea Eliade, *The Myth of the Eternal Return: Cosmos and History* (Princeton, NJ: Princeton University Press, 1971).

22 Suzanne Rose, "Following the Trail of Footsteps: From the Indian Notebooks to *Walden*," *New England Quarterly* 67, no. 1 (March 1994): 77–91. None of the half-dozen Earth Diver stories Thoreau copies into the notebooks feature a loon as the diver, and the main element—the creation of a world from a bit of mud brought from the bottom of a boundless sea—is absent in the loon episode.

23 In chapter 3 of *Thoreau and the American Indians* (Princeton, NJ: Princeton University Press, 1977), Robert Sayre argues *Walden* is a vision quest, a framework that certainly matches the broad outlines of retreat to the marginal edges of his community, his spiritual insight, and his return, though there is little evidence that Thoreau himself framed his experience in terms of this widely shared, though highly variable, Native ritual. Thoreau took notes on the traditional Ojibwe story about the origin of the robin, which centers on a vision quest, from Edwin James, ed., *A Narrative of the Captivity and Adventures of John Tanner* (New York: Carvill, 1830), 305, in his notebooks (IN 8:359), near the end of his drafting of *Walden*.

24 Bringhurst translates and comments on traditional Haida literature in *A Story as Sharp as a Knife: The Classical Haida Mythtellers and Their World* (Vancouver, BC: Douglas and McIntyre, 1999). Accounts of the ceremonial nature of Native mythology are numerous, including many by Native writers from Charles Eastman to Vine Deloria Jr. to Paula Gunn Allen to Winona Laduke. This view was not a feature of the nineteenth-century accounts available to Thoreau, though it certainly aligned with transcendental approaches to classical mythology.

25 N. Scott Momaday, *The Way to Rainy Mountain* (Albuquerque: University of New Mexico

Press, 1976), 84. Basso draws on Clifford Geertz's term "local knowledge" in framing the cultural landscape he learns to see from his Apache mentors in *Wisdom Sits in Places* (1996). Brooks draws on her Abenaki heritage in applying the concept of a place-world to early Native history in New England in *The Common Pot* (2008).

26 The Creek ceremony of the Busk is described by William Bartram in his *Travels in North America* (Philadelphia: James and Johnson, 1791), 507–8. Thoreau took extensive notes from this volume in Indian Notebook 4 but didn't copy the description of the Busk.

27 Lydia Willsky-Ciollo, "Apostles of Wilderness: American Indians and Thoreau's Theology of the Wild," *New England Quarterly* 91, no. 4 (December 2018): 551–91.

28 Rifkin, *Settler Common Sense*, 95.

Chapter 4: Indians in Massachusetts

1 Renée L. Bergland, *The National Uncanny: Indian Ghosts and American Subjects* (Hanover, NH: University Press of New England, 2000), 115; she cites Jack Campisi, *The Mashpee Indians: Tribe on Trial* (Syracuse, NY: Syracuse University Press, 1991), who in turn cites Russell Peters, *The Wampanoags of Mashpee: An Indian Perspective on American History* (West Barnstable, MA: Indian Spiritual and Cultural Training Center, 1987). For a detailed account of Mashpee in the nineteenth century, see Daniel Mandell, *Tribe, Race, History: Native Americans in Southern New England, 1780–1880* (Baltimore, MD: Johns Hopkins University Press, 2008), esp. 35–38; Mandell also claims a visit by Thoreau, citing Peters. See also Lisa Brooks's chapter on Mashpee in *The Common Pot: The Recovery of Native Space in the Northeast* (Minneapolis: University of Minnesota Press, 2006). There are a number of histories of Mashpee and other Wampanoag communities written by Wampanoag people. Peters's *The Wampanoags of Mashpee* is the most extensive; Earl Mills Sr. and Alicja Mann's *Son of Mashpee: Reflections of Chief Flying Eagle, a Wampanoag* (North Falmouth, MA: World Studio, 1996) and Joan Taveres Avant's *People of the First Light: Wisdoms of a Mashpee Wampanoag Elder* (West Barnstable, MA: West Barnstable Press, 2010) offer rich accounts of the Mashpee community. Linda Coombs has written and spoken extensively on Wampanoag history, with a particular focus on correcting misconceptions about the nature of early contact between English colonists and Wampanoag people. See her "Holistic History: Including the Wampanoag in an Exhibit at Plimoth Plantation," in *Dawnland Voices: An Anthology of Indigenous Writing from New England*, ed. Siobhan Senier (Lincoln: University of Nebraska Press, 2014), 473–76, and *Colonization and the Wampanoag Story* (New York: Crown Books, 2023).

2 Mark Rifkin poses this question in reference to *Walden* in particular in *Settler Common Sense: Queerness and Everyday Colonialism in the American Renaissance* (Minneapolis: University of Minnesota Press, 2014), arguing that this occlusion is part of the state of exception that made Native communities largely invisible in Massachusetts (111–13).

3 Jean M. O'Brien, *Firsting and Lasting: Writing Indians Out of Existence in New England* (Minneapolis: University of Minnesota Press, 2010); Laura Dassow Walls, *Henry David Thoreau: A Life* (Chicago: University of Chicago Press, 2017), 327.

4 Most scholars locate Wampanoag territory as beginning south of Boston. As discussed in chapter 1, a number of Wampanoag scholars, including Jessie Little Doe Baird, argue that Concord, Cambridge, and Boston are on traditional Wampanoag territory, the Massachusetts tribe being better understood as a political structure within the Wampanoag nation. This view is persuasive but not universally accepted.

5 Walls, *Henry David Thoreau*, 67.

6 William Apess's writings are collected in *On Our Own Ground: The Complete Writings of William Apess, a Pequot*, ed. Barry O'Connell (Amherst: University of Massachusetts Press, 1992). Two more-recent excellent biographies of Apess help contextualize his writing: Drew Lopenzina, *Through an Indian's Looking-Glass: A Cultural Biography of William Apess* (Amherst: University of Massachusetts Press, 2017), and Philip F. Gura, *The Life of William Apess, Pequot* (Chapel Hill: University of North Carolina Press, 2015).

7 Daniel Mandell has written two detailed histories of Native New England after King Philip's War: *Behind the Frontier: Indians in Eighteenth-Century Eastern Massachusetts* (Lincoln: University of Nebraska Press, 2000) and *Tribe, Race, History*. See also Jean O'Brien, *Dispossession by Degrees: Indian Land and Identity in Natick, Massachusetts, 1650–1790* (New York: Cambridge University Press, 1997).

8 It is possible that Thoreau and Ricketson contemplated visiting Mashpee. In his letter to Ricketson on October 1, 1854, Thoreau writes, "I have sometimes thought of visiting the remnant of *our* Indians living near you" (emphasis in original). It is more likely that the visits to the Smiths and Simon (discussed below) fulfilled this idea (*Corr* 2:248).

9 For a detailed account the Native community in New Bedford in the nineteenth century, see Russell G. Handsman, Kathryn Grover, and Donald Warrin, "New Bedford Communities of Whaling: People of Wampanoag, African, and Portuguese Island Descent, 1825–1925," National Park Service, 2021, https://www.nps.gov/nebe/learn/historyculture/upload/NEBE_Ethnographic_1825-1925_FY22_508.pdf.

10 Walter Harding, in *The Days of Henry Thoreau: A Biography* (New York: Knopf, 1965), describes *Cape Cod* as "Thoreau's sunniest book" (361). In *The Environmental Imagination: Thoreau, Nature Writing, and the Formation of American Culture* (Cambridge, MA: Harvard University Press, 1995), Lawrence Buell notes that *Cape Cod* complicates Thoreau's reception as an environmental saint. Walls, in *Henry Thoreau: A Life*, argues that as he revised the *Cape Cod* manuscript, he "deepened the dark undertones" (282).

11 John Lowney, "Thoreau's *Cape Cod*: The Unsettling Art of the Wrecker," *American Literature* 64, no. 2 (June 1992): 239–54; Alex Moscowitz, "Economic Imperception; or, Reading Capital on the Beach with Thoreau," *American Literary History* 33, no. 2 (Summer 2020): 221–42; Katie Simon, "Affect and Cruelty in the Atlantic System: The Hauntological Argument of Henry David Thoreau's *Cape Cod*," *ESQ* 62, no. 2 (2016): 244–82.

12 Lowney, "Thoreau's *Cape Cod*," 246; Michael C. Weisenburg, "Beyond the Borders of Time: Thoreau and the Ante-Pilgrim History of Cape Cod," *Thoreau beyond Borders: New International Essays on America's Most Famous Nature Writer*, ed. François Specq, Laura Dassow Walls, and Julien Nègre (Amherst: University of Massachusetts Press, 2020), 40–54.

13 Thoreau's hand-traced map of Cape Cod is available at the Concord Free Public Library, https://concordlibrary.org/special-collections/thoreau-surveys/157. It was likely derived from the 1844 *Topographical Map of Massachusetts* by Simeon Borden.

14 Christa Holm Vogelius, "Cape Cod's Transnational Bodies," in Specq, Walls, and Nègre, *Thoreau beyond Borders*, 32.

15 William Apess's writing is gathered in the landmark collection edited by Barry O'Connell, *On Our Own Ground*. "An Indian's Looking-Glass" is the last chapter of Apess's *Experiences of Five Christian Indians of the Pequot Tribe* (Boston: James B. Dow, 1833), 117–62.

16 William Apess, *Indian Nullification*, 170; O'Connell, *On Our Own Ground*, 170.

17 Mandell, *Tribe, Race, History*, 131; Brooks, *Common Pot*, 168.

18 Apess, *Indian Nullification*, 176.

19 Audra Simpson, *Mohawk Interruptus: Political Life across the Borders of Settler States* (Durham, NC: Duke University Press, 2014).

20 William Apess, *Indian Nullification of the Unconstitutional Laws of Massachusetts Relative*

to the Marshpee Tribe; or, *The Pretended Riot Explained* (Boston: Jonathan Howe, 1835), in O'Connell, *On Our Own Ground*, 163–74, 203.
21 William Apess, "Eulogy on King Philip," in O'Connell, *On Our Own Ground*, 275–310.
22 Philip Deloria traces the complicated negotiations of Native people entering the modern settler world in the postbellum era in *Indians in Unexpected Places* (Lawrence: University of Kansas Press, 2004); people like Attean, Polis, and Attaquin show that Thoreau had several examples available to him in the 1850s.
23 The story of Wampanoag revitalization is a long one; more recent highlights include the federal recognition of the Mashpee and Aquinnah tribes in 2006 and the Wampanoag language recovery project that began in the early 2000s under the leadership of Jessie Little Doe Baird. For an excellent account of this project, see the documentary by Anna Makepeace, *We Still Live Here—Âs Nutayuneân* (2011), https://www.makepeaceproductions.com/wampfilm.html.
24 Leanne Betasamosake Simpson, "Land as Pedagogy: Nishinaabeg and Rebellious Transformation," *Decolonization: Indigeneity, Education and Society* 3, no. 3 (2014): 1–25; Brooks, *Common Pot*.

Chapter 5: Lost in the Maine Woods

1 Walter Harding, *The Days of Henry Thoreau* (Princeton, NJ: Princeton University Press, 1964), saw Polis as one of Thoreau's few unambiguous heroes, whereas Richard Bridgeman, *Dark Thoreau* (Lincoln: University of Nebraska Press, 1982), argues that Thoreau was disappointed in Polis and quickly lost interest in Indians after his final trip to Maine. Robert D. Richardson Jr., *Henry David Thoreau: A Life of the Mind* (Berkeley: University of California Press, 1984), and Richard Lebeaux, *Thoreau's Seasons* (Amherst: University of Massachusetts Press, 1984), see a more ambivalent relationship. Among more recent studies of *The Maine Woods*, Joseph J. Moldenhauer, in his introduction to the Princeton edition of *The Maine Woods* (Princeton, NJ: Princeton University Press, 1972), suggests Thoreau was disappointed in Neptune and Attean but found Polis a kindred spirit in navigating between the woods and the village—a view shared by Michael Stoneham in "Remeasuring Thoreau: *The Maine Woods* and Thoreau's Evolving Appreciation of the Racial Other," *Concord Saunterer* 27 (2019): 68–88. Tom Lynch, "The 'Domestic Air' of Wildness: Henry Thoreau and Joe Polis in the Maine Woods," *Weber Studies* 14, no. 3 (Fall 1997): 38–48, and Linda Frost, "The Red Face of Man, the Penobscot Indian, and Conflict of Interest in Thoreau's *The Maine Woods*," *ESQ* 39, no. 1 (Spring 1993): 21–47, place more emphasis on the Penobscots themselves; the former points to the guides' immersion in traditional spirituality, and the latter foregrounds Penobscot political struggles over the tribe's land base and education. Jessie Bray has examined Thoreau's transcultural exchanges, while Lisa Brooks, *The Common Pot: The Recovery of Native Space in the Northeast* (Minneapolis: University of Minnesota Press, 2008), notes that Thoreau's "romantic reveries" are interrupted by his guides' very contemporary concerns. Jake McGinnis has argued in "A Smack of Wilderness: Affect and Enchantment in Thoreau's First Taste of the Maine Woods," *Concord Saunterer* 26 (2018): 28–53, that Thoreau's "enchantment" with the Maine wilderness shifted his thoughts regarding the Penobscot people. The collection *Rediscovering the Maine Woods: Thoreau's Legacy in an Unsettled Land*, ed. John J. Kucich (Amherst: University of Massachusetts Press, 2019), offers a range of approaches to Thoreau's legacy in this region.
2 Joseph Nicolar, *Life and Traditions of the Red Man: A Rediscovered Treasure of Native American Literature*, ed. Annette Kolodny (1893; repr., Durham, NC: Duke University Press, 2007).

I use the accepted Penobscot spelling of Thoreau's first guide's name, Joseph Attean, rather than Thoreau's phonetic "Aitteon." Joseph Nicolar may well have been on Indian Island when Thoreau visited: born in 1827, he was nineteen during the Katahdin trip and thirty during the trip with Polis. The "very intelligent Indian" Thoreau mentions as a source for several Penobscot definitions is identified only as the governor's son-in-law, likely Tomer Nicolar, Joseph's father, though Jeffrey S. Cramer, in *The Maine Woods: A Fully Annotated Edition* (New Haven, CT: Yale University Press, 2009), offers several other possibilities among the Nicolar family (301). Given the person's level of education and willingness to teach tribal tradition, it's possible (though impossible to prove) that rather than Tomar, this was Joseph Nicolar himself.

3 Robert Sayre discusses this at length in *Thoreau and the American Indians* (Princeton, NJ: Princeton University Press, 1977). See also Frost, "Red Face of Man," 21–47. Rachael DeWitt sees this anti-progressive narrative in more philosophical terms, tracing Thoreau's emerging "epistemic humility" in his three essays in "Thoreauvian Disappointment: Losing the Plot in *The Maine Woods*," *ESQ* 68, no. 4 (2022): 487–522.

4 Several studies have treated geography and U.S. expansionism in the nineteenth century. Martin Bruckner, *The Geographic Revolution in Early America: Maps, Literacy, and National Identity* (Chapel Hill: University of North Carolina Press, 2006); Anne Baker, *Heartless Immensity: Literature, Culture, and Geography in Antebellum America* (Ann Arbor: University of Michigan Press, 2006); and Hsuan Hsu, *Geography and the Production of Space in Nineteenth-Century American Literature* (New York: Cambridge University Press, 2010), all trace manifestations of space in Thoreau's era, though none discuss *The Maine Woods* specifically. Richard Schneider has examined the influence of Swiss geographer Arnold Guyot, who argued for the natural course of westward settlement, on Thoreau's "Walking," in "'Climate Does Thus React on Man': Wildness and Geographic Determinism in Thoreau's 'Walking,'" in *Thoreau's Sense of Place: Essays in American Environmental Writing*, ed. Richard Schneider (Iowa City: University of Iowa Press, 2000).

5 Charles T. Jackson, *Second Annual Report on the Geology of the State of Maine* (Augusta, ME: Luther Severance, 1838), 48. Jackson wrote three reports between 1837 and 1839; the second closely describes the river route Thoreau followed to Katahdin. Jackson was the brother-in-law of Ralph Waldo Emerson.

6 Joshua Bellin, "In the Company of Savagists: Thoreau's Indian Books and Antebellum Ethnology," *Concord Saunterer* 16 (January 2008), 1–32.

7 Wai Che Dimock, *Through Other Continents: American Literature across Deep Time* (Princeton, NJ: Princeton University Press, 2006); Paul Giles, *The Global Remapping of American Literature* (Princeton, NJ: Princeton University Press, 2011), 70–96.

8 Tom Lynch, in "'Domestic Air' of Wildness," situates Thoreau's *Maine Woods* essays in the context of an emerging American discourse of wilderness. For an account of the removal of Native peoples from newly formed national parks, see Mark Spence, *Dispossessing the Wilderness: Indian Removal and the Making of the National Parks* (New York: Oxford University Press, 1999). Richard Judd has traced Thoreau's role in the twentieth-century wilderness preservation movement in *Finding Thoreau: The Meaning of Nature in an American Environmental Icon* (Amherst: University of Massachusetts Press, 2018).

9 The literature on myth in Thoreau and transcendentalism more broadly is extensive. Mircea Eliade's work on sacred, or mythic, time remains foundational; see *The Eternal Return: Cosmos and History* (1954; repr., Princeton, NJ: Princeton University Press, 2019) and *The Sacred and the Profane: The Nature of Religion* (1957; repr., New York: Harcourt Brace Jovanovich, 1987). For a cogent account of myth in Thoreau's work, see Robert Richardson's

biography, *Henry David Thoreau: A Life of the Mind* (Berkeley: University of California Press, 1986), 230–33. Philip F. Gura offers a good discussion of the competing strains of progressive and mythic time in *American Transcendentalism: A History* (New York: Hill and Wang, 2007).

10 Mark Rifkin, *Beyond Settler Time: Temporal Sovereignty and Indigenous Self-Representation* (Durham, NC: Duke University Press, 2017), ix.

11 The term "wood-eater" is from Ebeneezer Emmons, *Report on the Quadrupeds of Massachusetts* (Cambridge, MA: Fulsom, Wells, and Thurston, 1840), which Thoreau reviewed in "A Natural History of Massachusetts"; other sources Thoreau would have read offer variants and cite both Narragansett and Abenaki languages. I am indebted to Jeffrey Cramer of the Thoreau Institute for this citation. I have been unable to locate the source of "moose-men."

12 Annette Kolodny's introduction to Nicolar's *Life and Traditions of the Red Man* offers a cogent history of the Penobscot nation in the nineteenth century. For a fuller account, see Pauleena MacDougall's *The Penobscot Dance of Resistance: Tradition in the History of a People* (Amherst: University of Massachusetts Press, 2004).

13 Fannie Eckstorm, *Old John Neptune and Other Maine Indian Shamans* (Portland, ME: Southworth-Anthoensen Press, 1945), 29.

14 Sarah Winnemucca, *Life among the Piutes: Their Wrongs and Claims* (New York: G. P. Putnam, 1883); David Cusick, *Sketches of the Ancient History of the Six Nations* (Lewiston, NY: n.p., 1828).

15 Darren Ranco, "Toward a Native Anthropology: Hermeneutics, Hunting Stories, and Theorizing from Within," *Wicazo-Sa Review* 21, no. 2 (Autumn 2006): 61–78.

16 Sylvia Winters, "On How We Mistook the Map for the Territory, and Reimprisoned Ourselves in Our Unbearable Wrongness of Being," in *Not Only the Master's Tools: African-American Studies in Theory and Practice*, ed. Lewis R. Gordon and Jane Anna Gordon (Baltimore, MD: Paradigm, 2006), 107–72, cited in Rifkin, *Beyond Settler Time*, 22.

17 Annette Kolodny, "A Summary History of the Penobscot Nation," in Nicolar, *Life and Traditions of the Red Man*, 20.

18 Evan T. Pritchard, *No Word for Time: The Way of the Algonquian People* (San Francisco, CA: Council Oak Books, 1997). Chris Sockalexis's essay recounts a portion of the Thoreau-Wabanaki 150th Anniversary Tour in 2014 described in the preface; it is included in Kucich, *Rediscovering the Maine Woods*, 23–37.

19 Frank Speck, "Penobscot Tales and Religious Beliefs," *Journal of American Folklore* 48, no. 187 (January–March 1935): 3.

20 There are many accounts of Native American storytelling and oral literature; David Murray's *Forked Tongues: Speech, Writing, and Representation in North American Texts* (Ann Arbor: University of Michigan Press, 1991) remains a thorough introduction. For a wide range of Algonquian oral literatures carefully situated in their tribal contexts, see Brian Swann, ed., *Algonquian Spirit: Contemporary Translations of the Algonquian Literatures of North America* (Lincoln: University of Nebraska Press, 2005).

21 Kolodny, introduction to *Life and Traditions of the Red Man*, 75.

22 Micah Pawling, *The Wabanaki Homeland and the New State of Maine: The 1820 Journal and Plan of Survey of Joseph Treat* (Amherst: University of Massachusetts Press, 2007), 59, 131.

23 James Francis, in "Carrying Place: Penobscot Language, Land, and Memory," in Kucich, *Rediscovering the Maine Woods*, 215–22, also describes watching Chris Sockalexis work a piece of flint "harvested from the belly of the cow moose, from Kineo," and marveling at how "each strike of the stone echoed through the fabric of time" (218). See also Francis's forward to David S. Cook, *Above the Gravel Bar: The Native Canoe Routes of Maine* (Solon,

ME: Polar Bear, 2007).

24 Lisa Brooks, in *The Common Pot*, details the efforts of different Native groups in what is now New England to reclaim tribal space during the colonial and early national eras. She cites the Abenaki dictionary compiled by Joseph Laurent, the Odanak/St. Francis chief, in 1884 as a compelling example of how naming the land establishes it as native space (250–53). One feature of the recent wave of Penobscot revitalization was the creation of a detailed map of place-names in the tribe's traditional territory, *Iyoki Eli-Wihtamak^w Katahkimawal / This Is How We Name Our Lands*. It is available for sale at the tribal museum at Indian Island, ME, and the Maine Historical Society, Portland, ME—an artifact of cross-cultural diplomacy.

25 Kolodny, "Summary History of the Penobscot Nation," 4.

26 Frank Speck, "Penobscot Shamanism," *Memoirs of the American Anthropological Association* 6, no. 3 (1920): 252; Abby Langdon Alger, *In Indian Tents* (Boston: Roberts Brothers, 1897), 82; Eckstorm, *Old John Neptune*, 98.

27 Alger, *Indian Tents*, 101–5; Francis, "Carrying Place," 219.

28 Speck, "Penobscot Tales," 22–23. Walter Harding cites a conversation between Thoreau and Harvard librarian Thaddeus William Harris making this point in *The Days of Henry Thoreau: A Biography* (Princeton, NJ: Princeton University Press, 1962), 310.

29 The scholarship on Native literature from the Northeast has been growing steadily. Some key examples include Bernd Peyer, *The Tutor'd Mind: Indian Missionary Writers in Antebellum America* (Amherst: University of Massachusetts Press, 1997); Robert Warrior, *The People and the Word: Reading Native Nonfiction* (Minneapolis: University of Minnesota Press, 2005); and Brooks, *The Common Pot*. A number of works have drawn on an increasingly wide range of literacies and texts, including Kristian Bross and Hilary E. Wyss's *Early Native Literacies in New England: A Documentary and Critical Anthology* (Amherst: University of Massachusetts Press, 2008). Betty Booth Donahue's *Bradford's Indian Book: Being the True Roote & Rise of American Letters as Revealed by the Native Text Embedded in "Of Plimoth Plantation"* (Gainesville: University of Florida Press, 2011) recovers a Wampanoag perspective embedded within Bradford's history of Plymouth. Siobhan Seiner's *Dawnland Voices: An Anthology of Indigenous Writing from New England* (Lincoln: University of Nebraska Press, 2014) draws together a wide range of literature long treasured among Native communities.

30 Jackson, *Report on the Geology of the State of Maine*; John S. Springer, *Forest Life and Forest Trees* (New York: Harper and Bros., 1851); James Russell Lowell, "A Moosehead Journal," in *Fireside Travels* (Boston: Ticknor and Fields, 1864).

31 Daniel Webster, "Bunker Hill Monument Address" (1825), in *The Works of Daniel Webster*, vol. 1 (Boston: Little, Brown, 1858), 59.

32 Charles G. Leland, *Algonquin Legends of New England: Myths and Folk Lore of the Micmac, Passamaquoddy, and Penobscot Tribes* (Boston: Houghton Mifflin, 1884), 130–33. Thoreau does not record the Penobscot name Polis bestowed on him; given his propensity for jokes, it may well have meant something quite different. It is clear, however, that Thoreau took this as an honor.

Chapter 6: Succession

1 For a broad history of the Dakota up to the Dakota Uprising, see Jessica Dawn Palmer, *The Dakota Peoples: A History of the Dakota, Lakota and Nakota through 1863* (Jefferson,

NC: McFarland, 2008). Gary Clayton Anderson gathers a range of first-person accounts of the Dakota Uprising in *Through Dakota Eyes: Narrative Accounts of the Minnesota Indian War of 1862* (Minneapolis: Minnesota Historical Society Press, 1988). Pekka Hämäläinen, *Lakota America* (New Haven, CT: Yale University Press, 2019), offers a rich account of the upper Midwest during the contact era.

2 Laura Dassow Walls, *Henry David Thoreau: A Life* (Chicago: University of Chicago Press, 2017), 437.

3 Annie Dillard, *Pilgrim at Tinker Creek* (New York: Harper's, 1974), 178.

4 Bradley P. Dean offers a cogent history of the "Wild Fruits" manuscript in the notes to his edited volume *Wild Fruits: Thoreau's Rediscovered Last Manuscript* (New York: W. W. Norton, 2000), 278–86. As Dean notes, his was a highly collaborative project, built on previously unpublished work on the manuscript by a number of scholars.

5 Thoreau sent "Wild Apples" to the *Atlantic Monthly* shortly before his death; "Huckleberries" was assembled by Leo Stoller from the "Wild Fruits" manuscript and published as a small book by the Iowa University Press in 1970.

6 Lance Newman, "Thoreau's Materialism: From *Walden* to *Wild Fruits*," *Nineteenth-Century Prose* 31, no. 2 (Fall 2004): 94. Kathryn Cornell Dolan focuses on Thoreau's advocacy for a local, sustainable food system in *Beyond the Fruited Plain: Food and Agriculture in U.S. Literature, 1850–1905* (Lincoln: University of Nebraska Press, 2014).

7 This hands-on, immersive pedagogy is a long way from Alcott's intuitive conversational method of the Temple School; it builds on his own teaching with John in the late 1830s and the field trips he took with his students. Alcott had recently taken a leadership role in Concord's public schools and repeatedly pressed Thoreau to write a handbook on the Concord landscape to use with students. This may well have been on Thoreau's mind. See Walls, *Henry David Thoreau*, 461–62.

8 Samuel Hearne, *A Journey from Prince of Wales Fort in Hudson's Bay to the North Ocean* (London: L. Strahan and T. Cadell, 1795); John Franklin, *Narrative of a Journey to the Shores of the Polar Sea in 1819, 20, 21 & 22* (Philadelphia: H. C. Carey and I. Lea, 1824); John Tanner, *Narrative of the Captivity of John Tanner* (New York: G. C. & H Carvill, 1830); William Wood, *New England's Prospect* (London: n.p., 1639); Roger Williams, "A Key into the Language of America," *Collections of the Massachusetts Historical Society* 3 (1794): 203–39.

9 Paul Le Jeune, *Jesuit Relations for 1639*, in *The Jesuit Relations and Allied Documents*, vol. 16 (Cleveland, OH: Burrows Bros., 1908), 190. Thoreau's work serves as the foundation of a more recent scientific study of Indigenous uses of the many species of *Vaccinium* in North America. See Kim E. Hummer, "Manna in Winter: Indigenous Americans, Huckleberries, and Blueberries," *Horticultural Science* 48, no. 4 (Spring 2013): 413–17.

10 Thoreau here references the Native American, or Know-Nothing, Party, which briefly flourished in the 1850s on a platform of Protestant nativism directed primarily against Irish Catholic immigrants; it adopted Native American iconography and helped sponsor an early Native American newspaper edited by George Copway, the Ojibwe writer and activist whose history of the Ojibwe Thoreau owned. Thoreau's allusion is a dismissive one, as befits his sympathetic stance toward his Irish immigrant neighbors, though it's important to note that he shares with the party a settler desire to claim status as a "native" in this land, with little interest in working with Indigenous communities. For a good discussion of the Know-Nothing Party in Concord, see Robert Gross, *The Transcendentalists and Their World* (New York: Farrar, Strauss and Giroux, 2021).

11 The American cranberry, *Vaccinium macrocarpon*, is native to eastern North America; what Thoreau terms the European cranberry, *Vaccinium oxycoccos*, is classified as a more

broadly dispersed species found across the northern hemisphere, of which *macrocarpon* is a subspecies. Both are cultivated.

12 The growing field of affective ecocriticism is useful in theorizing how emotional bonds are integral to reshaping the relationship between humans and the environment. Kyle Bladlow and Jennifer Ladino's collection *Affective Ecocriticism: Emotion, Embodiment, Environment* (Lincoln: University of Nebraska Press, 2018) offers a rich introduction to the field; Alexa Weik von Mossner's *Affective Ecologies: Empathy, Emotion, and Environmental Narrative* (Columbus: Ohio State University Press, 2017) is a rich study that applies cognitive neuroscience to environmental literature and film.

13 Glen Sean Coulthard, *Red Skin, White Masks: Rejecting the Colonial Politics of Recognition* (Minneapolis: University of Minnesota Press, 2014), 12–13. On Native dispossession and the creation of national parks, see Mark Spence, *Dispossessing the Wilderness: Indian Removal and the Making of National Parks* (New York: Oxford University Press, 1999).

14 Most accounts of the manuscript "The Dispersion of Seeds" focus on Thoreau's engagement with Darwinian science, including Laura Dassow Walls's *Seeing New Worlds: Henry David Thoreau and Nineteenth-Century Natural Science* (Madison: University of Wisconsin Press, 1995) and Michael Berger's *Thoreau's Late Career and "The Dispersion of Seeds"* (Rochester, NY: Camden House, 2000). The collection of essays edited by Branka Arsić, *Dispersion: Thoreau and Vegetal Thought* (London: Bloomsbury, 2021), explores the book's implications for New Materialist readings of Thoreau.

15 Thoreau's manuscript, titled "The Dispersion of Seeds," was edited and published by Bradley P. Dean as *Faith in a Seed: "The Dispersion of Seeds" and Other Late Natural History Writings* (Washington, D.C.: Island Press, 1993).

16 Randall Fuller, *The Book That Changed America: How Darwin's Theory of Evolution Ignited a Nation* (New York: Viking, 2017), 58–99, 145.

17 Walls, *Henry David Thoreau*, 474.

18 Arsić, "Thoreau's Vegetal Ontology," 7, and Antoine Trainsel, "Thoreau's Garden Politics," 52–69, both in Arsić, *Dispersion*.

19 Juliana Chow, *Nineteenth-Century America and the Discourse of Natural History* (New York: Cambridge University Press, 2021), 143–45.

20 William Howarth, *The Book of Concord: Thoreau's Life as a Writer* (New York: Viking, 1982), 10; Cristin Ellis, *Antebellum Posthuman: Race and Materiality in the Mid-Nineteenth Century* (New York: Fordham University Press, 2018), 82. Ellis follows Wai Chee Dimock in tracing Thoreau's shift toward a more gradualist approach to social change in his later works—a kind of "passive resistance" that worked on deeper time frames. See Dimock, *Through Other Continents: American Literature across Deep Time* (Princeton, NJ: Princeton University Press, 2006).

21 Chow, *Nineteenth-Century America*, 159–61. See also Charles Pickering, *The Races of Man: Their Geographical Distribution* (Botson: Little and Brown, 1848), and Arnold Guyot, *The Earth and Man: Lectures on Comparative Physical Geography, and Its Relation to the History of Mankind* (Boston: Gould, Kendell, and Lincoln, 1849).

22 Charles Loring Brace, *Races of the Old World: A Manual of Ethnology* (New York: Charles Scribner, 1863), 505, 512–13; Fuller, *Book That Changed America*, 200–203.

23 Curtis Runnels, "Henry Thoreau, Archaeologist?," *Concord Saunterer* 27 (2019): 42–67.

24 Ross Martin, "Fossil Thoughts: Thoreau, Arrowheads, and Radical Paleontology," *ESQ* 65, no. 3 (2019): 424–68.

25 Ellis, *Antebellum Posthuman*, 90–92.

26 For a detailed account of this little-known episode in Metacom's Rebellion, see Jenny Hale

Pulsipher, "Massacre at Hurtleberry Hill: Christian Indians and English Authority in Metacom's War," *William and Mary Quarterly* 53, no. 3 (1996): 459–86. One of the murderers was Daniel Hoar, the great-great-grandfather of Thoreau's close friend and travel companion Samuel Hoar. Thoreau never mentions the episode, and it may have been one that Hoar family members were reluctant to share, but Thoreau certainly read Daniel Gookins's account of the episode in his "History of the Christian Indians," in *Transactions and Collections of the American Antiquarian Society*, vol. 2 (Cambridge, MA: Harvard University Press, 1836), 423–534; notes from the volume appear in the Indian Notebooks (3:53–54). In her history of Concord, Ruth R. Wheeler, *Concord: Climate for Freedom* (Concord, MA: Concord Antiquarian Society, 1970), identifies (though with minimal evidence) the location of Hurtleberry Hill as Mt. Misery in Lincoln.

27 Gary Clayton Anderson, *Little Crow: Spokesman for the Sioux* (St. Paul: Minnesota Historical Society Press, 1986). For a thorough account of the long Dakota revival, see Waziyatawin, *What Does Justice Look Like? The Struggle for Liberation in Dakota Homeland* (St. Paul, MN: Living Justice Press, 2008). Diane Wilson's novel *The Seed Keeper: A Novel* (Minneapolis, MN: Milkweed Editions, 2021) is a key literary event in this revival, tracing the legacy of Dakota refugees from the Dakota Uprising into the twenty-first century, using traditional seeds as the medium and metaphor of the tribe's resurgence.

28 Leanne Betasamosake Simpson, *Lighting the Eighth Fire: The Liberation, Resurgence, and Protection of Indigenous Nations* (Winnipeg: ARP Books, 2008), 14, 211.

Index

Abenaki: 42, 50–3, 55
Aboriginal: 13–14, 86, 98–9, 122, 180
Acton, Mass., ceremonial site: 28, 198n2
Affective ecocriticism: 179, 214n12
African Americans: xvi, 9, 12, 16, 20, 30, 84, 96–8, 118–9, 124, 135
Aggasiz, Louis: 74, 183
Alcott, Bronson: 101, 183–4, 213n7
Alcott, Louisa May: 108
Alfred, Taiaiake: 7–8
Algonquins (Ontario tribe): 79
Algonquians (cultural group): 68–71, 80; *pukwudgees* or little people: 111
Anderson, Joyce Rain: xiv–v
Animal studies: 100–2. *See also* "more-than-human"
Anishinaabes, prophecy of the Eight Fires: 187, 191. *See also* Ojibwes
Apess, William: xiv, 1, 6, 13, 17, 117, 129–36; "Eulogy for King Philip": 136; "An Indian's Looking-Glass for Whites": 130; *Indian Nullification*: 129–36; *A Son of the Forest*: 130, 135–6, 195n16
Apples: 53–5, 86, 99, 180–1
Archaeology: 12, 25, 33–4; of Concord: 197n1
Armstrong, Jeanette: 82
Arrivant: 195n13. *See also* Settler colonialism
Arsić, Branka: 21, 38–9, 41, 49–50, 184, 200n20, 214n14
Attaquin, Solomon: 136–7; hotel: 115, 136–7

Attean, Joseph: 4, 6, 19, 84, 139, 141, 145, 149, 154, 156–8, 164–5
Aupaumut, Henry: 64

Baird, Jesse Little Doe: 196n22, 197n1, 207n4, 209n23
Balthrop-Lewis, Alda: 21, 109
Bancroft, George: 3
Barad, Karen: 102
Bartram, William: 76, 207n26
Basso, Keith: 91, 112–3, 156, 206–7n25
Bellin, Joshua: xv, 2, 20, 59, 75, 93, 144, 202n15
Bennett, Jane: 21, 38
Beothuks: 66
Bergland, Renée: 3, 39, 115
Berkes, Fikret: 71
Black: *see* African Americans
Blackhawk, Ned: 193n3
Blake, Harrison: 58–9
Botany: 8–9. *See also* "Thoreau: science: phenology"
Boudillion, Daniel: 197n1, 197n3
Brace, Charles Loring: 183, 186
Bringhurst, Robert: 112, 206n24
Brooks Joanna: 17
Brooks, Lisa: xiv, 18, 41–2, 91, 112–3, 132–3, 137, 198n4, 200n27, 208n1, 212n24
Bross, Kristina: 17, 195n18, 212n29
Brown, John: xii, 185
Bruchac, Margaret: 17, 52, 196n19, 201n33
Bruyneel, Kevin: 13, 19, 34, 196n25, 204n1
Bryant, William Cullen: 74
Buell, Lawrence: 123, 209n10

Burbick, Joan: 39
Byrd, Jodi: 3, 7, 19, 33, 196n25

Cafaro, Philip: 14–15, 21
Cajete, Gregory: 81, 203n23
Caldwell, Duncan: 194n5
Captivity narratives: 22, 201n33
Case, Kristen: 21, 38, 102
Channing, Ellery: 11–12, 123–4
Charlevoix, Pierre-François: 79
Cherokee Nation: 3, 20, 26
Child, Lydia Marie: 3
Christian Indians: 17, 125
Christy, Arthur: 194n6, 202n6
Civil disobedience: 134
Clamshell Bank, Concord: 28, 99, 200n26
Commons: 180–1
Concord River: 28, 36; meaning of Musketaquid: 31
Contact zone: 17–18, 199n18
Coombs, Linda: xv, 196n24, 207n1
Cooper, James Fenimore: 3, 46
Copway, George: 59, 73, 194n6, 213n10
Corntassel, Jeff: 7–8
Coulthardt, Glen Sean: 83, 181
Culbertson, Thaddeus: 76
Cusick, David: 73, 110

Dakota Access Pipeline protests: 18
Dakotas: 24, 169–70, 190–1
Darwin, Charles: 74; Darwinism: 123, 129, 173, 181–5, 189–90
Dawes Act: 5. *See also* Indian Boarding Schools
Dean, Bradley: 174, 213n4
Decolonization: xiii–xiv, 83, 92, 154, 193n2
Deer Island: 29
Deforestation: 43
Delawares (Lenape): 68, 79
Deloria, Philip J.: 3, 21, 33, 137, 209n22
Deloria, Vine, Jr.: 102
Dimock, Wai Che: 145, 152, 163, 214n20
Donahue, Brian: 28
Donohue, Betty: 17, 195n18, 212n29
Douglass, Frederick: xii
Dugan, Elisha: 97–8
Dunbar-Ortiz, Roxanne: 194n3
Dustan, Hannah: 22, 50–3, 201n33

Earle, John Milton: 119, 198n4
Eckstorm, Fannie: 151–2, 157
Ecocultural contact: 38, 50, 65, 86, 150–1, 163–6
Edge community: 94–5, 205n9; cultural edge: 95. *See also* Ecocultural contact
Eliade, Mircea, and sacred time: 111, 210n9
Eliot Bible: 34, 117, 145
Ellis, Cristin: 185, 189, 214n20
Emerson, Ralph Waldo: 1, 25, 27, 30–1, 36, 123, 146; "Eulogy for Henry Thoreau": 1, 78, 137; "Historical Discourse on Concord": 30–1, 92; Introduction to "Natural History of Massachusetts": 33; "Letter to Martin van Buren": 3; "Musketaquid" in opening of *A Week*: 39; *Nature*: 108; *Representative Men*: 135
Environment: 6, 9–10, 14–15, 18–19, 23, 27, 38, 70–7, 81–3; pre-contact: 43, 52, 64–5, 127; environmental movement: xiii, 6, 18–19, 91, 95; restoration: 127; tourism: 116, 137–8, 164 ; preservation: 146, 210n8. *See also* ecocultural contact
Ethnography: 2, 5, 10, 13, 19, 68–70
Evolution: 183–4. *See also* Darwin
Exploration, literature of: 62–4, 124

Finley, James: 21, 38, 193n2
Fleck, Richard: 60, 74, 202n6
Francis, James: 18, 156, 161, 193n2, 196n23, 211n23
Franklin, Benjamin: 33
Fuller, Margaret: 3
Fuller, Randall: 183–4, 186
Fuller, Richard: 35

Garrison, William Lloyd: 134
Gazaille, Brian: 39
Genocide: 30
Geography: 42, 56, 200n25, 210n4
Geology: 39, 48
Ghosts: 25, 26–7, 35, 39, 42, 51–3, 56, 90
Giles, Paul: 146
Gluskape / Klose-kur-beh: 153–4, 157–62, 167
Gookin, Daniel: 55, 64, 198n3
Gosnold, Bartholomew: 62–3, 124
Great Fields, Concord: 28, 31–2

INDEX 219

Gross, Robert: 20, 95
Groundnuts: 63, 86–9, 113–4
Gura, Philip: 17
Guyot, Arnold: 186, 210n4

Hale, Horatio: 117
Halttunen, Karen: 200n25
Harding, Walter: 208n10, 209n1
Haudenosaunee / Iroquois: 73, 77. *See also* Mohawks, Onondagas, Senecas, Tuscaroras
Hawthorne, Nathaniel: 1, 50–1, 203n21
Heckewelder, John: 68, 75, 80, 110
Herring Pond Wampanoags: 5–6, 122
Higginson, Thomas Wentworth: 184
Hoar, Daniel: 29, 198n3
Hoar, Edward: 29, 106, 198n3
Hoar, John: 29, 35
Howarth, William: 60, 78, 185, 204n26
Humboldt, Alexander von: 5
Hunter, John: 80
Hurons: 68, 84; Feast of the Dead: 39, 50, 70, 80, 200n20
Hurtleberry Hill Massacre: 29, 190, 215n26

Icelandic sagas: 124
Indian hating: 31
Indian wisdom: 2, 7, 9, 16, 21, 27, 37–8, 41, 53, 89–90, 98–9, 167, 176
Indigeneity: xvi, 7–8, 10, 13, 30, 32–3, 83, 88–90, 99, 109, 173, 179–82, 187
Irish Americans: xvi, 9, 16, 96, 105, 124, 195n13, 205n9
Irving, Washington: 33

Jackson, Charles: 144, 166, 210n5
Jacobs, Margaret: 92, 204n4
Jesuit Relations: 66, 68, 70, 72, 75–6, 78, 89, 110, 178
Johnson, Edward: 65
Johnson, Linck: 39, 124
Johnson, Rochelle: 21, 38
Josselyn, John: 64–5, 88, 178

Kaiser, Albert: 74
Katahdin Woods and Waters: xii, 193n2
Kimmerer, Robin Wall: xiv, 7–8, 82, 90
King Philip's War: *see* Metacom's Rebellion

King, Thomas: 92, 204n5
Know-Nothing Party / Native American Party: 178–9, 213n10
Kolodny, Annette: 17, 155, 157
Krewac, Patty: 193n3

Lakotas: 76, 169
Latour, Bruno: 21, 102, 205n13
Lejeune, Paul: 84
Lemire, Elise: 20, 96
Leopold, Aldo: 94–5
Line Three protests: 18
Longfellow, Henry Wadsworth, *Hiawatha*: 3; *Evangeline*: 53
Longue durée: 48, 128, 145, 154
Lopenzina, Drew: 17
Loskiel, Peter: 79
Lovewell's Fight: 46
Lowell, James Russell: 149, 166
Lowney, John: 124
Luccarelli, Mark: 39
Lyell, Charles: 48

Maine Woods: xi–xii, 140–1, 150, 156, 162, 164–5, 167–8
Mahicans: 64, 82
Maȟpíya Lúta Owáyawa / Red Cloud Indian School: xv
Mandell, Daniel: 132–3, 135, 195n16
Manifest Destiny: 20, 30, 105, 108, 111, 124, 127, 144, 148. *See also* Savagism and Settler colonialism
Martin, Ross: 188–9
Massachusetts tribe: 28
Mashpee Wampanoags: 6, 23, 64, 115–6, 125, 129–39, 194n8; Environment: 133; Revolt: 117, 130–9, 209n23. *See also* Wampanoags
Maungwudaus / George Henry: 10, 195n14
Maushop: 64
Medieval American literature: 146
Metacom: 66, 117, 136
Metacom's Rebellion / King Philip's War: 15, 29, 31–2, 35, 66
Meteoulin: *see* Shamanism
Mielke, Lauren: 205n11
Mohawks: 42, 165
Mohegans: 64
Momaday, N, Scott: 112

Montagnais / Innu: 68, 72
Montauks: 64
Mooney, Edward: 108–9
Moosehead Lake: 5
More-than-human world: 8–9, 20, 21, 41, 44, 51–3, 56, 70, 83, 87, 93, 100–6, 148–50, 161, 173, 182, 187, 189
Morgan, Lewis Henry: 74–5, 77, 203n20
Morton, Samuel George: 5, 74–5, 77, 144
Morton, Timothy: 21, 108
Musketaquid: xii, xvi–xvii, 5, 25, 27–9, 30–1, 35, 40, 42, 47, 65, 82–3, 92, 114, 179, 182–3, 188–9
Moskowitz, Alex: 124
Myth: 41, 49, 56, 73, 75, 81, 106–14, 146–7, 210–11n9

Nabokov, Peter: 48
Narragansets: 63–4
Nashaways: 35
Nashobahs: 29, 31–2, 35, 118, 198n3
Naticks: 118
National parks and preserves: xii, 146, 181, 205n10
"Native": xvi, 173, 175
Native American and Indigenous Studies: xiv, 17–19; Indigenous animal studies: 102
Native Americans: Agriculture and land management: 28, 43, 63–5, 69, 70–2, 79, 82, 132, 182. *See also* Three Sisters; Boarding schools: 202–3n16; Ceremonies: 70, 99, 113; burial: 49–50, 200–1n32; and landscapes: 28, 64, 198n2; Concord, nineteenth-century: 9, 25, 29, 109–10, 198n4; Diplomacy: 42, 154, 156, 164, 206n19, 212n24; Foodways: 61, 63, 70, 89, 99, 128; History: 27–30, 37, 41–2, 48, 52, 62–5, 73, 148, 152; Language: 10–11, 68, 76, 81–2; Oral traditions: 17, 48, 72–3, 76, 112, 195–6n19, 211n20; Origins: 72–4; Pedagogy: 164; Religion: 63–4, 70, 80–1, 84, 157; Science: 81, 203n23. *See also* Traditional ecological knowledge; Social norms: 69; In Southern New England: 198n2; Sovereignty: 17–18, 20, 33, 83, 133–4, 141, 150–2, 154, 164; Time: 52, 56, 152–4, 166–7

Native American Graves Protection and Repatriation Act (NAGPRA): 200–1n32
Native American Party: *see* Know-Nothing Party
Nature: 21, 23, 37, 39, 41, 45, 54, 80, 87, 97, 100, 104, 108, 123, 127, 150, 157, 173, 177, 182, 185
Naturalization: 8, 15, 37, 40, 46–7, 50, 53–4, 89–91, 99, 103, 105–6, 128–9, 179–80
Neighboring: 93–4, 100–2
Neptune, John: 151, 155–7, 161, 165–7
Neptune, Louis: 4, 144
New England history: 25–27, 30, 39, 42, 48, 51, 65
New Materialism: 21, 38, 49, 53, 56. *See also* More-than-human world
Newman, Lance: 20–21, 175, 205n9
Nicolar, Joseph: xiv, 17, 23, 141, 152–62, 166, 210n2
Nipmucs: 27–8, 118
Nott, Josiah: 74–7

O'Brien, Jean: xiv, 7, 18, 19, 26–7, 30, 35, 89, 197n25
Occom, Samson: 64
Object-Oriented Ontology: 38. *See also* New Materialism
Ojibwes: 10, 68, 73–4
Onondagas: 67
Oral literatures: 17
Ortiz, Simon: 81–2
Osages: 72, 80

Pantheism: 21, 105, 108, 149–50
Parkman, Francis: 3–4
Passaconaway: 42, 55–6
Pawtuckets: 28, 42
Penacooks: 42
Penobscots: xi, xiv, 4–6, 9–11, 18, 23–4, 55, 67, 96, 109–10, 140–68, 196n23, 212n24; and Thoreau: 19
Petrulionis, Sandra: 20
Peyer, Bernd: 17, 195n18
Place: 23–4, 34–7, 41–2, 54, 63, 80–4, 86–7, 89–90, 156, 173–4, 189; and naturalization: 40, 89, 111; place-world: 91, 112–3, 156

Playing Indian: 3, 15, 21, 33–4, 49, 110, 182
Plotinus: 41
Polis, Joseph: 4–6, 10, 84, 137, 141, 145, 157–8, 164–6
Powwows: *see* Shamanism
Pratt, Mary Louise: 199n18
Pratt, Richard Henry: 74
Praying Indian Villages: 29, 119, 202–3n16

Queerness: 111

Race: 2, 4–5, 30, 40, 49, 74–5, 99, 105, 120–2, 128, 172, 180–2, 184–9
Ranalli, Brent: xv, 2, 205n15
Ranco, Darren: 18, 153, 196n23
Ricketson, Daniel: 5, 67, 116–7, 119–20
Rifkin, Mark: 3, 19, 92, 114, 148, 152, 197n25, 207n2
Romanticism: xiii, 19, 26, 30, 33, 45
Rose, Suzanne: 29, 59–60, 74–5, 112, 201n4, 202n6, 206n22
Rowlandson, Mary: 35
Runnels, Curtis: 188

Salt, Henry: 74
Sagan, Dorian: 102
Samoset: 109–10
Sanborn, Franklin: 59–60, 74, 183
Sattelmeyer, Robert: 7, 60
Savagism: 2–4, 6, 8, 16, 20, 22, 32, 39, 45, 56, 58, 72–7, 83, 120, 145, 163, 185. *See also* Settler colonialism
Sayre, Robert: xxiii, 39, 46, 53, 58–60, 75, 77, 142, 203–4n26, 206n23
Schact, Paul: 205–6n16
Schneider, Richard: xv, 2, 20, 39, 53, 210n4
Schoolcraft, Henry Rowe: 5, 72, 74–6, 110, 144
Senecas: 77
Senier, Siobhan: xiv, 17, 18
Settler colonialism: 3, 19, 32–3, 65–7, 70–7, 83–4, 89–90, 92–3, 105, 114, 124–9, 148; and ghosts: 27, 37, 39, 41, 44–6, 49, 56, 71, 90, 172–3, 177–8, 188–9; settler nativism: 179. *See also* Savagism
Shamanism: 55–6, 70, 72, 80, 141, 151
Shattuck, Lemuel: 25–7, 31–2, 40, 92
Silko, Leslie Marmon: 48

Simon, Katie: 124
Simons, Martha: 5, 9, 120–2
Simpson, Audra: 11, 133
Simpson, Leanne Betasamosake: 137, 191
Smith, Linda Tuhiwai: 193n3
Smith, Sepit and Thomas: 5, 119–20
Sockalexis, Chris: xix, 154, 193n2, 211n18
Solnit, Rebecca: 20
Speck, Frank: 155, 157, 161
Springer, John: 166
Squaw Sachem: 28, 31
Squier, Ephraim: 5, 73, 77, 110
Stone, John Augustus: 3
Succession: 43, 49, 170–1, 182–90
Swann, Brian: 17, 196n19, 211n20

Tahattawan: 4, 21, 26, 30–1, 33, 42
TallBear, Kim: 13, 89, 102
Tedlock, Dennis: 17, 195–6n19
Thoreau, Henry David: Abolitionism: xii–xiii, 4, 7, 15, 19, 20, 84, 194n5; American Association for the Advancement of Science: 68, 81; Arrowheads and other stone tools: 12, 21, 25, 33–4, 188–9; Birth house: 31; Capitalism: 15, 20–21, 23, 27, 47–8, 91–4, 124, 163, 180, 189; Concord River survey: 47–8; Early writing: 26, 33; Education: 175, 177, 180, 213n7; Environmentalism: 19, 27, 43, 104–5; Fish creel near Walden Woods: 12–14; History: 3, 21–2, 34–7, 38–40, 44–5, 47–8, 52, 56, 87, 142–7; Hunting: 148–9; Indigenous project: 7, 10, 15–16, 87–8; Memorial to Tahattawan: 34; Minnesota trip: 24, 78, 169–70; Mourning: 22, 27, 36, 49–50, 51–2, 55–6, 104, 170–2; Phenomenology of place: 14, 111; Poetry: 87–9, 113–4; Religion: 15, 19, 21, 45, 47, 53, 55–6, 79–80, 108–9, 177, 179; Science: 10, 19, 21, 23, 24, 38, 71, 81, 88, 97, 167; botany: 177; geology: 39, 48; human geography: 42, 56, 156 ; phenology: 7, 10, 98, 111, 174, 184; Two Thoreau problem: 20; Woods-burning: 106;
Thoreau, Henry David Works: "The Allegash and East Branch": 9, 142, 145–6, 150–67; *Cape Cod*: 123–9; "Che

Thoreau, Henry David, works: (*continued*)
suncook": 9, 11, 142, 145, 148–50, 181;
Dispersion of Seeds: 24, 78, 170–4, 181–5; "Huckleberries": 174, 190; Indian Notebooks: 5, 10, 21, 22, 43, 57–85, 88–9, 110, 172, 176–8, 194n6, 201n1, 203–4n26; proposed book: 58–60, 77–8, 84, 187–8, 203n21; transcriptions: 202n6; Journal: 78; Kalendar: 24, 78, 111, 174, 190; "Ktaadn": 4, 142–7; "Life without Principle": 4–5; *The Maine Woods*: xi, 23, 125, 141–68; "Natural History of Massachusetts": 6–7, 21, 27, 32, 33–8, 98–9, 176; Natural History Notebooks: 60, 78; "Resistance to Civil Government": 4, 79, 135; "Slavery in Massachusetts": 23; "The Succession of Forest Trees": 174, 182–4; *Walden*: 5, 9, 14, 22–3, 59–60, 79, 86–114, 205–6n16; "A Walk to Wachusett": 32, 35–7; "Walking": 14, 22–3, 78, 106–114; *A Week on the Concord and Merrimack Rivers*: xi, 22, 26–7, 39–56, 59, 66; "Wild Apples": 86, 99, 173–4, 180–1; *Wild Fruits*: 10, 24, 78, 170–81, 190, 213n4
Thoreau, John Jr.: 26–7, 33–4, 56
Thoreau, John Sr.: 32, 36, 171–2
Thoreau, Sophia: 123
Thoreau-Wabanaki Anniversary Tour: xi–xii, xix, 193n1
Three Sisters agriculture: 9, 28, 80, 91
Time: 14, 40, 111, 128, 141–7, 166, 185, deep: 146–8, 155; ceremonial: 147; mythic: 56, 111, 157; thick: 147–8, 155

Traditional ecological knowledge: 7–9, 10, 13–14, 58, 70–2, 81, 84, 121
Treat, Joseph: 155–6
Truth, Sojourner: xii
Tuck, Eve, and Wang Yang: 193n3
Tuscaroras: 73

Virtue ethics: 14–15, 21
Vitalism: 189. *See also* New Materialism

Wabanakis: 109, 144, 151, 165
Walls, Laura Dassow: 21, 33, 96, 123, 184, 204n6, 208n10, 214n14
Wampanoags: xiv–xv, 5, 33–4, 63–4, 66, 137; language reclamation: 18, 196n22; and Thoreau: 19. *See also* Herring Pond, Mashpee
Wanalancet: 42
Warrior, Robert: 17, 18, 195n18
Weaver, Jace: 7, 18, 32, 83
Webster, Daniel: 137, 166
Weisenberg, Michael C.: 124
Wheeler, Bill: 97
Wild, the: 23, 43–6, 86–8, 90, 94, 97–100, 105–6, 108, 111
Wilderness: 14, 53, 78, 144, 210n8
Williams, Roger: 63, 75, 176, 178
Willsky-Ciollo, Lydia: 21, 114
Winters, Sylvia: 154
Wolfe, Patrick: 3, 19, 30, 33, 84, 197n25
Womack, Craig: 18
Wyeth, N. C.: 95
Wyss, Hilary: 17, 195n18